Encyclopedia of Human Servic

MW00786807

Encyclopedia of Human Services

Master Review and Tutorial for the
Human Services-Board Certified Practitioner
Examination (HS-BCPE)

*Become a Human Services-Board Certified
Practitioner (HS-BCP) and take your career
to the next level. This book can improve your
performance in any human services course!*

Howard Rosenthal

Routledge
Taylor & Francis Group

NEW YORK AND LONDON

First published 2014
by Routledge
711 Third Avenue, New York, NY 10017

and by Routledge
27 Church Road, Hove, East Sussex BN3 2FA

Routledge is an imprint of the Taylor & Francis Group, an informa business

© 2014 Taylor & Francis

The right of Howard Rosenthal to be identified as author of this work has been asserted by him in accordance with sections 77 and 78 of the Copyright, Designs and Patents Act 1988.

All rights reserved. No part of this book may be reprinted or reproduced or utilised in any form or by any electronic, mechanical, or other means, now known or hereafter invented, including photocopying and recording, or in any information storage or retrieval system, without permission in writing from the publishers.

Trademark notice: Product or corporate names may be trademarks or registered trademarks, and are used only for identification and explanation without intent to infringe.

Library of Congress Cataloging-in-Publication Data

Rosenthal, Howard, 1952–
Encyclopedia of human services : master review and tutorial for the human
   services-board certified practitioner examination (HS-BCPE) / by Howard Rosenthal.
      pages cm
   1. Social service—Examinations, questions, etc.   2. Human services—Examinations,
questions, etc.   3. Social work education.   I. Title.
   HV11.5.R67   2014
   361.0076—dc23   2014002348

ISBN: 978-0-415-70769-5 (hbk)
ISBN: 978-0-415-53812-1 (pbk)
ISBN: 978-0-203-10960-1 (ebk)

Typeset in Sabon
by Apex CoVantage, LLC

Printed and bound in the United States of America by Publishers Graphics,
LLC on sustainably sourced paper.

Contents

Acknowledgments

The Human Services-Board Certified Practitioner (HS-BCP) credential isn't just sitting on the launching pad ready to take off; it's already in orbit. Moments before I sat down to write this very paragraph, I spied several articles with information related to the fact that the National Board for Certified Counselors Foundation (NBCCF) is awarding scholarships to HS-BCP credential holders who wish to pursue a career in counseling. The intent is to increase the number of human services practitioners who become counselors. What a wonderful idea. This upbeat and innovative study guide for exam preparation is being released at the ideal time.

I want to acknowledge a host of key individuals who assisted behind the scenes to make this book a reality. First, there's my wife Patricia, who's the Associate Director of the School of Social Work and Director of Field Education at the University of Missouri–St. Louis. Next, my two sons, Paul and Patrick, who put up with my incessant work on the book, all the while providing technical assistance when necessary. Paul, by the way, built the entire computer used to compile this book from scratch, as well as my last text. Nice job, dude!

Professor Joanne Galanis of the St. Louis Community College at Florissant Valley Library deserves special mention for helping with research assistance, as she has for so many of my books. Private practice therapist and adjunct professor Vicky Aitken of St. Louis Community College at Florissant Valley came up with a host of valuable suggestions. Hats off to Amy Bird, manager of the St. Louis Community College at Florissant Valley Access Office, who, with the help of my former human services student, Lisa Dye Myers, created questions related to disabilities.

Needless to say, the vignettes created by experts Marla Berg-Weger, Julie Birkenmaier, Ed Neukrug, Hannah Neukrug, Tricia McClam, and Marianne Woodside proved invaluable.

I would be remiss if I didn't mention my wonderful editor, Anna Moore, who is always there when I need her. Ditto for the entire Routledge, Taylor & Francis Group staff.

Finally, I want to thank all my human services students who have taught *me* so much over the years. Special thanks go to student Johanna White, who took on assignments related to this text that went well beyond the call of duty.

The HS-BCP has come of age. It's your turn to snare this valuable credential. I say go for it.

Chapter 1

Who Else Wants to Say, "I Passed!"?

As I stepped out of the Capitol Plaza Hotel in Jefferson City, Missouri, on April 8, 2011, into the scorching hot 95 degree afternoon sun, I couldn't help feeling terrific. It was truly one of those magical moment days to remember. Perhaps 90 percent of the folks at the American Counseling Association of Missouri (ACAM) Annual Conference, where I had just given a presentation, seemed to know me. Never mind the fact that I only recognized a handful of their faces, at best. The title of my workshop was "Sixteen Sure-Fire Ways to Publish Your Counseling or Self-Improvement Book."

My final words of the presentation emphasized that a book author should always be working on something new and exciting, and also have a project on the back burner. I suggested that most authors let their minds travel around the globe, when genius (that creative idea for the perfect book) is most likely right in front of their noses.

Having shared that gem of wisdom, honesty compels me to admit that I was personally clueless: I didn't have the slightest idea what my next frontier was going to be for my subsequent book project. Author, heal thyself!

As we battled the intense heat radiating off the parking lot on the way to the car, my son, Paul, who was with me to help sell books, said, "Wow, dad, you're a celebrity."

"I assure you, Paul, I'm not a celebrity."

"No, you really are dad. Everybody knows you. Look at how many people wanted your autograph. Several even insisted they wanted to get a picture of you with them."

Okay, I had to admit, I did silently chuckle at the folks who wanted a photo taken with me. Were they really asking *me*? I mean, you're kidding, right? The first time something like that ever happened, I looked around the room to see if TMZ, the paparazzi, or perhaps *People Magazine* were hot on the tail of a movie idol or rock star who had accidentally wandered into the seminar room.

Let me be clear that my notoriety had nothing to do with the workshop I had just presented. So why was I enjoying this mini-celebrity status and, more importantly, why should you care? How in the world is it going to help you? Well, if you can sit tight for just a few moments, you have my word as a gentleman, a scholar, a professor, and the program coordinator of a college human services program that my story is going to benefit you far more than you could ever imagine.

The Strangest Exam Secret

It all started over 15 years ago when I set out to create a set of licensing materials that would help counselors pass a test known as the National Counselor Examination (NCE) to secure state licensing or snare National Certified Counselor (NCC) status.

I thus penned a unique book I titled *Encyclopedia of Counseling*. Now you're probably thinking I'm going to say the sales of the book took off like a fighter jet on steroids, but that would be a lie. In reality, the text came out of the starting blocks with all the vigor of a turtle with ankle weights strapped to its feet. But, fortunately, as time went by, that slow-moving tortoise began to gain some serious speed.

The pivotal turning point seemed to occur when one day, I received a message on my answering machine from a counselor educator (a professor who teaches or trains counselors) asking where her students could purchase "The Purple Book." Several moments later, I punched up my email only to discover a message from another counselor who also wanted to buy a copy of "The Purple Book." What in the world was "The Purple Book?" I punched the term into a search engine and discovered **that counselors writing on Internet discussion groups and chat rooms from coast-to-coast were talking about** *my* **book!**

The only explanation was that my friend, the slow-moving turtle, put the pedal to the metal and kicked into passing gear. A grassroots movement began to take hold that I, as the author, didn't even see happening. Permit me to explain. In the second edition of the *Encyclopedia of Counseling,* we used a purple cover. (The first edition used a green, black, and white color scheme.) At about the same time my book was coming of age, a pharmaceutical company, AstraZeneca, was advertising a drug called Nexium for heartburn and billed it as "The Purple Pill." Counselors put a twist on the ad, and my *Encyclopedia of Counseling* had become "The Purple Book."

Why was the book becoming so popular? Simple, I actually made exam prep (dare I say it) fun and easy to understand. That's right, studying became enjoyable. I never believed that education needed to be dry, dull, and boring, and my book went on to prove it. *The greatest exam secret is that studying and exam prep can actually be a pleasant experience and something you'll look forward to doing.*

My style in the *Encyclopedia* (um, excuse me, I mean "The Purple Book") was upbeat and, at times, humorous. For years now, I've been in meetings or conferences where I've heard teachers remark, "I'm not here to entertain the students." Truth be told, I very often heard the exact same thing from professors when I was a student. But you know what: I typically stroll into classes I'm teaching on the first day and tell my students, "A lot of teachers will tell you they aren't here to entertain you, but actually, I *am* here to entertain you!"

The *Encyclopedia* was merely my engaging teaching style in print, and readers loved every minute of it. How do I know? Great question! I could tell you that on many occasions, I'd punch the keyword "counseling" into Amazon or other top booksellers and there I'd spy the *Encyclopedia* sitting pretty in the top five spots—often number one! In the 2010 Routledge Counseling and Psychotherapy catalog, *Encyclopedia* was the number one seller in the "Top Ten List." In 2011, it captured the number two spot, beating out works by many of the top counseling and psychology authors in the world. Yes, success leaves clues, but here is my most convincing argument. Over the years, I've received numerous emails from readers who suggested they were sad when their study process ended. Say what? That's correct, you read it right; counselors were enjoying the exam preparation process so much they didn't want it to end. Some readers even used the word "grieving" to describe their reaction.

Now Here's What's in It for You!

Several days after the conference, I still didn't have any idea what my next literary mission would be, but then it happened. I was lecturing to one of my classes about a new credential: the Human Services-Board Certified Practitioner (HS-BCP). A young woman blurted out, "What's the name of the study guide for the test, Dr. Rosenthal?"

"Oh, you don't understand," I replied, "the credential is brand new. I've already checked, nobody has written a study guide yet."

"Well, you should write one, Dr. Rosenthal. You always seem to have a way to make the material interesting." Now, keep in mind that this student, and most likely the rest of the class, had no idea that my *Encyclopedia of Counseling* had become the darling of the counseling licensure and certification movement. So, little did my student know, but she just carved out my next literary frontier! Or, as a cowboy might have said to my student in the days of the Old West, "Much obliged, ma'am!"

The Encyclopedia of Human Services: You Will Be Riding on the Coattails of a Winner!

The book you have in your hot little hands is simply a clone of my "Purple Book," except it's geared toward the Human Services-Board Certified Practitioner Examination, aka the HS-BCPE. Successfully completing this examination allows you to become a Human Services-Board Certified Practitioner (HS-BCP).

Yep, you'll be using the same great strategy, but tailored to the personal needs of the human services practitioner (namely, you!) who's interested in snaring board certified practitioner status.

So what's really different about this master review and tutorial from study guides of yesteryears?

The answer: plenty. First, I'll take you by the hand and teach you the material ever so slowly using very tiny baby steps. I'll use an a, b, c, d question-and-answer format. Unlike traditional exam prep guides and textbook questions, many of my questions and answers are "ringers" in the sense that they are purposely jam-packed with vital information to help you successfully tackle *other* questions on the actual exam. So, as a simple example, I might say, "William Glasser created reality therapy with choice theory, Carl R. Rogers is the father of the person-centered approach. Who created psychoanalysis?" Notice that the question itself is providing you with key gems of wisdom. The other reason I do this is to help you answer future questions in the book that are more difficult. That said, the very best way to use this book is to begin with question one and work through each and every question in order without skipping a single question.

As a bonus, I'll provide repetition and alternative explanations when necessary. **Unlike other works, this book will not limit itself to a single definition. Often, several descriptions of the same concept will be provided in regard to must-know concepts.**

One Weird Trick Improves Your Memory in One Evening

You're innocently surfing the Internet when you see one of those infamous ads, like "One Weird Trick Allows You To Lose 20 Pounds In 7 Days," or "One Ridiculously Simple Strategy Gives A 65 Year Old Woman Smoother Skin Than Her Teenage Grand Daughter," or some such nonsense. Scams—all of them—each and every one of them. You click the link and, lo and behold, the person running the ad has an expensive miracle product to sell you.

Nevertheless, I do have a fabulous strategy—although I don't know how weird it is—to improve your memory and you won't even need to send me an extra $39.95 to learn the secret. It's so simple that, unlike the aforementioned advertisers who are exaggerating,

I'm being modest in the sense that you could most likely learn this technique in less than a single evening.

First, let me assure you that I began dabbling in memory devices (also called mnemonic strategies) because I was *not* blessed with a photographic or even a particularly good memory. My brother, for example, has savant-like memory characteristics. You can ask him what the high and low temperatures were on a certain date in our hometown 30 years ago and he'll quote you the temperature right down to the exact degree. He can often tell you precisely what he had for dinner on that day to boot!

I once had a mathematics professor who, on the first day of class, would ask everybody to say their name and tell something about themselves. As soon as everyone in the class had spoken, he would repeat back everybody's name and information, such as "Jane Smith, a philosophy major," or "Sam Jones, an employee at the shoe store." His recollection rate for 30 plus students was 100%.

If you possess a memory like my brother, or perhaps my former math professor, I can safely say you don't need my memory-boosting tips. If, on the other hand, you're a mere mortal like the rest of us, who can't remember what you had for breakfast or what your human services theories and skills instructor said just 5 minutes ago, then my ideas will work wonders for you. Have you ever heard the old adage, "Imitation is the most sincere form of flattery?" After I began pushing memory devices in my exam prep materials, some of my competitors began doing the very same thing. Hey, what can I say but thanks for helping me change the face of exam preparation.

I firmly believe the most effective memory device is to associate the difficult-to-recall principle with something that's easy to remember. Serious associations often work well, but at other times, the silliest ones can be the best. Also, keep in mind that the memory device only needs to make sense to you. If it doesn't work for somebody else, well, that's just tough bananas.

I'll be giving you a few examples throughout this book but, again, you may need to create personalized ones for yourself if the ones I suggest don't cut the mustard for you. Here are a few quick examples:

- How do you remember which way to reset your clock when the time changes? Here's one of the most common memory tricks ever invented. Simply: spring forward, fall back. Get it?
- You're studying about Ivan Pavlov's famous experiment in which a dog hears a bell that's presented before some meat and is conditioned to salivate to the bell when the meat isn't present. How do you remember that the conditioned stimulus in the experiment (or CS) comes before the unconditioned stimulus (the US)? That's easy. Repeat after me: C comes before U in the alphabet. Again. C comes before U in the alphabet. Thus, the CS comes before the US in the experiment. Nice!
- Sticking with Pavlov's experiment, how do you remember whether the meat is the CS or US? Yes, this stuff can seem insanely complex, but try this. In the US, we eat a lot of meat. Go ahead and repeat it out loud. Just shout, "In the US, we eat a lot of meat." Your family won't think you're abnormal. Actually, they might, but you really need to pass this exam, so who cares! Once again, "In the US, we eat a lot of meat." When you see the US (the unconditioned stimulus), it's the meat in the experiment. Case closed. I doubt that you'll ever forget it again.
- A cholesterol test yields two readings, the LDL and HDL cholesterol levels. How do you remember which type of cholesterol is the good kind (and thus you want to raise the number) and which is bad (and therefore you want to lower the statistic)? Hey,

that's easy enough. Let's personalize this one. My first name (Howard) begins with H and it's a darn good name, and therefore HDL, which also begins with an H, must be the good cholesterol. And you thought exam prep was always going to be difficult.

• How do you remember that primary groups are targeted toward prevention? That's easy enough: Primary starts with a "p" and so does the word prevention.

FAQ: For the Future Human Services-Board Certified Practitioner (HS-BCP)

Question: Why in the world would I want to secure the Human Services-Board Certified Practitioner (HS-BCP) credential? It sounds like a lot of work.

Answer: I tell my undergraduate human services students with some degree of sincerity that, "Everybody nowadays has a degree, a technical certificate, or both. What do you have that the other candidates for the job don't?"

Now, of course, I'm exaggerating just a teeny bit, but in this rough and tumble highly competitive economy, the more credentials you have, the better. This credential will help separate you from the rest of the pack. I like to think of the HS-BCP as your trump card to better opportunities. In this case, more letters after your name really is better. The credential makes you stand out as a serious practitioner in the field. One of the best of the best. Hmmm, I like that phrase.

Question: Wait just a minute. I asked my supervisor and the head of my human services agency what each of them thought of the HS-BCP credential—and yes, I explained what the letters meant—and neither of them even heard of it! What would you say to that?

Answer: Hey, no surprise. When I first secured my certificate as a National Certified Counselor (NCC) and Licensed Professional Counselor (LPC), nobody ever heard of those credentials. I remember the psychiatrists I worked with asking me why I put the letters LPC and NCC after my name. Today, counselors are beating the doors down to secure these academic badges of honor. As another example, in the early years of credentialing for counselors, I saw a client whose insurance company—one of the largest insurance companies in the country—was unwilling to pay me for conducting the sessions. I thus went all the way up to the vice president of the insurance firm who said, "I'm sorry, Rosenthal, but you're wrong, counselors aren't licensed. Only psychiatrists and psychologists are licensed, and we only pay licensed providers."

"Oh, I get it," I replied, "so those certificates behind my desk are just a hallucination." The bottom line is it takes a while for any new credential to become popular. My advice: Get your HS-BCP now and avoid the rush! Everybody will know what it is soon enough. Give it some time. Just think of it as investing in your future.

Question: My agency employs licensed psychologists, licensed clinical social workers, and counselors who are engaged in the practice of psychotherapy. Will my HS-BCP certification be the same as their licenses?

Answer: No. First, licenses are conferred by the state and, in this case, the certification is given by an organization. Although some social workers are licensed with a bachelor's degree, licensed social workers (who perform therapy) and licensed counselors need a master's degree, and a psychologist needs a doctorate. Post masters or doctoral supervised experience, and specific exams, are then necessary to snare one of these licenses. Moreover, licensed practitioners can often provide psychotherapy, diagnose clients, take insurance or managed care payments, and, in some cases, administer complex psychological and educational tests. In a nutshell, a license will usually be a more advanced credential. But look at it this way: If you wish to advance your professional status, licensing would be an excellent goal. And, even if you're a licensed professional in another profession with a masters or doctorate, the HS-BCP would still be highly recommended.

Question: I've been trying to read up on this credential and I'm thoroughly confused by all the letters: CCE, NOHS, HSE, etc. Can you decipher all this for me?

Answer: One thing you learn in a hurry in the human services, mental health, and social services field, is it's inundated with alphabet soup terminology in the form of numerous abbreviations and acronyms.

Let me see if I can break it down for you in regard to the task at hand. Again, the credential you're trying to snare is the Human Services-Board Certified Practitioner (HS-BCP). The exam you're gearing up for is the Human Services-Board Certified Practitioner (HS-BCP) Examination, also written as HS-BCPE. The credential and exam are offered by the Center for Credentialing and Education (CCE), as well as the National Organization for Human Services (NOHS)—formerly known as the National Organization for Human Services Education (NOHSE). Just for the record, NOHSE was created in 1975 at the 5th Annual Faculty Development Conference of the Southern Regional Education Board (SREB). Since NOHS is the major organization for human services practitioners, you'd do well to secure a membership. The aforementioned organizations also consulted with the Council for Standards in Human Service Education (CSHSE). This organization is the sole body that accredits human services educational programs nationwide.

The CCE has contracted with Applied Measurement Professionals, Inc. (AMP) to assist with the administration, as well as the scoring of the exams. In short, AMP will help you schedule the date, time, and location of the exam.

And, oh yes, HSEs are folks like me—Human Services Educators—who are employed in human services education programs.

Question: My college instructors use the term human services worker, while you keep using the term human services practitioner. Perhaps I'm splitting hairs, but what in the world is the difference?

Answer: Like your instructors, I've been using the term human services worker in the classes I teach and in our literature given to students for years. Other experts prefer the term human services professional. In reality, you'll see (and hear) all the aforementioned terms and they all describe the same thing: somebody who's providing human services. Nevertheless, since this certificate is championing the word practitioner, my guess would be that this terminology will become the norm in the coming years. I'll switch back and forth when I use the terms in this work to avoid sounding redundant.

Question: Hold on, you're moving a little too fast for me. How do I know if I'm even qualified to apply for the exam?

Answer: The CCE has a complete *HS-BCP Application Packet* that's 11 pages long, so I'll be summarizing just a tad here. First, you'll need a sealed official transcript verifying you have a degree from a regionally accredited college, university, or state-approved community or junior college. If you possess an associate's degree, you must *also* have a minimum of 3 years and 4,500 hours experience. **Of the hours required for any level of education, 50% must be acquired post degree. So, in the case of the associate's degree, at least 2,250 hours (or half the required number of hours) must be acquired after you received your degree.** Post degree simply means you received the experience <u>after</u> you received the degree. If you climbed up the food chain and secured a bachelor's degree, the experience drops to 2 years, with a minimum of 3,000 hours, at least 1,500 hours amassed after your degree. And, if you hold a master's degree or higher, just 1 year, including a minimum 1,500 hours of experience—at least 750 earned after the degree—will put you in the driver's seat to take the exam. If you snared your degree outside the US, you'd need to have your degree/degrees evaluated. See the *HS-BCP Application Packet* for specifics.

Question: Again, I'm a neophyte and have never applied for a certificate before. I'm assuming when you talk about experience, I can't count the years I flipped fries at a fast food burger joint or the six months I put silicone spray on car tires at the wash where I worked.

Answer: You guessed right; making tires shine and performing fast food preparation really would not qualify as bona fide human services work. As you shall see in just a moment, your experience will need to be approved.

Question: Like you, I teach in a human services program. Which category do I fit into?

Answer: As a Human Services Educator, or HSE, you'd indeed fall into a degree category just like a student and, therefore, you'll have to produce a sealed transcript, as well. Nevertheless, in lieu of the experience requirement, a letter on the institution's academic stationery from your department chair, provost, or academic vice president confirming your involvement with the human services education program is required.

Question: How will I submit documentation of my experience to the CCE to prove I have the qualifications to take the exam?

Answer: An excellent question indeed, and now you'll see why fast food work or employment at the local car wash isn't going to help! Included in your HS-BCP Application Packet, you'll find a page titled "HS-BCP Verification of Experience Form." This form is used to verify your work as a human services practitioner. The majority of the form is completed by an individual known as the "experience verifier." An experience verifier could be your supervisor, a human resources official, or someone with similar authority at your work site. It's legal to photocopy the form if you've worked in more than one workplace setting (since you'll need one from each place you worked). When the form is completed, you (the applicant) and your experience verifier will both sign the form. Information on the form should be printed in blue ink.

Question: I graduated from an accredited CSHSE program. Do I get any bonus points or special perks?

Answer: The answer is an unequivocal yes, although I haven't seen the term "bonus points" in the clinical literature as yet. If you graduated from a CSHSE or former CSHSE accredited program, you will <u>not</u> need to complete a Verification of Experience Form. If you're unsure if you fall into this category, go to www.cshse.org/accredited.html to see the list of current and previously accredited institutions. Ditto for HSEs working in colleges or universities, who are also exempt from filling out this form whether they attended a CSHSE school or not.

Question: So, if I graduated from a CSHSE accredited program, all I need to do is pass the exam and submit a final official transcript verifying the degree?

Answer: Yes, and follow the HS-BCP *Code of Ethics*.

Question: So I'll have the HS-BCP forever?

Answer: Like virtually every other professional credential, you'll be required to take continuing education (CE) courses, often called continuing education units or CEUs. Recertification requirements state you'll need 60 clock hours of continuing education and a minimum of 6 hours must be related to ethics every 5 years. Official documentation of the hours is required, and you'll receive a log to track your education. There's also a $35 yearly fee for the credential. Human services educators can use teaching as part of this requirement. All readers should go to www.cce-global.org/hsbcp/maintain for additional details.

Question: I attended a college that didn't have CSHSE accreditation, but did have CSHSE member status. Will that be beneficial?

Answer: Here again, yes, it will. You'll need to pass the exam, submit an official transcript with the degree, and show you've met all coursework requirements. You could take the exam prior to graduation and use field experiences that occurred prior to, during, and after graduation.

Question: Alright, say I'm still enrolled in a CSHSE member school or CSHSE accredited program; when can I take the exam?

Answer: If you're enrolled (and in good standing) and you have 15 semester hours or 22 quarter hours or less until graduation, or if graduation was within 6 months of the date the application was submitted to CCE, you'd be good to go for the test.

Question: I have a degree in sociology rather than human services. Will this be a problem?

Answer: A problem? Well, let me be diplomatic and just say it could be a tad more complicated! If you have a degree in the fields of human services, social work, counseling, marriage and family therapy, psychology, or criminal justice, you're just fine and can skip my answer here. If you *don't*, keep reading, my friend.

If you don't have a degree in the aforementioned areas, you'll need a minimum of 15 semester hours (or 22.5 quarter hours) of coursework in one or more content areas. There are 11 content areas: 1. Interviewing and Intervention Skills, 2. Group Work, 3. Case Management, 4. Human Development, 5. Ethics in the Helping Professions, 6. Social and Cultural Issues, 7. Social Problems, 8. Assessment/Treatment Planning, 9. Intervention Models/Theories, 10. Human Behavior, and 11. Social Welfare/Public Policy. Moreover, at least two semester hours (or three quarter hours) must fall into area number 5, related to ethics. Two more semester hours (or again, three quarter hours) will need to fall into area number 1, interviewing and intervention, and finally, two semester hours (or three quarter hours) must be completed for number 3, the case management content area.

Question: I still have additional questions. Is there a way I can contact the CCE directly?

Answer: Absolutely! General information appears on their website at www.cce-global. org. You could also e-mail them at cce@cce-global.org. Their telephone number is 336-482-2856 and their fax number is 336-482-2852. Finally, you can contact them via snail mail at 3 Terrace Way, Greensboro, NC 27403-3660, USA.

Question: Say I complete my application packet and send everything in. How long will it be before I know if I'll be allowed to take the HS-BCPE?

Answer: It generally takes about six weeks.

Question: Where is the exam actually administered?

Answer: There are approximately 175 centers in the US. You can schedule an exam by going to www.goAMP.com and clicking "Candidates," or by calling 888-519-9901. The exam is never administered on major holidays. And, oh yes, a word to the wise. Be on time. If you arrive more than 15 minutes late, you won't be admitted. If you need additional information on exam scheduling, you can contact Applied Measurement Professionals (AMP), 18000 W. 105th St. Olathe, KS 66061-7543 or call them at 913-895-4600. You could also fax them at 913-895-4650.

Question: What if Mother Nature hits us with 12 inches of blinding snow and lots of power outages on the day I'm scheduled to take the exam?

Answer: Gee, aren't you positive! Go to the Applied Measurement Professionals, Inc. (AMP) website at www.goAMP.com to see if the assessment center is closed and then get out and help your neighbors with snow removal!

Question: Is it a pencil-and-paper exam or will I take the test on a computer?

Answer: The exam is a computer-based test. Nevertheless, typing or keyboarding skills are not necessary.

Question: Is it free to take the exam?

Answer: Surely, you jest! I mean, wow, you're new to credentialing, aren't you? Virtually all exams for licensing and certification charge a fee. I hesitate to put the current fee in this book since things change, but here goes. At the current time, the fee is $195 US dollars. If your educational institution is a CSHSE member and coursework requirements are satisfied within the program, you receive a 15% discount and will pay $165 US dollars. If your school is CSHSE accredited, then you'll receive a 30% discount and will pay $136 US dollars. You'll also be charged an annual maintenance fee of $35 US dollars. HSEs pay the $195 fee.

Question: I'm deaf and in a wheelchair. Can AMP accommodate hearing-impaired candidates?

Answer: Yes, the centers are equipped with telecommunication devices for the deaf (TDD). Any examinee in a wheelchair should let AMP know this prior to the exam. If you have a disability, you'll need to let the CCE know at least 45 calendar days before the exam. There's actually a form titled "Candidates with Disabilities" in your application packet. There's no additional charge for the special arrangements. You'll need a diagnosis and documentation of your disability and the documentation can't be more than five years old. You'll receive a written statement back from CCE regarding your situation. If you need special accommodations, you're required to call AMP at 888-519-9901 to schedule your test. Online scheduling won't be available in this instance.

Question: English is really my second language and thus I'll need a longer testing time. Is this a problem?

Answer: The aforementioned form includes a request for "Candidates for Whom English Is a Second Language." ESL applicants will be charged an additional fee for extended testing time.

Question: Can you give me the history of this exam on the head of a pin?

Answer: Sure. A norming version of this exam was first administered in July 2010, and the final administration was in October 2010. Over 1,900 human services workers applied during this grandfathering period. The first non-norming or pass/fail version was administered in February 2011.

Question: What can I expect when I finally come face-to-face with the exam?

Answer: The exam consists of 10 case vignettes. Vignettes are short stories or discussions regarding a client's issues or a client's family situation. So, you'll read the vignette and then answer 10 multiple choice questions on each one. The answer format is always the same. You'll choose a, b, c, or d as an answer choice and **you'll have three hours to complete the exam**.

Question: Hold on. That comes to 100 questions. Isn't that a huge number of questions?

Answer: Not really. In our field, some certification exams have double that number.

Question: How long are the vignettes?

Answer: No exact length is specified; nevertheless, some might be a tad longer than students and practitioners might expect. For example, the sample vignette in the *Human Services-Board Certified Practitioner Exam Candidate Handbook* consists of nine short paragraphs. According to my recollection from when I took the exam, that might be one of the longer ones.

Question: It's obvious that the better part of this book uses a question-and-answer format. I'm fairly certain that if your questions were nine paragraphs long, I'd be too confused to learn the material. What are your thoughts on this issue?

Answer: As I hinted at earlier: I agree 100%. Very long questions are not conducive to learning. Most of my questions will be considerably shorter than those on the actual exam, although I'll let you tackle a few longer ones just to get the hang of the exam. But just to give you a taste for the actual exam, I also have a brief section of the book where top textbook authors in the field were kind enough to create some vignettes that likely parallel the ones you could see on an actual exam.

Question: Please be honest with me, Dr. Rosenthal. Couldn't I personally look up all the information in this book without purchasing and reading this text?

Answer: Sure, but it would most likely take you hundreds of hours, you'd need to consult stack after stack of books, and you'd most likely develop massive eye strain from endless searches on the Internet. Finally, you'd use a sizable chunk of change to buy gasoline for those numerous visits to see your former professors. It could conceivably take you years to accomplish this task. Glance at a few of my questions and answers, and you'll see what I mean.

Question: Wow, I just checked and you do have a ton of questions and answers in this guide. Do you absolutely, positively guarantee that you'll cover every single question that will appear on the real exam?

Answer: I absolutely, positively guarantee you that I *won't cover* every question on the test. First, let me be frank and tell you that nobody (except the test authors) knows precisely what's on the exam. Anybody who tells you otherwise is just trying to gain access to your wallet, purse, piggy bank, credit card, or PayPal account! In fact, if you're taking the exam and you spy a question that *is* identical to one of mine, I'd say it's your lucky day and the moment the exam ends, I'd run—don't walk—to purchase a lottery ticket!

Question: So, let me make sure I'm clear. If your questions won't be exactly like those on the exam, is it at least safe to say that most of them will be very similar?

Answer: In a few cases, yes; in many or most instances, no. First, my questions are tutorial; they teach you the material. They also build on each other, so the answer to the current question is based on what you learned in an earlier question in this book. In addition, my questions impart key information or explain the material in a different manner, while the real questions on the exam will not. Or, to put it as simply as possible, my questions are teaching you at the same time I'm asking you to wrestle with an answer. Just as a quick example, I might say: In human services, we use three averages—the mean, the median, and the mode—to summarize assessment data related to the client. The mean is the most useful. Which answer—a, b, c, or d—doesn't describe the mode? On the real exam, it would be highly unusual for the authors to volunteer something helpful regarding the mean.

Question: Hold on. I'm still not ready to move on. You haven't convinced me yet. Instead of using short questions and answers, have you ever thought of writing a book composed of questions that you feel might be virtually identical to the ones on the real exam? In fact, the book could merely consist of a ton—I mean lots and lots—of practice exams with long vignettes precisely like the exam we'll actually be taking.

Answer: For sure I've thought about it, possibly more than anybody who'll ever read this text! In fact, this difference is precisely what's separated my works from those of others. In the counseling field, where I've worked extensively, many authors and companies have tried it. Some of those folks' study guides are now out of print. Here's the problem: I might create 10,000 questions and, even if you have a super-human computer memory and really could memorize all those answers, what happens when you encounter question 10,001 and it's different? Since you only memorized the answers and didn't understand the principles, you'd still most likely miss the question. Also, once again, using very long vignettes/case histories wouldn't be conducive to teaching you the material. Humans learn best in small chunks. But to repeat: I do have a section in this text where top human services practitioners let you wrestle with a few vignettes that should be very similar to the actual exam.

Question: Hmm. I guess I'm starting to see your point. Have you ever tested your theory on human services students just to ensure your position is accurate?

Answer: Oh yes! For many years, I've taken my own human services students and given them the exact exam or quiz I administered to my previous class. Now stay with me here: This is very important. I don't mean I gave them a study guide; I mean I gave them the <u>exact test</u>. Next, they took the real or current exam, which was a parallel version of the same exam. By a parallel version, I mean an exam that covers the same material, but has different questions. Last year's practice test seemingly didn't provide any grade enhancement whatsoever when compared to students who didn't get the old exam. *You must understand material and use critical thinking skills. Trust me when I say, just attempting to use rote memory to recall every possible question they might ask you isn't the royal road to an impressive exam score. A headache or severe anxiety, maybe!*

Question: I don't always agree with your answers in this book. Do you absolutely, positively agree with all your own answers?

Answer: First, you really do have an issue with this absolutely, positively thing, don't you? Anyway, to answer your question—and this will no doubt be the most unusual statement in the entire book—no, I do not! I'd agree with the answer I give 99.9% of the time, but there will be an occasional exception.

I'll give you the answer that I firmly believe is most likely to be accepted by experts and textbooks in the field. You might not agree with it, and I might not agree with it, but that's irrelevant for the purposes of the exam.

As I've said earlier, most folks love my exam prep materials. Nevertheless, once in a while, I'll receive an email from somebody who says something like, "I didn't agree with what you said about such and such." Truth be told, I personally might not agree 100% with what I said either! I do know, however, that this particular theory or explanation is espoused by the major theorists and textbooks in the field and that's why it appears in my book. The same goes for verbiage or terminology I use in this text. Sometimes, my readers question my use of jargon, verbiage, or terminology, and here again, it might not be what I'd choose to say, but since the experts and the scholarly works rely on it (translation: the way you'll most likely see it on an exam), that's what I'm using. Onward!

Question: I notice you have a lot of questions on some topics and just one or two on others. I'm assuming this means there will be more questions on these topics on the actual exam. Am I correct?

Answer: Nope, certainly not in every case!

Question: Stop. That doesn't make sense! Please tell me more.

Answer: Why should I have 50 questions and answers in this book that everybody knows? As stated earlier, I've been teaching human services for many years. During that time, I've discovered a number of topics many students seem to struggle with or have a tough time grasping the material. Sometimes, they just need alternative explanations or lots of repetition. Finally, there are areas where the textbooks and many of the classes I've seen just don't seem to cover issues that might show up on the exam. I'm going to put some extra firepower on these subjects. Does that make sense?

Question: In my opinion, every field has a dirty little secret. Please be honest enough to share the dirty little secret related to exam preparation.

Answer: Geez, you're using the term "dirty little secret," and readers are worried about *my* use of terminology? Okay, if there's one thing that folks don't know (and certainly don't want to hear), it's simply that you'll most likely study a wealth of material that won't be on the exam! Sorry, but that's the truth, the whole truth, and nothing but the truth. In fact, it might be accurate to say that **most of the material you study won't be on the exam!** Okay, the secret's out. I actually said it. In our field, this is often true for certification exams, licensing exams, oral and written board exams, and comps, or university comprehensive exams. You have to study a lot of extra material because you don't know exactly what's on the version of the exam you'll be taking. But think about it for a moment. This phenomenon occurs in other fields. When you took your written test to secure your driver's license, wasn't there some material you memorized that didn't make its way onto the exam? Yes? That's what I thought!

In fact, let's take this a step further. I'd say about one out of every two or three people will say something like, "Darn, I studied a boatload of material about behavior modification (or it could be child development, or supervision, or adult abuse, or agency program review, or anything else) and there wasn't a single question on the exam related to that topic."

Congratulations, I tell them, your experience of the exam was totally normal.

Question: I want more information on the actual examination. Just exactly what does the exam cover?

Answer: According to the CCE, the exam will assess your knowledge from four key areas: 1. Assessment, treatment planning and outcome evaluation; 2. Theoretical orientation/interventions; 3. Case management, professional practice and ethics; and 4. Administration, program development/evaluation and supervision.

Question: Will each of the four areas have the same number of questions?

Answer: Apparently not. When I took the exam, the assessment, treatment planning and outcome evaluation section had 25 questions; the theoretical orientation/interventions questions numbered 22; there were 37 questions related to case management, professional practice and ethics; and, finally, administration, program development/evaluation and supervision checked in as the lowest area with just 16 questions. Add $25 + 22 + 37 + 16$ and, presto, you get 100 as the best possible score.

Question: How is the exam graded?

Answer: You'll receive a listing by mail for the maximum score you posted for each area, as well as your total score (i.e., how many questions you answered correctly in each of the four exam areas). As an example, say there were 25 questions related to assessment, treatment planning and outcome evaluation, and you answered 18 correctly. The sheet will show you this, and it will also delineate your total or overall score for the entire exam, say, 75 out of 100 questions answered correctly. **Your total raw score determines whether you passed or failed. The raw score for the current version needed to pass is 66. The CCE reports they actually only grade 90 of the 100 questions; the other 10 questions are only there for field testing to see if they might be suitable for future exams. You won't know which questions are graded and which are not**

graded, so do your best on every question! Also, the CCE didn't guarantee me that 66 would always be a passing score, nor did they guarantee me that the number of questions in each area would remain static on future versions of the exam. Nevertheless, this gives you an idea of the basic structure of the exam, as well as what might be required. Assuming you passed, your HS-BCP certificate will be mailed to your home address in six weeks. If you didn't pass, you can take the exam again, but you'll need to wait at least three months after your last exam date. As it stands now, you could take the exam three times during the three-year period that your exam application remains open with the CCE.

Question: Do I ever need to mark more than one answer?

Answer: No.

Question: Should I ever leave an answer blank?

Answer: Yes, when the moon turns into cream cheese! There's no penalty for guessing. If a sane person doesn't know the answer, he or she should guess. Let's think about this logically for a moment. Assume you don't have a clue what constitutes the correct answer. Statistically speaking, if you guess, you still have a 25% chance of getting the answer correct.

Question: Okay, let's look at the worst case scenario. Say I flunk the exam. Now what?

Answer: First, try going in with a positive attitude! But, to answer your question, you're allowed to take the exam a maximum of three times. Nevertheless, you must wait at least three months between exams.

Question: Help, I'm scared stiff. I hate exams and have a terrible case of test anxiety. Any suggestions?

Answer: Really? Let's just say you and everybody else reading this sentence have that problem. Okay, I'm being a bit sarcastic, and perhaps exaggerating just a little, but test terror is extremely common. The good news is that strategies to abate this difficulty work extremely well. Think about it for a moment. What would you recommend for a client experiencing test anxiety? Most likely, counseling. In addition to traditional counseling, helpers use techniques such as relaxation training, systematic desensitization, creative visualization, guided imagery, hypnosis, and biofeedback. The good news is that some community colleges, colleges, and universities offer free counseling services to current or past students, so you won't need to break into your piggy bank. If your counseling or psychology center cannot assist you, ask them for an appropriate referral.

There are a lot of good audio relaxation programs on the market, although I'm partial to the *Test Anxiety Prevention* audio CD I created (gee, there's a surprise). No, seriously, it's excellent. The CD is part lecture and part guided imagery, just like if you actually came for help at my office. It's been successfully used by thousands of counselors nationwide. Now, although my audio program is targeted at counselors, it will undoubtedly work wonders for human services exams. Call 1-800-634-7064 to get your hands on a copy.

Question: Let's say I go to counseling and use your audio CD and still have a little anxiety, then what should I do?

Answer: Nothing! According to a notion called the Yerkes-Dodson Law, a tinge of anxiety might actually boost your exam score!

Question: Since you actually took the exam, what was your personal feeling about the difficulty of the test?

Answer: Well, quite frankly, I don't know if I'm the best person to ask since, as a Human Services Educator, I eat, sleep, live, and breathe this stuff all day long. Nevertheless, if pushed for an answer, I'd have to say it wasn't the most difficult exam I ever took, but on the flip side, it clearly wasn't slam dunk easy. Many of the questions were extremely challenging. My final answer: A study guide or exam prep book would have been nice!

Question: Now, of course, I'd never cheat but . . .

Answer: Well, needless to say, *you* would never cheat, but let's just say someone else who's reading this was going to play the game this way. I could only describe their behavior as dumb, dumb, dumb, and, well, you know what I'm going to say. First, if you were caught, you'd be disqualified from ever receiving your HS-BCP credential. If there's any misconduct, your scores will not be reported, nor will your money be refunded.

But wait, I want to deal with this issue just a little bit more in-depth to show you how incredibly stupid dishonest behavior can truly be. Let's say that you get to question 52 and you just don't have a clue what the answer is. You decide to go get a drink of water and your eyes kind of, sort of, accidentally glance over at the guy's computer screen next to yours and notice that he marked choice d for the answer to question 52. You go back to your computer terminal and, well, let's just say you click d as the best choice. There's only one problem with your logic. While your question is asking about something related to child abuse, the guy next to you (unbeknownst to you) is taking the exam to become a real estate appraiser and is wrestling with a question about a home heating and cooling system! Hello, is anybody in there? Answer: not so much!

Question: I was always taught to be prepared. I'll be armed with extra pens, pencils, erasers, and a calculator. Wouldn't you agree this is a good idea?

Answer: Strongly disagree: a very bad idea! My advice: Just walk in with your wallet and keys. If you have a coat or other items, the folks at the testing site will place the items in a room outside of the testing room. The folks at the site may ask you to pull your pockets out to verify that you've totally emptied the contents.

No notes; documents, such as books or articles; or electronic devices, such as a calculator, PDA, or cell phone are permitted. The only things you should bring to the actual testing site are two forms of identification. Now listen closely: At least **one of the IDs** will need to sport a photograph. Just for the record, both of the IDs with your name should be current, so if you're 29 years of age, that old driver's license acquired the same day as your sweet 16 birthday party won't get you in the door. At least one of the IDs must be a driver's license, passport, military ID, or state identification card with your picture. **The second form of ID** will need to have your current name and your signature. Most folks rely on a social security card, student ID, an ID card from your place of employment, or a credit card.

Finally, pencils and a single sheet of scratch paper will be given to you when you enter the testing room and the scratch paper must be returned to the supervisor when you're finished with the exam. Keep in mind that audio and video surveillance devices monitor the testing site for security reasons at all times.

Question: Wait a moment. You just said current name. I just went through a divorce and my last name has changed. What do you want me to do, bring a copy of my divorce decree to the testing center?

Answer: Yep!

Question: You're kidding, right?

Answer: No, ma'am, I assure you I'm absolutely serious. Somebody who was just married and experienced a name change should bring their marriage license. In some cases, a court order might be necessary.

Question: I'll be bringing a bottle of green organic tea and a health food bar to keep energy levels high. Do you see this as a good idea or not such a good idea?

Answer: This one definitely falls into the "not such a good idea" category. Drinking, eating, or smoking is against the Assessment Center's rules.

Question: I always feel better when my boyfriend is around to give me moral support. I know he would most likely not be allowed in the testing room, but don't you think they would allow him to sit in the reception room?

Answer: Ditch the boyfriend, at least for the brief period of time you're in the exam! No friends, relatives, or guests are allowed in the testing room or the reception area.

Question: Do you believe in very long exam preparation study sessions, or do you feel shorter ones are more effective?

Answer: I'm totally convinced that short sessions are much more valuable than long ones and, indeed, psychological research backs me up on this. Also, I'm not a fan of last minute cramming. A concise review the day of the exam, or the evening before the exam, works well. Also, make sure you scope out precisely where the exam site is located well in advance of the actual date and get a good night's sleep the night before.

Question: I want to take the exam six months from today. Is that reasonable?

Answer: Hats off to you! I'd like to see everybody take at least six months or more so they don't have to cram or feel rushed. In terms of preparation time, longer is better than shorter. I've known a lot of folks who took comprehensive exams and only prepared for a few weeks, but that certainly isn't ideal.

Question: What exactly is the Exam Booster section of this book?

Answer: I think you're really going to like my answer, so thanks for asking! Imagine that you gathered all your notes from your college human services classes. Next, you added all the most important points in your textbooks and key information from other major works used in the field, and looked up any material you didn't understand. Finally, you constructed a sentence, or just a few sentences, to explain nearly *all* the major topics on the head of a pin. Could you have accomplished this yourself? Sure, but a lot of you value having a life. Also, I've been performing and teaching human services work since many of you (or your big brothers and sisters) were in diapers, so I might have a slight advantage in terms of compiling the material!

First, read all the questions and answers. Next, **the Exam Boosters section of this text is a must read**. It makes one heck of a good review that you can read several nights prior to the exam or even on the day of the exam.

Question: Any final words of wisdom?

Answer: Yes, if this book helps save you even one point on the exam and you pass, then it was worth my time writing it and your time wading through the numerous questions and answers. Imagine holding a business card that has the letters HS-BCP after your name. And what about that cool framed certificate on your office wall? Wow. It feels pretty darn good, doesn't it?

Chapter 2

Assessment, Treatment Planning, and Outcome Evaluation

1. The founder of human services was

    a. Sigmund Freud.
    b. Anna Freud.
    c. Harold McPheeters.
    d. Jane Addams.

(c) Just think of this question as a warm up pitch or perhaps a practice swing since the real exam *won't* have questions of this ilk, but you didn't think I was going to let you read this book without knowing who created our discipline? On the actual exam, you'll be given a description of the client's current situation and often past history (called a vignette) and then you'll be expected to answer 10 questions. The vignettes can be rather lengthy, say seven or eight short paragraphs. However, I'll often use shorter questions to teach you key exam material. It's easier to remember material in this way. So who's the father or mother of human services? How many of you chose Sigmund Freud? Come on, fess up. Well, just because you've heard a name or term thousands of times doesn't mean it's the correct answer! Sigmund was the father of psychoanalysis—also called analysis—which is a personality theory and a type of treatment. Your exam might well call his model psychodynamic, but more on that later. Anna Freud, his daughter, helped popularize child analysis and ego defense mechanisms. Jane Addams has been dubbed as the mother of social work and was the first American woman to snare the Nobel Peace Prize. She's often praised for starting Hull House in Chicago, Illinois—the first settlement house in the US. So your answer—drum roll, please—is psychiatrist Dr. Harold L. McPheeters. Yes, a psychiatrist, and not a social worker, created human services. Dr. McPheeters has a delightful sense of humor and when I spoke to him once, he told me that he isn't considered the most important *founding father* in the family since one of his relatives was the father of the yellow school bus! I guess you're never a hero in your own court, or in your own family.

2. During your first visit, you will conduct a psychosocial history. This can also be called an intake interview or an initial assessment. A psychosocial history includes information about the past, as well as the present, that could have an impact on the client and your approach to treatment. You discover that Victoria is a 29-year-old married female who has two children, Lauren, 3, and Lydia, 9. She is crying throughout the entire interview and you can never recall seeing a client this depressed. You should

    a. ask her forthrightly if she is suicidal.
    b. not ask her if she is suicidal since this could put the idea in her head.
    c. use a person-centered interview approach to conduct the psychosocial assessment.
    d. use a Rogerian client-centered interview approach.

(a) When conducting a comprehensive psychosocial history, sometimes known as an initial assessment or evaluation, you'll examine the client's perception of the problem; her emotions and behavior; her goals, support systems, social functioning, family interaction, medical issues, environmental and cultural factors, stressors, coping strategies, and motivation; and resources to help her. Basically, you'll take a cook's tour of the client's circumstances. The aforementioned information will be amassed from interviews and observations with the client and family members. The client's chart (also called a record) can be helpful since it could contain feedback from other agencies and might even have psychological or diagnostic tests.

Okay, first things first: The fact that Victoria has two children ages 3 and 9 has about as much to do with this question as the price of mustard at the local grocery store! Comprehensive exams often provide you with lots of irrelevant information that has nothing to do with answering the question, so as they say (whoever they are), just suck it up and get use to it. **If you believe there's any—and I do mean any—chance a client is suicidal, you should forthrightly ask the client if he or she is contemplating hurting or harming themselves.** For years, books and courses taught us that asking the client if he or she was suicidal could put the idea in the client's head. Today, we know that's wrong—I mean dead wrong. I, for one, would like to get my money back from all those courses that gave me the misinformation. As for choices c and d, they mean the same thing. Person-centered, client-centered, Rogerian, nondirective, and self-theory all refer to a style of helping where the helper is <u>not likely</u> to ask a lot of direct questions, such as "Are you suicidal?" Although the nondirective style is excellent, most experts feel it's *not* the best choice in a suicidal crisis. **Exam booster: If a client has multiple problems but has thoughts or feelings related to hurting himself/herself or others, the suicidal/homicidal urges should always be addressed first!**

3. Victoria, mentioned in the last question, says "yes" when you ask her if she has thought about killing herself. Your next step would be to

    a. spend the next 15 minutes of the interview showing her accurate empathy.
    b. spend the next 15 minutes of the interview showing her sympathy.
    c. ask her if she has a plan to commit suicide.
    d. open your resource guide and give her the name of a reputable psychiatrist since psychiatrists prescribe psychotropic medications.

(c) The worst thing you can do is to say something like, "Why would a mother like you with two great children want to kill yourself?" The next crisis intervention step is always the same: inquire about the suicide plan. Some experts refer to this step as *conducting a lethality assessment* (i.e., how likely is it that the client will try to harm herself). The more specific the plan, the greater the likelihood that the client will make an attempt. We'll take a look at choices a, b, and d, all incorrect I might add, in future questions. **Also, keep in mind that many of the terms I mention in these questions are discussed in the Exam Boosters section of this book. Translation: The Exam Boosters chapter is a must read!**

4. Victoria mentions that she has a plan, but the lethality level seems low and her plan indicates that she will not try to hurt herself for another 6 weeks. Your **best immediate** *plan of action would be to*

    a. refer her to a competent clinical psychologist.
    b. refer her to a competent licensed counselor.

    c.   refer her to a competent licensed clinical social worker.

    d.   have her sign a no-suicide agreement and create a safety plan.

(d) Now for those of you who are new to this comprehensive exam business, let me give you some information you may not want to hear! These exams typically feature a host of questions with answer choices that are technically *all correct* like my question above. Horrors! These are what we call best-answer questions. Although none of my answer stems would be totally wrong, read the question carefully. You'll note that it says *immediate plan of action*. Thus, the best answer would be d: to have the client sign a no-suicide agreement or contract. Some state ethical bodies require this step. There's a recent conflict in the field whether the worker should call it a contract (the traditional name) since it's not a legal document. Hence, you might want to tell your client that it's a no-suicide agreement rather than a no-suicide contract. How do you like that for political correctness? I doubt whether your exam will split hairs on this one, but if they offer you both choices, I'd go for the no-suicide agreement terminology.

5.   When you write up Victoria's no-suicide agreement, you should

    a.   give her the number of the suicide prevention hotline.

    b.   not give her the number of the suicide prevention hotline since it is unethical to burden them with your client's problems.

    c.   use a written rather than an oral agreement if you are seeing her face-to-face.

    d.   choices a and c.

(d) Always give clients the number of the suicide prevention helpline/hotline in your area. A lot of clients who say they would "never call that stupid suicide prevention center" often do call! And just for the record, although any contract or agreement is better than none, written agreements are generally considered superior to oral ones. Nevertheless, life is never perfect and if this were a situation where you were contacting the client only by phone, then an oral agreement would certainly be better than nothing. Give the client a copy of the agreement whenever possible. When a client is even moderately suicidal, it's best if another individual can stay with that particular client.

6.   After you have Victoria sign a no-suicide agreement, you

    a.   should refer her to a licensed clinical social worker for psychotherapy.

    b.   should refer her to a licensed therapist and a psychiatrist.

    c.   should refer her to a licensed marriage and family counselor so the children can be helped, as well.

    d.   could perform any of the choices above. They are all ethical and appropriate.

(b) In our field, we often assume our client's problems are caused *only* by psychological, social, and environmental facts, but often we're wrong. What if Victoria's suicidal feelings and depression are being spawned by a brain tumor, a thyroid condition, or a blood sugar problem? Well, it's possible, isn't it? Thus, for the well-being of the client and to cover yourself ethically, a referral should always be made to a psychiatrist (a medical doctor, an MD or DO) or, at the very least, a general medical doctor. Here again, all the choices are decent, but clearly b is the overall winner!

7.   Patrick is a 33-year-old construction worker who came to the states from the Democratic Republic of the Congo, Africa. His presenting complaint, voiced during the initial assessment, is that his current employer is discriminating against him. In human

services, the presenting complaint is also known as the presenting problem, and is the reason the client gives you for wanting treatment. Your supervisor tells you that you should help Patrick improve his cognitive skills to better cope with this situation. Your best course of action would be to use

    a.   an alloplastic approach.
    b.   an emic approach.
    c.   an etic approach.
    d.   an autoplastic approach.

(d) No, *all* my answer stems won't end in the word "approach," though it's beginning to look that way, isn't it? Now let me teach you some big words and admit that most human services workers armed with a master's degree might be challenged by this question, so don't lose any sleep over it if you didn't have a clue how to answer. All the answers describe decisions the human services worker must make when working with **diversity. The terms alloplastic and autoplastic are very common in multicultural circles. Autoplastic means the client must change himself or herself.** A great memory device is simply to remember that when you drive an <u>auto</u>mobile, you're in control. You make the changes by hitting the brake, the accelerator, or turning the steering wheel. The same goes for <u>auto</u>hypnosis, often called self-hypnosis. You're hypnotizing yourself. Thus, in an autoplastic approach, Patrick would need to change his own thinking and coping skills. The thing about these memory devices is that they only need to make sense to you—nobody else. Moreover, often the ones that are the silliest or humorous work best. Try to create your own when mine just don't seem to work for you. And as for emic and etic, hold your horses. We'll get around to it, I promise.

8.   The next day, you are assigned to a new supervisor who disagrees with your previous one. She vehemently believes that Patrick's assessment (from the previous question) indicates that he should not try to change himself, but rather attempt to change the policies of the company who is discriminating against him. You would use

    a.   an alloplastic approach.
    b.   an emic approach.
    c.   an etic approach.
    d.   an autoplastic approach.

(a) Come on now, you didn't really think I was going to leave you hanging with an explanation of autoplastic (also called autoplasty) and not tell you what alloplastic (also known as alloplasty) means? **Alloplastic is roughly the opposite of autoplastic. Instead of trying to change the client, the client should work to change the environment, such as an unfair policy.** We'll visit the emic and etic distinctions down the road in later questions.

9.   Lee is a new client from the People's Republic of China. Your supervisor teaches multicultural courses at the local community college. She insists you rely on an etic approach. In essence, this means

    a.   you will assess and treat Lee just like you would a client of any race, creed, color, or background.
    b.   you would study as much as you can about Chinese culture and use that knowledge to assess and treat the client.
    c.   you will only focus on present moment issues.
    d.   you will rely on an ahistoric form of treatment regardless of what the assessment reveals.

(a) **When using the etic approach to multicultural intervention, you treat all clients in the same manner.** Here's a memory device that's worked for many of my students. When we speak of etiquette, we're referring to treating all people in a kind manner. Take a look at choice c. Strategies that focus on the present moment, or the here-and-now, are called **ahistoric** approaches.

10. You are working as a food stamp worker for the state. One of your clients calls and tells you that she has physically abused her 5-year-old son and he has marks on his face. You should

   a. tell no one, as human services practitioners practice relative confidentiality.
   b. tell no one because human services practitioners adhere to the policy of absolute confidentiality.
   c. report it to the child abuse hotline since NOHS ethics stipulate you should do so and it is a law in every state in the US.
   d. report it to the child abuse hotline since NOHS ethics stipulate you should do so.

(c) To answer this question, you need to know about the CAPTA (say what?) and the difference between **absolute and relative confidentiality.** Absolute implies that no matter what's occurred, the human services worker will not break confidentiality. Relative, on the other hand, dictates that there are times (such as when a client is going to hurt herself or somebody else) that you <u>will</u> be expected to break confidentiality. To be sure, the National Organization of Human Services (NOHS) Ethical Guidelines would champion the idea of making a child abuse report, so choice d isn't a bad answer. Nevertheless, since 1974, child abuse reporting has been the law—Public Law 93-247 or the Child Abuse Prevention and Treatment Act (CAPTA), later updated in 2003 to the Keeping Children and Families Safe Act. The bottom line: Choice c is the best answer of the bunch.

11. You want to start a new charitable human services agency for clients who need shoes and clothes. You should contact

   a. the state committee for licensed social workers.
   b. an attorney who has a good understanding of the IRS 501 (c) (3) code.
   c. the state committee for licensed professional counselors.
   d. an attorney who sports JD, MSW after her name.

(b) If you chose choice b, give yourself a gold star! Believe it or not, it's the IRS—yep, the good old Internal Revenue Service—that sets the standards for non-for-profit (possibly called not-for-profit or nonprofit on your exam) charitable agencies. Agencies/organizations that meet the code can receive tax-deductible contributions and tax-exempt status. Before you decide to start your agency, I suggest you check your piggy bank. Why? The answer is easy. The IRS is going to hit you with a filing fee for the 501 (c) (3) application. This will set you back either $400 or $850, depending on the projected income of your agency. More repetition on this later, just in case it's your first time hearing about it.

12. You are working as a case manager at a human services agency. Last year, you received your Associate of Applied Science (AAS) degree in human services. Your first client of the day is Sally, a 37-year-old mother of three children. Her youngest son, Andy, who is in the third grade, needs help with his anxiety. You should

   a. refer him to a child psychologist you do not know personally who is listed in your resource and referral list for your agency.

b. refer him to a child psychologist who is on your board of directors and has an excellent reputation. She is listed in your resource and referral list for your agency.

c. refuse to make the referral since you only have a two year degree and this would clearly be unethical.

d. All of the above could be correct. More information is necessary to answer the question.

(a) Once again, the fact that Sally is 37 and the fact she's your first client of the morning is about as relevant as knowing what Sally read off the back of her cereal box that morning. Forget it. A lot of neophytes in our field will mark choice b as the correct answer, but surprise, the correct choice is a. Board members should not make a profit from their work on the board. Thus, even if this board member is the best child psychologist in the world, you should opt for choice a. Reality check: A psychologist on your board of directors should not be listed and you should speak with your supervisor about having the board member removed from the referral bank. And just for the record, choice c is so inappropriate, it's off the charts! Human services workers can, do, and should make referrals on a regular basis.

13. You have secured a job with the children's division as a child abuse treatment worker. Child abuse and neglect workers are often called protective service workers. After your home visit to Mr. Clifford's house, you complete your initial assessment. You are convinced the kids should be removed, as the house is not fit for the children to live in. You should

a. write the family court and ask that the children be removed.

b. refer the client to a licensed social worker, since human services workers cannot ethically write the court and ask that the children be removed.

c. write the civil court and ask that the children be removed.

d. Choices a and c are both correct.

(a) Hint: Don't read things into the question that are not there! A lot of human services practitioners will read this question and leap to the conclusion that the children are in imminent danger and the police should be called. Well, with all due respect, I see two problems with that logic. First, the question *doesn't say that*, and second, you're not given the option to call the cops as an answer choice. Sorry folks, but the truth, the whole truth, and nothing but the truth, is that on exams, you can only play with the cards you're dealt; namely, the answer choices the test provides! Family courts rule on decisions related to the family and children, including custody. A human services worker (with the blessing of his or her supervisors) can write the court for action at any time—no license necessary. A home visit to a client's house where the children were removed previously might reveal the opposite of the situation delineated in this question: Although the children are currently in placement, the parent is now ready to take the children back and the worker could write the court asking for this action. Civil courts (see choice c) deal with cases where an individual or company feels they have been financially or physically hurt by another individual or company, such as a credit card company dispute or compensation related to an auto accident.

14. Melissa is a college graduate who is currently out of work and has never been satisfied with any job. Melissa would like career counseling and you tend to agree this would be beneficial. The best referral would be

a. a board certified psychiatrist.

b. a licensed clinical social worker (LCSW).

    c.   a masters level sociologist.
    d.   a licensed professional counselor (LPC).

(d) In general, a professional counselor would have more training in vocational and career counseling than the others listed, just as a psychiatrist (always a medical doctor) mentioned in choice a would have the most training in medication management.

15. Terry is caring for her grown daughter. After you complete an initial assessment on the family, you firmly believe that Terry's grown daughter is suffering from bipolar disorder which was once called manic depression. In this situation, the best referral for her treatment would be

    a.   a psychiatrist.
    b.   her personal physician, because any family doctor or internist can prescribe psychiatric medicine.
    c.   an I/O (also abbreviated I-O) psychologist.
    d.   a social worker with the MSW or PhD degree.

(a) The best answer would be choice a, **a psychiatrist—a medical doctor armed with a DO or MD degree who's an expert in medication management for emotional disorders.** Truth be told, choice b is correct in the sense that *any* family doctor or internist can indeed prescribe these medicinals. However, since a psychiatrist prescribes psychiatric drugs all day, and has specialized training in this area, he or she would be the best option. If you're scratching your head wondering what an I/O psychologist is, the I/O is simply an abbreviation for industrial organizational. HOW TO THINK LIKE THE EXPERTS WHO CREATED THE EXAM: There's a fairly good chance that at least some of you reading this book are sitting there thinking, "I don't agree with Rosenthal's answer. I believe that bipolar disorder could be better treated via a social worker who could do therapy with Terry's daughter or perhaps the condition could be dealt with using an over-the-counter natural remedy." Well, guess what: You may be right! But the trick on comprehensive exams is to *think like the folks who put the test together.* In about 99 out of 100 cases, you're best off going with the answer that <u>most</u> mainstream textbooks would support, and clearly, that would be choice a. The mental health establishment views bipolar disorder (formerly known as manic depression or manic depressive illness) as a condition that's best treated with prescription medicines. **Exam hint:** Client's symptoms can sometimes be caused by side effects of medications and, thus, a worker would do well to investigate this when assessing a client.

16. Terry's daughter (cited in question 15) could best be treated by

    a.   Rogerian therapy.
    b.   natural colloidal lithium, available at some health food stores and Internet sites without a prescription.
    c.   prescription lithium, often accompanied by an antidepressant medication.
    d.   cognitive behavioral therapy, also known as CBT.

(c) If you missed this question, it's time to slow down and read the answer to question 13 once again. Lithium is a trace mineral, or so-called rare earth, which helps treat and possibly prevent mania (an overly excited mood) seen in clients with bipolar disorder. Unlike most psychiatric medicines, a physician will often require blood tests since very high lithium levels can be dangerous, such as causing kidney damage. Although lithium has been the treatment of choice for years, it's becoming more common to prescribe it along with an antidepressant. CBT (choice d) is a powerful form of talk therapy that's especially valuable for clients with depression; although, it can be used with virtually any problem. In reality, any of these choices *might* be beneficial for the client, however, choice c is the one most textbooks would recommend.

17. Karen's husband teases her and this upsets her greatly. Based on your knowledge of behavior modification and extinction, you explain to Karen that the best way to handle this is to ignore him. You should mention that

  a. this technique is guaranteed to always work.
  b. this technique works in about one out of five cases.
  c. if this doesn't work, you will need to send Karen and her husband to couple's counseling, since counseling is very helpful.
  d. her husband's behavior will generally get worse before it gets better so she needs to keep ignoring him until it gets a lot better or goes away totally.

(d) Yes, in animals and humans, we see a phenomenon known as a **response burst** or **extinction burst,** in which the behavior escalates (translation: gets worse!) before it gets better or goes away. You must explain to the client that if she gives up during the phase where the behavior has escalated, the teasing may remain at a level which is higher than at the beginning of the treatment. P.S. Per choice a, ethically, you should never guarantee that a technique will always work—NEVER! If the technique fails (or you see other difficulties in the marriage), then by all means go with choice c and make a marriage counseling referral.

18. Ted was sexually abused by a Catholic priest when he was 11 years old. His stepson just had his 11th birthday and Ted is feeling tremendous emotional insecurity. He stopped taking his son to church and pulled him out of the Catholic school he was attending. His son was very fond of the school and he had many friends there. He does not want to switch schools. The most likely diagnosis is

  a. Ted is having a psychotic break from reality.
  b. Ted is using mind altering drugs and has not admitted this to you.
  c. Ted's son's birthday has consciously or unconsciously raised unresolved issues related to his own sexual abuse as a child.
  d. Ted has a severe case of pica.

(c) Psychosis, the term in choice a, is used to describe an individual who suffers from hallucinations, delusions, and thought disorder. To put it simply, a psychotic individual is out of touch with reality. Certainly, based on the minimal amount of information given in the question, we have no reason to believe Ted is psychotic. **Pica, featured in choice d, occurs when a client ingests non-nutritive objects, such as pencils or perhaps chalk!** The take away message here is that, **often, a victim of sexual abuse has feelings resurface when a child or stepchild reaches the age when their own sexual abuse occurred.**

19. Your new client tells you that her son is flunking nearly every subject in high school. The client's chart indicates that her son's IQ is 123. Based on this, you would assume that

  a. the client's son is mentally challenged and does not have a high enough IQ to graduate.
  b. the client's son has a rather high IQ and should be able to pass high school unless he has a learning disability.
  c. you cannot trust a single IQ test. Several IQ tests need to be administered.

d.   the client's son's IQ is normal and high school might be very easy or it could be difficult. His motivation is the only issue.

(b) This young man has a rather high IQ since **100 is the average IQ** and the average range is from 85 to 115. Clearly, his lack of intellectual prowess isn't the issue here.

20. You are working with a 72-year-old woman who is having a difficult time taking care of herself. She is adamant that she loves her home and does not want to be placed in a nursing home. Your best course of action would be

a.   to investigate the home health care agency in town to find out about their services.
b.   to investigate the assisted living facility down the street.
c.   either choice a or b.
d.   to place her in a nursing home despite her wishes, since her well-being is the real issue.

(a) Okay, to answer this question, you'll need to know the difference between three key options: a nursing home (also known as a senior care facility), assisted living, and home health care. Often, a nursing home will offer nursing home services *and* assisted living services. A nursing home generally caters to a person who can't be cared for at home. Medical care is a central theme in such facilities and, in many instances, the residents need a lot of attention. In most nursing facilities, a doctor supervises the services. Most clients in an assisted living facility (also called assistive living, residential care, or a personal care community) will have more independence than a person receiving nursing home services. The individual may need help with things like bathing, using the bathroom, or preparing a meal. Hence, if a person needs help with **small things**, the assisted living option is best. Unlike the other two options, home health care providers actually come to the client's residence. Housekeeping, meal preparation, physical therapy, shopping, and even transportation may be provided. **Since home health care is the only option where the client will remain in the home—and all you know from the question is that the client prefers to stay in her home—choice a makes the most sense.**

21. Bret's physician reports that his smoking is threatening his life. You are assigned as his human services worker to use behavior modification to help him quit. Your <u>first</u> step would be

a.   to perform a baseline.
b.   to spend some time talking about the exact reasons he began smoking to look cool as a teenager.
c.   to put him through a series of deep relaxation exercises.
d.   to refer him to a group down the street for clients who wish to quit smoking.

(a) The group down the street might be a good option as an adjunct to your behavior modification, but in behavior modification (aka behavior mod) the first step is always the same: take a baseline. Since you're assigned to do the intervention, choice d would not be the desired answer.

22. The best way to take a baseline is simply to

a.   ask Bret how many cigarettes he smokes in a day.
b.   tell Bret not to smoke under any conditions. Abstinence is necessary for all addiction treatments. It doesn't matter if it is alcoholism, cocaine, or smoking.

    c.   ask Bret to chart the number of cigarettes he smokes every day for a week.

    d.   refer Bret for MMPI or Minnesota Multiphasic Personality Inventory. It is one of the finest personality tests ever created.

(c) A baseline measure is best achieved by charting the incidence of the behavior without treatment or behavior modification for a reasonable period of time; say 5 to 7 days. By the way, the MMPI is a powerful personality test, but it won't give you a baseline measure of Bret's smoking.

23. Mindy lost her mother to cancer a month ago and is experiencing intense grief. She indicates that she really likes and respects you as her caseworker. She asks you to go to the zoo with her because she feels it might really cheer her up. You should

    a.   agree to go to the zoo inasmuch as it could be beneficial for the client.
    b.   tell her there is a good chance the answer will be yes, but you do need to ask your supervisor.
    c.   agree to go with her, but bring a fellow caseworker along, so she could never make sexual or romantic accusations against you that could ruin your career.
    d.   thank her for the offer, but politely turn it down because you know that it could be in violation of human services worker/client boundary issues.

(d) This question spotlights one of *the big issues in human services work*: dual relationships. (On your exam, dual relationships could be called multiple relationships.) An exam without a question on dual relationships? Hey, I don't think so! A dual or multiple relationship occurs when the human services worker has a relationship with the client which goes beyond the professional one. Examples: You're dating the client. The client is your accountant. Your client is a plumber and he is installing a new kitchen sink for you. Your client is your first cousin. You visit your client's home on weekends because she has a swimming pool and your kids love to swim. All of these are examples of violating professional boundaries.

24. An example of a dual relationship would be:

    a.   You meet a client at a permanency planning and review team (PPRT) meeting held at another agency because her three children are in foster care.
    b.   You drive the client to another agency because she needs energy assistance help to get her gas heat turned on in her apartment.
    c.   You drive the client to her counseling session because she cannot afford public transportation.
    d.   You drive the client to the museum of transportation because you both enjoy looking at antique autos and trains and she needs a break from the stress of her family.

(d) And, yes, on the real exam, some questions, like this one, will be a lot easier than others. Experts frown on dual relationships because they get in the way of objectivity. How so? Well, try this on for size. Imagine you're dating a current client (a huge no, no) and she comes in one day and tells you she has a new dating partner and it *isn't you*! Will you still be unbiased in terms of your interventions? Hello, I don't think so! Let's say your client is a painter and she paints your apartment and you don't like the job. Will you be capable of treating her in an unbiased manner? Again, don't bet the farm on it! Finally, choice a introduces PPRT meetings. These meetings are composed of a team of multidisciplinary experts (e.g., a caseworker, child abuse protective treatment worker, therapist, pastoral counselor, and hospital social worker) and they are intended to abate foster care drift. Foster care drift occurs when there's no permanent plan to place the child in a stable environment or return the child to his or her home. Measures such as **PPRT meetings were instituted to eliminate foster care drift, as some children were even lost (not a misprint) in the system! Nobody knew where some of these children were placed.**

25. Armand is worried that his 10-year-old son, Quinn, has attention deficit hyperactivity disorder, also known as ADHD. Armand tells you he "wants Quinn tested." During some of your home visits, you have noted that the child could be displaying some psychotic behavior. You should refer Quinn to _____ for a complete psychological evaluation.

    a. a clinical psychologist
    b. a licensed counselor
    c. a social worker with experience in behavioral problems
    d. an LMFT or LMT

(a) Choice a is the best response since, in general, clinical psychologists have more training in psychological personality testing than any of the other choices. Now remember, you're not going to try to read into the question. Indeed, the licensed counselor *could be trained* to perform the tests, but in most instances, counselors are not as well trained in personality testing as clinical psychologists. Again, ask yourself: What answer would most textbooks provide? As far as choice c goes, most social workers have no training in psychological testing and MSW programs typically have no courses devoted to administering psychological measures. In 1955, Lucky Strike, a top selling cigarette, used the slogan LSMFT, or "Lucky Strike means fine tobacco." It became a very popular ad and slogan. Mental health boards dropped the "s" and came up with LMFT. The meaning it will have on your exam has nothing to do with smoking Luckies, as they were called, though somehow I get the feeling you might have figured that one out on your own! Try licensed marriage and family therapist. Hint, hint: Common abbreviations and acronyms often show up on certification exams.

26. You are a case management supervisor for a non-for-profit agency which is in serious financial trouble. The organization is doing wonderful work, but your executive director, who is the head of the agency, has confided in you that she is unsure "how long she can keep the agency doors open to clients." Your supervisor has asked you to try to raise money. You share the situation with your case manager and tell her to take some positive action to help the financially struggling agency. Her best course of action would be to

    a. eliminate the sliding scale for poor clients as soon as possible.
    b. charge some of the wealthier clients who use your service a fee that exceeds the going rate for services. After all, these clients can certainly afford it.
    c. send a letter asking for a contribution to people in the neighborhood who have never contributed.
    d. send a letter to your donor list asking for a contribution.

(d) With the recent economy and state budget cuts, this scenario has become all too real for a lot of agencies, so let's look at each choice separately. First, a sliding scale (or income sensitive scale) is used to give clients who can't afford the full rate a discount. Hence, just to use a hypothetical example, let's say your agency charges $50 per hour for a given service. Your sliding scale might dictate that if the family's income is below $50,000 a year, they can secure the service for just $25 per hour. The scale might indicate that if the family income is below $15,000 a year, the same service costs just $5.00 per hour. Sliding/ income sensitive scales do vary from agency to agency. Choice b is considered unethical. If a multi-millionaire athlete or movie star struts into your office, you're not permitted to charge $500 for that $50 service. The going rate (i.e., the full fee) is the maximum you can charge. Choice c is wrong because it's harder (and often more expensive) to get people who have never given before to donate than it is to get people who have donated (choice d) to open the wallets once again. A donor list is simply a fancy term for people who have made contributions to your agency in the past.

27. Based on the situation described in the previous question, you, as the supervisor, instruct your case manager to create a letter aimed at securing contributions.

    a.   You would reject the letter because your case manager used a P.S. at the end. You explain that this looks foolish and very unprofessional.

    b.   You would reject the letter because it was extremely short; less than a page to be exact.

    c.   You should praise his use of the P.S. in the letter.

    d.   Choices a and b are correct.

(c) First, keep in mind that medium and large agencies have fundraisers or directors of development who are experts at writing letters like these. They may even hire outside experts to draft the letter. However, at an itsy-bitsy, small struggling agency, the person writing the letter could be YOU! Most of the time, short letters with short paragraphs or even a lot of bullet points work well, and—surprise—the P.S. is a must with research showing it's often one of the most-read portions of the letter. **I've included questions such as this because assessment and evaluation on your exam will generally apply to client situations, but the test will also include questions that focus on the agency itself.**

28. You ask a client a question during an initial interview. She becomes quite angry and says, "Why do you keep asking me these silly questions?" The best way to respond would be to

    a.   use the behavior modification technique of extinction and ignore her so she won't say it again. Just go on to the next question.

    b.   be honest with her and tell her that you don't agree with all the questions the agency requires, but you must ask them.

    c.   respond with, "You have some serious anger issues. Would you like to talk about them?"

    d.   explain to the client the reason why you have asked the question.

(d) I just want to talk about choice a for a moment. When you ignore a behavior, that's indeed a type of behavior modification we call extinction. However, a lot of practitioners don't know that the behavior usually get worse (yikes!) before it gets better. Although I mentioned this previously, the repetition won't hurt you. We call the increased negative behavior an extinction burst or response bursting. So, in extinction, the behavior gets worse before it gets better. The final choice generally works the best.

29. Mrs. Rather has been going through years of treatment and now her physician has explained she is terminally ill. When a patient is going to die, the words "terminally

ill" are often used to describe the situation. The doctor states she will no longer be providing any medical care intended to actually treat Mrs. Rather, but mentions that Mrs. Rather will be in dire need of medication to deal with the pain. The best referral would be

a. a hospice program.
b. a home health care nurse.
c. a hospital critical care unit.
d. a hospital ER, since ER units can handle end of life pain issues.

(a) **By definition, hospice programs deal with terminally ill clients who the physicians are reasonably sure will die.** Hospice care can be provided in the home or at a facility such as a hospital. **Hospice attempts to keep the patient comfortable and as pain free as possible, rather than trying to cure the individual.**

30. During your first visit, your client, who is from a foreign country, expresses a desire to become as US citizen. A person who is in the country but was born in another country might be called a **foreign national** on your exam. The process of becoming a US citizen is known as **naturalization.** Neither you nor your supervisor (who is also the executive director) is very knowledgeable about the process of attaining US citizenship. An executive director—who can also be called a president—is the top employee at an agency. To secure information, it would be best to contact

a. the Department of Justice.
b. the State Department of Social Services.
c. the State Department of Mental Health.
d. the local suicide prevention hotline, because they often have a large resource and referral bank.

(a) Just for the record, the Department of Social Services generally deals with public assistance such as TANF (temporary assistance for needy families), food stamps, Medicare, and child abuse services. The Department of Mental Health, choice b, logically deals with mental health services. Surprisingly, choice d isn't a bad answer. Suicide and crisis help lines often have a terrific data bank chocked full of resources and referrals. **Nevertheless, the good old Department of Justice runs the Immigration and Naturalization service.**

31. You are the type of helper who likes to intervene in a situation and then move on to another situation. You should secure a job as

a. a treatment worker.
b. an intake worker.
c. a program or clinical director.
d. a resource and referral coordinator.

(b) The best fit would be the intake worker. In some organizations, the intake worker completes the psychosocial assessment or initial evaluation and—bam—the client moves on to a different worker for treatment services (assuming the intake worker decides the client's case should remain open). A program or clinical director would typically be supervising intake and treatment workers, or even their supervisors. And, logically, the resource and referral employee is trying to find other services which might be appropriate to help the client.

32. Key mistakes when engaging in crisis intervention include

   a. focusing primarily on the past or spending a lot of time on small talk.
   b. being nondirective.
   c. choices a and b.
   d. none of the above.

(c) Crisis intervention works best when a practitioner is more active directive than he or she would be in a situation that isn't crisis oriented. The focus is centered primarily on the current crisis.

33. Cary's dad has recently been diagnosed with Alzheimer's disease. All of these are signs of Alzheimer's disease *except*

   a. frequent bouts of mania.
   b. memory loss that is negatively impacting the client's life.
   c. difficulty remembering how to drive home.
   d. confusion with dates and the passage of time.

(a) **Alzheimer's disease is not the leading cause, but the most common form of dementia. It's a progressive degenerative condition (i.e., it usually gets worse as time goes on)** that isn't a normal part of aging. Mania (in choice a) is characterized by racing thoughts, overactivity, delusions, and euphoria.

34. Your supervisor recommends you implement bibliotherapy with Cary. This would consist of

   a. Cary and her dad seeing a neurologist together.
   b. Cary and her dad seeing an audiologist.
   c. Cary reading a book you recommend on Alzheimer's disease and how it impacts family members.
   d. having Cary's dad take an IQ test to see if his intellect has been compromised.

(c) **Bibliotherapy consists of reading books and pamphlets that can be therapeutic.**

35. Nelson is disabled and is having trouble finding employment. You explain to Nelson that

   a. the unemployment rate for individuals who are disabled would be the same as for those who are non-disabled.
   b. the unemployment rate for individuals who are disabled would be lower than it is for those who are not disabled. Finding Nelson a job should prove extremely easy.
   c. the unemployment rate is over 90% for persons who are disabled. It is nearly impossible to find work and you should explain this to Nelson in the first session.
   d. the unemployment rate for individuals who are disabled is higher than the rate of unemployment for those who are non-disabled.

(d) According to the Bureau of Labor Statistics, the average unemployment rate for individuals who were non-disabled in 2011 was 8.7%. In that same year, the average unemployment rate for individuals who were disabled was 15%. However, while it would be correct to say that it could be more difficult to help Nelson find a job than it would be for a client who isn't disabled, it certainly isn't impossible.

36. During your initial assessment of Nelson, it is obvious he uses a wheelchair. Which of the following may *not* be difficult for an individual such as Nelson who uses a wheelchair?

    a. Accessing standard computer equipment.
    b. Understanding questions that are being asking during an intake interview or psychosocial assessment.
    c. Navigating novel environments.
    d. Choices a and b describe situations that don't necessarily present a difficult problem.

(d) Choice a (using computer equipment) is typically not an issue. Why? Because it's not uncommon for individuals who use wheelchairs to have fine motors skills that are completely intact. Choice b illuminates the fact that using a wheelchair does *not* mean the client has a mental or intellectual impairment. Choice c could present some issues since a person using a wheelchair somewhere new will nearly always require investigation for access.

37. "Invisible" disabilities include all of the following *except*

    a. an anxiety disorder.
    b. attention-deficit disorder (ADD).
    c. blindness.
    d. post-traumatic stress disorder (PTSD).

(c) An invisible disability is a disability that's hidden or not readily apparent. If a person has an anxiety disorder, ADD, or PTSD, you'd most likely <u>not</u> know this unless you knew the person well or the person told you. Blindness is the correct answer because you can usually tell if a person is blind. **In search of the perfect answer? The exam will not always give you ideal or perfect answer choices! Take this question. I purposely had it written for me by a colleague who runs a program for college students with disabilities. You might protest that choice c isn't correct because there are times when you can't readily spot a person who's blind. Even if that's accurate, you'd still notice the other choices are all diagnoses that you can virtually never identify at first glance, which leaves choice c as the best, though possibly not perfect, answer.**

38. You are conducting an initial evaluation. Which of the following *could* be considered a disability under the ADA?

    a. Depression.
    b. Alcoholism/ or drug addiction.
    c. Color blindness.
    d. A broken leg.

(a) **Currently, substance abuse isn't considered a disability.** Color blindness doesn't substantially limit someone's life and a broken leg (as bad as it is) is temporary. Clinical depression, on the other hand, *could* be so debilitating, depending on the situation, that it's considered a disability by the ADA.

39. The Americans with Disabilities Act (ADA) prohibits discrimination on the basis of disability for which of the following?

    a.   State and local government.
    b.   Commercial facilities.
    c.   Employment.
    d.   All of the above.

(d) Verbiage comes right from the ADA! Very few entities would <u>not</u> be held to the ADA.

40. You just landed your first job in the field. Most experts would agree that

    a.   for an entry level position, you don't really need malpractice liability insurance.
    b.   even though you are securing an entry position, you should secure malpractice liability insurance.
    c.   you might need malpractice liability insurance for a hospital, but not for a hotline.
    d.   you might need malpractice for a hotline, but not for a hospital.

(b) Some places of employment (e.g., hospitals) will not let you get within 50 feet of your first client until you show them your malpractice policy! Are they really that strict? Yep, some places really are. Moreover, don't expect your agency to pick up the tab for your malpractice policy—a few agencies do and just as many, if not more, do not. I remember some years ago when I was the program director of a suicide prevention center and our insurance carrier told us that we were one of the few centers in the country at the time that paid for malpractice for all the phone workers, volunteers, and practicum students.

41. You are seeing Ms. Parsons for the first time. She is 88 years of age. Your supervisor recommends *aging in place*. You should

    a.   take her to visit a traditional senior care facility.
    b.   give her brochures from several senior care facilities.
    c.   discuss services available in which providers could come into her home to help.
    d.   give her brochures from several assisted living facilities.

(c) **The aging in place movement champions strategies that allow the individual to stay in one's own residence or remain in one's own home.**

42. All of the statements regarding the aging in place *village model* are correct *except*

    a.   individuals living in their own homes may receive shopping discounts.
    b.   individuals living in their own homes may have a list of community volunteers ready to assist them.
    c.   Mrs. Parsons (mentioned in the previous question) would need to take a complete psychological test battery consisting of IQ tests and personality inventories to receive services.
    d.   individuals living in their own homes may receive transportation services.

(c) According to the Association for the Advancement of Retired People (AARP), the village notion attempts to support the medical, social, spiritual, and functional needs of older adults who wish to remain in their own residences. This approach is viewed as **an alternative to traditional institutional care.** Community networks often provide the necessary services.

43. Your supervisor wants you to follow the WDEP approach to assess the client's treatment needs. Your supervisor is

    a. a strict Freudian.
    b. a strict behaviorist.
    c. a strict Rogerian.
    d. a reality therapist.

(d) Reality therapy pioneer Robert Wubbolding created a paradigm called WDEP that's very popular right now. (My memory device for the order of the letters is to use the well-known lubricant WD 40 and say, "<u>WD</u> works under <u>E</u>xtreme <u>P</u>ressure." Your challenge is to come up with something that works for you. WDEP might be your grandparents' initials.) Wubbolding asserts that the model helps therapists and clients understand the nature of reality therapy better.

In WDEP, the W stands for **wants**. For example, what does the **want** and how can the human services practitioner help him or her get it? The D addresses what the client is **doing** and if it is taking him or her in the right or wrong **direction**. The E is a place-holder for **evaluation**. This time, the TV therapists might have actually got it right when they say, "How's that working for you?" Finally, the P stands for the **plan** for changing behavior. *The emphasis is on responsible actions here, not what the client will eliminate.*

44. When you do reality therapy created by psychiatrist William Glasser, you do all of these **except**

    a. you accept no excuses when the client does not carry out the plan.
    b. make friends with the client.
    c. focus mainly on the past.
    d. focus primarily on the present.

(c) In reality therapy, when the past is discussed, it's generally focused on your successes and not your failures or traumatic memories.

45. As you approach the client's home for your visit to do your first assessment, you see a dog barking very loudly and jumping into the front glass door as if the animal is trying to get to you. The dog appears angry. The best plan of action would be to

    a. call the police. They deal with this routinely.
    b. call animal control. Keep the number handy for situations like this.
    c. call the humane society. Keep the number handy for situations like this.
    d. hold the door with your hand and ask your client to secure the pet.

(d) My dog acts like this five times a day and the most a guest might incur is some gentle licking, but you never know. Take the safe route.

46. You are seeing Miss Riley for the first time. She was very close to her mother who just passed away the night before. According to the Elisabeth Kübler-Ross model that posits stages of grief, you would expect Miss Riley to

    a. be in denial.
    b. display anger.

    c.   be in a stage of acceptance.
    d.   show several different emotions ranging from laughing to crying.

(a) Dr. Elisabeth Kübler-Ross, a Swiss-born US psychiatrist, came up with her ideas while working with terminally ill people. Denial is the first stage and, according to the theory, this helps the individual survive the loss. The client might remark, "This isn't truly happening."

47. Your new client, Bella, was told she only had a year to live. When you saw her for the last visit, she seemed to be in total denial. Now her mood has changed markedly. According to the five-stage Elisabeth Kübler-Ross model, she would

    a.   show anger.
    b.   show acceptance.
    c.   engage in bargaining such as saying, "God please. I'll never yell at my grandkids again if you let me live."
    d.   be in a deep psychological depression.

(a) The order of the stages is <u>d</u>enial, <u>a</u>nger (the correct answer for this question), <u>b</u>argaining, <u>d</u>epression, and <u>a</u>cceptance; often called the DABDA formula. Some practitioners believe the DABDA formula can be used for looking at the reaction of children going through a divorce, the break-up of a relationship, and persons giving up an addictive behavior. Basically, the model could apply to any situation where there's a major loss involved. Not all of the research supports this model or the sequences of the stages, and some people never make it to the final stage.

48. As you are conducting an assessment on your 23-year-old client, he tells you that he began taking an antidepressant medication because he was moderately depressed. Now, after taking the medicine for a month, he is having serious thoughts of suicide.

    a.   You should tell him that his suicidal feelings have nothing to do with the medication.
    b.   You should explain that all clients have suicidal feelings from time to time and you are glad to hear he is normal.
    c.   You should explain that some research indicates that some antidepressant medications can cause side effects. He should speak with his doctor immediately.
    d.   You should explain to him that he is trying to be very manipulative and although that approach may have worked with this last human services practitioner, it won't work for you.

(c) **Do not tell the client to stop taking his medication!** This isn't a game of let's play doctor. Most, if not all, of my readers are not licensed physicians. The latest research has concluded that some antidepressants can abet suicidal feelings in young adults ages 18 to 24 years and that it can occur as early as the first or second month of usage.

49. Harvey is a 29-year-old gay male. He explains that he has been gay as long as he can remember. He wants you (a heterosexual male practitioner) to "make him straight so he can marry a good woman." You

    a.   should work with him to help him obtain his goal. The client is always right.
    b.   would need a wealth of additional information before you could answer this question.

c. should explain that most ethical bodies and professional organizations do not believe in reparative therapy.

d. should refer him to a female therapist who understands the female mind.

(c) Some practitioners believe that this is one of the most controversial issues of our time. **Reparative therapy (also known as conversion therapy)** attempts to change an individual's sexual orientation. Since **homosexuality isn't considered a mental disorder,** it should not be treated or cured by reparative or conversion therapy, or a client given referrals for such services. **Gay affirmative therapy,** on the other hand, or helping clients to become comfortable with their current or preferred sexual orientation, is generally considered ethical.

50. You are working at a homeless shelter. You completed your assessment on a new client. The client is also working with a career counseling center. The career counseling center would like to see your assessment.

   a. Be polite, but explain to the career counseling center that this would be a violation of confidentiality.

   b. Send them the assessment. They are working with you to help the client.

   c. Send them the assessment, if and only if your client signs a release of information form to them provided by your homeless shelter.

   d. Ask them for a detailed list of reasons why they want the assessment and then discuss it with other workers at your agency in a case conference.

(c) **Before you give out or receive any information in any form, you'll need a signed release of information sheet (also known as a disclosure form at some organizations)** that your agency will provide and your client will sign. You need a separate release for *each source* requesting information. Hence, if the local mental health clinic wanted a copy of your assessment, an additional disclosure form made out to them would have to be signed by your client.

51. You are still working with the same client noted in question 52. While your client was staying at your homeless shelter, she went to the local university psychological center and received a complete psychological evaluation which is now part of *your record.* The career counseling center mentioned in the previous question believes the psychological center report could help them assist this client. You

   a. cannot give them this report.

   b. you can give them the report, but remember that your client's signature on a release of information or disclosure form is necessary.

   c. can discuss the university psychological report, but cannot actually give it to the career counseling center.

   d. should write in your record why the psychological evaluation would be helpful to the career center and then invite a representative from the career center to come read the report in your presence.

(a) Sorry, but if you or your agency didn't collect the information, then you can't give it away, even with the client's signature. Can the career center get their hands on this information? You bet they can! The career counseling center can ask the client to sign a release that goes directly to the university psychological center and if she says yes, then presto, it's a done deal.

52. In terms of the record, the face sheet is

   a. usually at the beginning of the record or in the inside cover.
   b. usually at the end of the record or attached to the back cover.
   c. not a legitimate part of the record.
   d. is part of the termination summary.

(a) The **face sheet,** most likely near the beginning of the chart, provides the client's name, address, contact information, gender, names of household members, and other basic information that can be found very easily. It's sometimes dubbed a family face sheet.

53. Lulu is being physically beaten by her husband. In terms of a legal document,

   a. a subpoena duces tecum would be the most valuable.
   b. a subpoena would be the most valuable.
   c. an order of protection would be the most valuable.
   d. all of the above would be extremely helpful and therapeutic.

(c) The **order of protection** is helpful if the client is being threatened or stalked. A **subpoena** orders a recipient to make a court appearance on a given time/date. A subpoena **duces tecum** takes things a step forward and orders that you bring records or documents to court.

54. During your psychosocial assessment, a client mentions that her 2-year-old toddler brings her doll with her everywhere and insists on sleeping with the doll. The most likely explanation is

   a. the child is autistic and cannot relate to people.
   b. the child is mentally challenged and is not stimulated by normal stimuli.
   c. the child is having abnormal separation anxiety from her mother (your client).
   d. the doll is merely a transitional object and this behavior is totally normal.

(d) Just for the record, a toddler is usually defined as a child between the ages of one and three. **Transitional object** is a common term used in child development and psychology. It refers to objects that curb anxiety and comfort the child. Some parents merely refer to them as security objects that calm the child down. These objects are predictable and are helpful when a child is physically separated from a parent, as well. I'll never forget my oldest son's stinky old teddy bear, affectionately named Teddy. He went everywhere with us. Anyway, one night he left Teddy at a store we visited that was many miles away from our home. It was late and the establishment was closed for the night. And to answer your question before you ask: Yes, I drove to the store after hours to rescue Teddy.

55. Mrs. Leonard is 96 years of age and has numerous health challenges and needs a doctor. *Ideally,* you should refer her to

   a. a geriatrician.
   b. a psychiatrist, since older adults often experience blue moods and depression.
   c. an internist.
   d. a physician who specializes in family practice.

(a) **A geriatrician is a doctor who specializes in geriatrics and working with older adults.** They generally are family practitioners or internists who receive at least an additional year of specialization related to working with elderly patients. The problem: We just don't have enough geriatricians to meet the need. While it's been said that the fastest growing segment of the population is 65 years of age or older, it's also been noted that the number of geriatricians appears to be decreasing. So if you're thinking of going on to medical school . . .

56. Pick the choice that could cause sterility.

    a.   The use of anabolic steroids for men.
    b.   Untreated Chlamydia.
    c.   Untreated gonorrhea.
    d.   All of the above.

(d) Sexually transmitted diseases may be called STDs or STIs (sexually transmitted infections) on your exam. Chlamydia is now classified as the most common STD. Treatment for these diseases usually consists of a course of antibiotics. Steroids (choice a), as almost everybody knows in this day and age, are used to increase muscle size, strength, and athletic prowess, but can have serious side effects.

57. A client talks to you for nearly 10 minutes. She is speaking so rapidly, you barely uttered a "go on" or "tell me more." At the end of the session, she thanks you and says she feels 100% better and you are a terrific helper. This can be explained by

    a.   catharsis.
    b.   counter transference.
    c.   cognitive behavior therapy, which is very effective.
    d.   solution focused therapy, which is very effective.

(a) **Catharsis conveys the notion that just talking about your problems can make you feel better** about them. Choice b, **counter transference, a common exam term, refers to a situation where the helper (yes, you!) has a psychological problem that's getting in the way of efficacious treatment** (for example, you fall madly in love with the client or, quite the opposite, you thoroughly dislike the client).

58. You are running a group to help clients struggling with anxiety issues. There are seven clients in the group. You would

    a.   generally keep one master chart with write-ups for everybody in the group.
    b.   generally have a chart for each of the seven clients and write something in each individual client's chart after each session.
    c.   only chart on a client if he or she says something significant. It is way too much work to keep a chart on each client in the group.
    d.   only need to write something if a client says she is going to hurt herself or hurt somebody else, or both.

(b) It may sound like a lot of work (and often it *is* a lot of work!) but normally each client has a chart, and when he or she attends a group or an individual one-on-one session with you, you'll record/document the session.

59. The _____ is the most useful average when assessing clients or programs.

    a.   median
    b.   mode

c.   mean
d.   standard error of measurement

(c) A common test question if there ever was one. **The mean is the arithmetic average you learned back in elementary school. You simply add up the sum of the scores and divide by the number of scores.** If you went bowling today and scored 200 the first game (nice!), 100 in the second game, and shot 150 in the final game, you'd have a series of 450. Divide the 450 series by three games and, bingo, your bowling average is computed as 150. **Although the mean is the most useful average, it's impacted by *extreme scores* also called *outliers*.**

60. In your human services class, the scores on the final exam are 21, 21, 46, 89, and 99. The top score in the class was 99 out of a possible 100 points. Find the median.

   a.   It is 89.
   b.   It is 21.
   c.   It is 46.
   d.   It cannot be computed without additional information.

(c) **The *median is the middle score* when you rank order the data from highest to lowest or lowest to highest.** Since 46 has two scores below it, as well as two above it, it would be the median.

61. Your outcome data for your program yielded scores of 21, 21, 46, 89, and 99. When you compute the mode, it would be _____.

   a.   150
   b.   87
   c.   46
   d.   21

(d) Don't complicate this! The **mode is simply the most frequently occurring score or category.** Is it really that simple? Yes, it really is that simple. A distribution is merely a set or collection of scores or numbers. In this example of scores, only one number—21—occurs more than one time, so 21 is said to be the mode.

62. **The mean, median, and mode might be called measures of central tendency on your exam.** Measures of central tendency are different ways of describing the average score in a distribution of numbers. Your exam shows you a complex graph and asks you to find the mode, or modal point. It would be the _____ on the graph.

   a.   highest point
   b.   lowest point
   c.   exact middle
   d.   point you could not see

(a) This is a rather typical comprehensive exam question. **The mode is the highest point on a graph. If it's a bar graph (also called a histogram), it will be the highest category or longest bar.**

63. In a batch of outcome data, the scores were 21, 21, 21, 32, 33, 36, 44, 44, 44, and 96. Since 21 and 44 both occur three times, this would be

    a.   a mistake. The data could not come out like this.
    b.   another example where 21 is the mode.
    c.   a bi-modal distribution.
    d.   a set of numbers where there is no mode because two numbers (21 and 44) both occur more than once.

(c) **By definition, a bi-modal distribution has two modes. If we graph a bi-modal distribution, it will look something like a camel's back because it will have two peaks. The term multi-modal is sometimes used when several modes are evident. All the statistics I'm mentioning could be used for outcome evaluations.**

64. Compute the range for the set of scores listed in the previous question.

    a.   21
    b.   75
    c.   36
    d.   39.2

(b) **To compute the range, you merely take the highest score and subtract the lowest score.** So, 96 minus 21 equals 75.

65. Appropriate methods for evaluating a group include

    a.   securing information on member satisfaction.
    b.   informally asking members after a given session what they liked or did not like about it.
    c.   showing a video account of the group to your supervisor.
    d.   all of the above.

(d) It's also acceptable to ask members what the leader could have done differently.

66. During your psychosocial assessment, Heinz reveals that he hears the voices of Abe Lincoln and George Washington in his head telling him what to do and how to make important decisions. Heinz notes that this does not bother him and he feels this is normal.

    a.   Heinz has an ego alien/ego dystonic condition.
    b.   Heinz has an ego syntonic condition or reaction.
    c.   Heinz has a rather typical ADHD or attention deficit hyperactivity disorder pattern.
    d.   Heinz has pica.

(b) Let's do a quick scan of the answer choices. **Ego alien or ego dystonic condition (choice a) occurs when a client has thoughts, feelings, and behaviors that are unacceptable.** Well, that's certainly not Heinz, so let's eliminate choice a. When thoughts, feelings, behaviors, and impulses don't bother the client, we often say they're ego syntonic, so that's the best answer choice. Pica, choice d, occurs when clients eat non-nutritive substances, such as chalk, clay, sand, or the wood of a pencil. Basically, items that aren't considered sources of food. This usually occurs in young children and could be caused by a lack of nutrients in the diet, such as iron. *If the child has ingested paint, a lead test should be performed since this can have serious damaging effects.*

67. Lance reveals during his initial assessment that he was sexually abused as a young child. The chances are

    a.   the perpetrator was an adult who was a total stranger.
    b.   the perpetrator was a child from the local high school he never met prior to the incident.
    c.   the perpetrator was somebody he knew as a child.
    d.   a and b are the best answers.

(c) **Over 90% of juvenile sexual abuse victims know the perpetrator.**

68. You are working in a hospital setting. The client's record indicates she is cheeking the medicine. This means

    a.   she is chewing the pills before swallowing and this is not appropriate for some medicines.
    b.   she is taking twice as many pills as she should to get a buzz off the medicine.
    c.   she refuses to open her mouth to swallow the pill.
    d.   she places the medicine in her cheek and never swallows it.

(d) The patient or client could be cheeking to stockpile pills to get high at a later date, or she might even be selling them. Other individuals just wait until the staff leave the room and then spit them out and simply throw them away.

69. An IEP team would most likely work with

    a.   prisoners in a half-way house.
    b.   abused women in a shelter.
    c.   a drug treatment center.
    d.   a school system that has children with disabilities.

(d) **IEP stands for Individualized Education Plan. The Individuals with Disabilities Educa**tion Act, or IDEA, stipulates that students with disabilities should be evaluated and given a unique educational plan. The team is usually multidisciplinary and could consist of teachers, speech therapists, human services practitioners, parents, psychotherapists, nurses, and school counselors, to name a few.

70. You are thinking of creating a task force to determine whether your community should build a homeless shelter. You give out 250 surveys to the members of the community and local human services personnel to see if they feel a homeless shelter might be useful. You receive 125 back by your required due date. Your return rate

    a.   is 50%.
    b.   is 100%.
    c.   cannot be calculated without a lot more data.
    d.   is a desirable 5%.

(a) The **return rate is the percentage of surveys you received completed after you distributed or sent out all the surveys. Since 125 is half of 250, your return rate is 50%. It's possible your exam could call the return rate a response rate.** *Key hint: I don't expect your particular exam to have any difficult statistical or mathematical problems. In fact, there's a small chance you won't need to compute anything. A knowledge of basic arithmetic and the human services principle should be enough to get you through with flying colors.*

71. A client says, "I am feeling very anxious and depressed now that my daughter turned 14." The best example of an interpretation would be

  a. "You were sexually abused at age 14, and hated your father; therefore, the fact that your daughter has turned 14 is intensifying your own anxiety and depression."
  b. "Tell me more."
  c. "I hear you saying you are nervous and down in the dumps."
  d. "That's very interesting. Please go on."

(a) **An interpretation occurs when you help a client see the true or real meaning of a behavior that's not obvious. Interpretations often link a client's current situation with the past. Interpretations are popular with psychoanalytic or so-called psychodynamic helpers.**

72. The client says, "I feel like the whole world is coming down on me. I lost my job, my kids are in trouble, and now my husband has left me." An example of paraphrasing would be

  a. "Go on please."
  b. "Tell me more."
  c. "You are getting hit with problems from your career, your children, and your marriage, and it just seems like too much to cope with at one time."
  d. "Maybe this goes back to that thing with your childhood where you always felt your mom never gave you the attention you needed."

(c) There are a lot of different ways you could respond to this client using the technique of paraphrasing. Mine is just one example. **Paraphrasing takes place when you (yes, you, the helper) state in your own words what the client has said.** This lets the client know you're listening and it helps him understand his feelings better. This technique is very popular with nondirective, client-centered, or person-centered Rogerian helpers. Choice d would be another example of an interpretation.

73. A client begins crying when she prepares to speak about her mother's death. Reflection (a technique where the helper restates or paraphrases the client's feelings) can be used even when the client has not said a single word. An example would be if the helper said,

  a. "Losing a loved one is very painful."
  b. "Please continue."
  c. "I lost my mother three years ago."
  d. "Why not explain to me precisely why you are crying right now."

(a) Here, just like the question says, the helper was able to reflect although the client hasn't said a single word. Words and phrases like "please continue," "go on," "umhm," "I see," "yes, I understand," and even a head nod, are known as **minimal encouragers.** You'll note I used quite a few of them as the *incorrect* answers on previous questions. **Minimal encouragers, just as the term implies, encourage the client to continue speaking and sharing information.** A word to the wise. If the helper doesn't rely on minimal encouragers enough, the client might feel she's being ignored. On the other side of the spectrum, if the helper interjects minimal encouragers at the speed of light, the client might feel his helper is being impatient. Choice c is an example of personal disclosure. Like minimal encouragers, personal disclosure shouldn't be overused. When a client says, "All my last worker did was talk about her own problems," you know the previous helper disclosed way too much, way too often, or both!

74. The best example of a tentative suggestion would be

   a. "Look dude, let's get serious. You have a gambling problem. Now do something about it."
   b. "I hear you saying that your gambling addiction is causing you a lot of problems."
    c. "I wonder how your life would be different if you sought treatment for your gambling addiction and began attending the gamblers anonymous group."
   d. "I gambled a lot years ago, but then I decided I needed inpatient treatment."

(c) **In a tentative suggestion, we buffer the suggestion or an interpretation so the client is more likely to accept it.** Or, as my students say to me, "You mean I should sugar coat it, Dr. Rosenthal." Well, that might not be a dictionary definition, but I believe my students understand the basic idea!

75. Mrs. Busch tells you during the interview that her son's room always smells like gasoline, glue, paint, or cleaning fluid. She found soaked rags under his bed with a strong chemical odor. He has watery eyes and his nose runs, though her pediatrician can find no medical reasons for these symptoms. Her son is too young to work on cars and she has never seen him work on small engines, such as lawnmowers. His behavior seems strange and he seems like he is "high."

   a. Her son is drinking vodka or addicted to video games.
   b. The most likely scenario is her son is smoking marijuana, often called pot, dope, weed, or a joint.
   c. Her son is definitely in a gang.
   d. Her son is probably using inhalants. This can also be described as huffing, dusting, or sniffing.

(d) Huffing fumes can even cause **Sudden Sniffing Death Syndrome,** in which the person can actually die (generally from cardiac arrest), even if this is the first time the substance is used. Air conditioning products, aerosol gas food sources, cements, and computer keyboard dust cleaners can easily be abused. A can of whipped cream, hair spray, or no-stick frying pan spray could be emptied into a bag or empty cola can and inhaled. Recently, some bath salts not intended for human consumption have been on the chopping block. It's been determined that, in the case of females, a pregnant mother who's huffing can do damage to her fetus.

76. You want to evaluate a client after treatment.

   a. Use a pre test and post test.
   b. Use a baseline chart and continue to chart until the treatment ends, and perform a second baseline.
   c. Both choices a and b are good ways to evaluate the client's progress, or lack of it.
   d. All you need is a valid post test.

(c) A lot more on the word baseline mentioned in choice b later. For now, just know that it means you measure the behavior without treatment. **Also, a pre test is simply a test you give prior to helping, teaching, or treating somebody. A post test is given after the process is completed.** So, if you were given a pre test, then went to a human services class and took the same exam as a post test, it would tell how much you learned or didn't learn.

77. A client in your caseload has an official psychiatric diagnosis. That diagnosis came from

    a. the National Organization of Human Services (NOHS) official diagnosis list.
    b. the official diagnosis list for Human Services-Board Certified Practitioners (HS-BCP).
    c. the DSM.
    d. the official diagnosis list published by the American Psychological Association (APA).

(c) **The official diagnostic guide for mental health professionals is the DSM, which stands for Diagnostic and Statistical Manual. It's published by the American Psychiatric Association, also known as the other APA.**

78. Your agency stipulates the exact questions you will ask to evaluate each client. This constitutes

    a. a nondirective or person-centered interview.
    b. a classical unstructured interview.
    c. a classical structured interview.
    d. a psychodynamic interview based on psychoanalytic principles.

(c) **In a structured interview, you ask the same questions for every client. This is great for continuity and research purposes. In an unstructured interview, you create the interview based on what you personally feel is necessary to ask. This means that if you're doing unstructured interviews, the order of the questions and even the questions themselves can change from client to client.**

79. A client who seems to benefit most from insight oriented therapy should be referred to

    a. a person-centered social worker.
    b. a psychologist who performs therapy with a psychoanalytic slant.
    c. a counselor who believes in CBT.
    d. a counselor who believes in solution focused therapy.

(b) **Psychoanalysis emphasizes insight (understanding something about yourself you didn't truly understand before), often based** on incidents which occurred in childhood. When an individual practices classical psychoanalysis and he or she isn't a physician, the analyst is often classified as a **lay analyst. CBT, or cognitive behavioral therapy, attempts to change thinking patterns. Person-centered therapy lets the client guide the topic of the therapy and champions the power of the client/helper relationship. Solution focused therapists try to change the client in a minimal number of sessions without promoting insight. Or, to put it a different way, you don't need to know why you're behaving in a certain way in order to change.**

80. You refer a client to an Alcoholics Anonymous (AA) group, also called a 12-step program. AA seems to work best with clients who are motivated to recover. AA teaches all these principles *except*

    a. alcoholism is a disease.
    b. alcoholism is a disease that, without treatment, will kill you.
    c. total abstinence on a day-to-day basis is advocated since alcoholism cannot be cured, but it can be controlled via social support and spiritual changes.
    d. an alcoholic can control his or her drinking using self-control, and no support.

(d) AA promotes the idea that support groups and sponsors are highly beneficial.

81. _____ is/are an example of collateral contact. To interact with a collateral contact, you will need the client to sign a release of information form. Some agencies call this a signed consent document or form.

    a. Contacting the client's family physician and her physical therapist for information
    b. Asking your client to show you a copy of her psychological test report
    c. Asking the client about his or her childhood
    d. None of the statements above

(a) **Collateral contacts can literally be defined as any person, agency, or organization that could share beneficial information or provide services for the client. Interaction with collateral contacts should be documented in the client's record; and remember that since you're getting the information from another source, it may or may not be accurate.**

82. _____ is an example of a leading question.

    a. "How may I help you today?"
    b. "Are you currently attending the community college?"
    c. "How are you feeling about your brother's decision to try inpatient treatment?"
    d. "Am I correct that you hated your father for turning his back on you and your family?"

(d) Leading questions can often alter the client's response, especially if you're working with young children.

83. _____ is an example of a statement or question which could abet False Memory Syndrome (FMS).

    a. "Look at your life. The evidence is clear; you must have been sexually abused as a child,"
    b. "You just said you were physically abused by your mother at the age of 9. Can you tell me about your feelings toward your mom at the time?"
    c. "I hear what you are saying. What do you think is the trigger for your bouts of severe depression?"
    d. "Would you like a referral for counseling?"

(a) **False memory syndrome occurs when you put an idea in a client's mind that might not be true! Avoid statements that could abet FMS like the plague. They are poor treatment/diagnosis and could result in an ethical violation.**

84. A good psychosocial history or initial assessment/evaluation of the client should include

    a. a discussion of the presenting problem, the client's symptoms, and who will be involved in the treatment.
    b. the client's current life situation (married, divorced, attending school, housing, job status, public assistance status, etc.).
    c. the history of the client's background, as well as the history of the presenting problem.
    d. all of the above.

(d) Of course, you also want to know the client's goals. What does he or she wish to achieve? **The presenting problem—a very common term in human services—is what brings the client to treatment** (e.g., she wants to get off public assistance, he wants to stop drinking).

85. The client remarks, "I am no longer bothered by the fact that my boyfriend and I broke up." _____ is a good example of confrontation.

   a. "You claim the breakup with your boyfriend is not having an impact on you, yet you are tearful each time we talk about it,"
   b. "Tell me some specifics about the breakup with your boyfriend,"
   c. "Was your boyfriend attending school or did he have a job?"
   d. "What was it that was so special about the relationship?"

(a) **Confrontation occurs when a helper points out differences between what a client says and what she does, or the way she thinks. In this case, the difference is revealed by her nonverbal behavior.**

86. The client remarks, "I love my children. They always come first in my life and I would never do a single thing to harm them." _____ is a good example of confrontation.

   a. "That's wonderful. Can you share some examples with me?"
   b. "I hear you. My children have always come first in my own life,"
   c. "I hear you, but just yesterday, child protective services removed your children because you left them alone while you were out using drugs and partying,"
   d. "Go on, this is very helpful to have you talk about this issue,"

(c) In the previous question, the focus was on discrepancies between the client's verbal and nonverbal behavior. In this question, the confrontation focuses on the difference between the client's verbalizations and her behavior.

87. A behavioral contract with a client

   a. is generally not a legal document, but they can be very helpful.
   b. is always a legal document, and they can be very helpful.
   c. can ethically be used only if the client is genuinely suicidal.
   d. could be ethically used with an adult, but never with an adolescent or a child.

(a) Take this simple example and let's use a touch of common sense here: Imagine that a client wanted to stop yelling at his children. You had him sign a contract saying he would lower the number of times he yelled at his children, and bring a chart you jointly created illuminating his behavior to the next session. The contract isn't a legal document (e.g., the state police won't be arresting him if he doesn't do it) and his behavior has nothing to do with having thoughts of killing himself (choice c). Contracts are often used with kids of all ages (choice d) and some agencies require them.

88. Your client was the victim of a robbery at gun point. All of these are common reactions *except*

   a. increased feelings of anxiety and anger.
   b. fear that wasn't present prior to the robbery.
   c. withdrawal, depression, and, in many cases, nightmares.
   d. uncontrollable laughter that never appeared prior to the robbery.

(d) The symptoms mentioned in choices a, b, and c are not just transient (a big word meaning something lasts for a short period of time) but can persist for a very long period (e.g., over a year). Initially, in a situation like this, or perhaps a school shooting, tornado, volcanic eruption, rape, flood, or terrorist attack, crisis intervention would be the intervention of choice.

89. Delirium tremens (DTs) is associated with

    a. eating disorders.
    b. alcoholism.
    c. post traumatic stress disorder (PTSD).
    d. learning disabilities.

(b) **Delirium tremens can occur when a client who has a high consumption of alcohol stops drinking and experiences withdrawal.** If this is going to take place, it will generally happen within about 3 or 4 days after the final drink. Symptoms include tremors, convulsions, paranoia, fear, an agitated state, fever, and hallucinations (seeing/hearing/feeling/tasting something that isn't there). **DTs can be life threatening and immediate medical attention is recommended.**

90. Korsakoff's syndrome can be caused by chronic or long term alcohol use. The cause is

    a. a vitamin B1 deficiency.
    b. a vitamin B3 (niacin) deficiency.
    c. a simple vitamin C deficiency.
    d. lack of sunshine resulting in a vitamin D deficiency.

(a) The syndrome is named after the Russian neurologist Sergei Korsakoff, who first described it in 1887. The primary symptom is amnesia, which is just a fancy term for an inability to remember or recall.

91. Your chart indicates your new client was adopted from a third-world country. She is suffering from Kwashiorkor. This is

    a. a protein deficiency.
    b. a carbohydrate deficiency.
    c. a common calcium deficiency.
    d. a deficiency of omega-3 fatty acids.

(a) **Kwashiorkor is generally present in third-world countries where there's a lack of foods which supply protein.** Some experts feel the problem starts with breast milk that lacks amino acids (the building blocks of protein). This type of malnutrition can stunt growth; induce weakness; alter hair and skin color; and cause liver damage, apathy, and stomach swelling (often called abdominal distension).

92. You are dealing with a juvenile offender and his family. The chances are good

    a. the child is from a loving family and no family intervention is necessary. Parenting has little to do with the child's behavior.
    b. that, surprisingly enough, he is doing quite well in school. Juvenile offenders, formerly called juvenile delinquents, generally like school and have unusually high grades.

c. the family is emotionally cold and the child is doing poorly in school. Family inter-
    vention would be necessary.
d. that, surprisingly enough, the child is most likely not using drugs or alcohol so no
    addiction treatment is necessary.

(c) **A juvenile offender, defined in most states as a youth under the age of 18 who perpe-
trates one or more legal violations, is often a substance abuser from an emotionally cold
family who's doing poorly in school.**

93. According to the **SOAP (subjective, objective, assessment, and plan) case report writ-
    ing format,** when you see the phrase "client reports" in the chart, this would be

    a. objective.
    b. subjective.
    c. an assessment.
    d. a plan.

(b) **Any time a record says "the client reports," "the client shared," "the client indicated,"
or "the client described," it would fall into the subjective category since these statements
are not proven, objective facts. SOAP notes are also popular in medical and health care
settings.**

94. In terms of the SOAP case report writing format, an objective statement could be any
    of these *except*

    a. the client shares, "I believe I did great in the job interview."
    b. "The client did not have on shoes."
    c. "The client's front window was broken and there was glass on the floor."
    d. "The client's toddler was crying throughout the interview."

(a) **An objective statement is something you saw, heard, counted, or measured.** It could
even be smell (e.g., the client's house smelled dirty and musty). Note that the A in SOAP
stands for assessment, such as a DSM diagnosis or the client's progress or lack of it. An
assessment summarizes the human services worker's clinical impressions and ideas about
the situation.

95. In the SOAP method of documentation, the P stands for a description of the plan.
    Examples of this would be

    a. "I will refer the client to the university psychology center for biofeedback."
    b. "I will need to build a better rapport with this client and refer her for medication
        management."
    c. "I will use a VR reinforcement scale to change the client's behavior."
    d. any of the above statements.

(d) **Biofeedback is a behavioral technique where sensitive electronic instruments (including
computers) are used to give the client biological feedback (e.g., hand temperature). Once
an individual has this feedback, he or she can often change seemingly unchangeable behavior, such as blood pressure or muscle tension.** If you don't know what VR reinforcement is,
keep on reading my friend—I promise we'll get there soon enough.

96. An important part of case management is follow-up services. Examples of good practice in this area include

    a. sending an email to the client after treatment ends.
    b. making a phone call to the client after all services have been provided.
    c. sending a letter to the client following the final interaction with him or her.
    d. all of the above actions.

(d) **The follow-up process allows you to check whether the client's changes are still evident. Follow-up also helps the worker evaluate the services that were provided. In addition, it opens the door if additional services with you or another worker might be helpful.**

97. Prognosis

    a. is essentially the same as diagnosis.
    b. means the same thing as recidivism/relapse.
    c. is an educated guess concerning the outcome of the situation (e.g., the client will be employed within 6 months).
    d. is a type of schizophrenia.

(c) **Prognosis is actually an attempt by the human services practitioner to predict the client's future related to the treatment process.**

98. An issue related to proxemics and treatment would be

    a. whether to refer to a psychologist for treatment or a psychiatrist who will likely believe the cause of the mental disorder is biological.
    b. how many sessions are needed.
    c. whether sitting too close to your client is making her uncomfortable.
    d. whether to use a personality test or not.

(c) **Proxemics is the study of how the distance between people (say the helper and the helpee) impacts behavior. Indeed, sitting too close to a client may make him or her feel very cramped and uneasy.** If you keep accidentally kicking the client, back off—you're too darn close!

99. If your supervisor decides to transfer the client to another worker, you will need to

    a. construct a transfer summary.
    b. just hand the case record to the new worker. No special write-up is necessary.
    c. keep it a secret from the client until the transfer is complete to keep anxiety at a low level.
    d. discuss the transfer in detail with the client; however, no formal transfer summary in the record is generally required.

(a) **The summary includes a discussion of what services you've provided thus far, suggestions for additional intervention, and a prognosis.**

100. Catchment area refers to

    a. clients who wish to change.
    b. clients who don't wish to change, but you can still help them.
    c. a place where clients can pick up communicable diseases.
    d. the area where your agency is allowed to provide services.

(d) Let me give you an actual example. If a homeless shelter is only allowed (or funded) to provide services to city clients, and your client lives in the county, the shelter could *not provide services to this client*. Catchment could even be based on postal zip codes. **Eligibility refers to whether the client qualifies to receive the service. The catchment area can be a part of this determination. Income and means tests (looking at assets, equity in an auto, mutual funds, a bank account, or other resources) can also be utilized.**

Chapter 3

Theoretical Orientation/Intervention

101. All of the following statements about psychotherapy are true *except*

 a. it is considered a curative procedure.
 b. it has been called talk therapy.
 c. it can be performed by a human services worker who has completed a two- or four-year human services degree, if he or she has the HS-BCP credential.
 d. it can be performed by a licensed clinical psychologist.

(c) Psychotherapy should be performed by a licensed social worker, counselor, or psychologist. Expect a certain number of exception questions on any comprehensive examination. On the other hand, don't expect the authors of your real exam to be so kind as to italicize the word *exception.*

102. All of the following experts would be qualified to perform psychotherapy on your clients *except*

 a. a licensed professional counselor (LPC).
 b. a licensed clinical social worker (LCSW) with training in psychotherapy.
 c. a licensed PhD clinical psychologist.
 d. a licensed psychiatrist.

(d) Surprised? Well, it's true. Modern psychiatrists are experts in medication management but are generally no longer trained to do psychotherapy.

103. Behavior modification primarily focuses on

 a. the client's behavior.
 b. the client's past, such as her childhood.
 c. your client's cognitions.
 d. an analysis of the client's emotions.

(a) **Behavior modification is also called functional analysis or applied behavior analysis (ABA).** This is really simple because, just as the name implies, **behavior modification focuses on behavior. Human services workers who are *not* licensed to perform psychotherapy are often qualified to implement behavior modification techniques, and that's why I'll be spending a lot of time on the topic in this book.**

104. The most popular technique in behavior modification is

 a. punishment because, contrary to popular belief, it is very effective.
 b. dream analysis because it allows you to understand the client's unconscious mind.

    c.   catharsis.

    d.   positive reinforcement, which is based on B. F. Skinner's operant conditioning.

(d) **The behavior is often called the antecedent and the reinforcement is the consequence.**

105. When conducting behavior mod (also known as behavior modification), you will use the technique of positive reinforcement very often. A reinforcer should

    a.   come immediately after the behavior in order to be effective.

    b.   be delayed for at least 60 seconds in order to be effective.

    c.   not be used in K-12 schools due to strict ethical guidelines.

    d.   only be performed by a licensed social worker (LCSW), licensed professional counselor (LPC), or by a doctoral-level licensed PhD or PsyD clinical psychologist.

(a) Hold on. Let's think about this one. It's 6 a.m. and you want your dog to go outside. She does. Great! Would you throw a treat outside for her at that very moment to reinforce her, or would you wait until you return from work at 5 p.m. that evening? If you think about it, it makes sense **that, within reason, the sooner you give a reinforcer, the better!**

106. Evelyn's 9-year-old daughter, Kelsey, is refusing to do her math homework each night. The best approach to treat this challenge from a behavior modification standpoint would be

    a.   to give Kelsey a piece of her favorite candy and then kindly ask her to complete the problem.

    b.   to ask Evelyn to smile and say to Kelsey, "Kelsey, please complete the problem."

    c.   to have Evelyn complete the problem and then smile at Kelsey and say, "Kelsey, please complete the problem."

    d.   to have Evelyn tell Kelsey she will give her a piece of her favorite candy as soon as she completes the math problem, and then follow through and actually give her a piece of the candy.

(d) **Again, good old behavior modification (aka behavior mod) is concerned with what takes place immediately after the behavior. Per choice a, if you give Kelsey the candy before she completes the problem, she might just never complete it!**

107. Which diagnosis or evaluation would <u>not</u> be suited toward a behavior modification paradigm?

    a.   Johnny is too anxious to give a speech in his high school class.

    b.   Five-year-old Sally refuses to wipe her feet before coming in the house when they are muddy.

    c.   Kelsey says she will not do her math homework.

    d.   Kelsey has weak ego strength.

(d) Here again, you probably have a better chance of winning the lottery than you do of the authors of your exam underlining the word <u>not</u>, but questions of the <u>not</u> variety are very popular on comprehensive exams, and it would be foolhardy to believe your exam would be the exception.

108. Behavior modification relies on operational definitions. All of these statements are operational definitions *except*

    a.   Tom has a co-dependent relationship with his ex-wife.
    b.   Brandon has a bad self-image.
    c.   Michelle wants to get off of TANF and secure a job in fast food.
    d.   choices a and b.

(d) You must be able to measure something or replicate it if it's operationally defined. Ever try to measure a co-dependent relationship or a bad self-image? Can't do it very well? Yeah, that's what I thought!

109. Pete is just 22 years old, but he is having lung problems because he smokes so much. He says he wants to quit (thus, smoking is considered his target behavior), but can't. According to behavior modification theory, your first step would be to

    a.   take a baseline measure of his smoking.
    b.   find pictures online that show the actual damage smoking causes to your lungs and allow Pete to examine them.
    c.   tell him that you really care about him and you will help him find out why he smokes so much, so he can quit.
    d.   use punishment as your initial or first approach.

(a) Behavior modification—as stated earlier in this book—begins by taking baseline data. Baseline data tells us how much or how frequently the behavior is taking place. Therefore, once we apply the intervention, we can see if the behavior mod procedure is helping, causing his smoking to stay the same, or causing it to get worse. That actually makes a lot of sense, doesn't it? It takes the guesswork out of the procedure.

110. The best method to secure baseline data would be

    a.   to have Pete chart the number of cigarettes he smokes every day for the next week.
    b.   to simply ask him approximately how many cigarettes he smokes in an average day.
    c.   to ask Pete to switch his brand of cigarettes for a week and see what transpires.
    d.   to refer Pete to a lay hypnotist for smoking cessation.

(a) Once again, for evaluation purposes, taking a baseline for a few days is more accurate than just tracking a behavior for a single day. In choice d, I've introduced the term *lay,* which, in this case, refers to a person who doesn't have the necessary degrees or specialized training to be performing the procedure or approach in question (in this instance, hypnosis).

111. When we chart a baseline, it is signified by

    a.   X.
    b.   A.
    c.   the abscissa and the ordinate.
    d.   the XY axis model.

(b) **The uppercase letter A is used to signify the baseline in a behavior modification procedure.**

112. In behavior modification, we signify the baseline using A. Treatment is signified by

    a. the letter X.
    b. the letter B.
    c. the letter X or B—more information is clearly necessary to answer this question.
    d. the letter T for treatment.

(b) **The uppercase letter B is used to signify the treatment phase in behavior modification.**

113. Every time 11-year-old Almeda completes a math problem, you give her a piece of her favorite candy. This is

    a. continuous reinforcement, and it is recommended at the beginning of treatment.
    b. continuous reinforcement, and it is never recommended at the beginning of treatment.
    c. a rather typical cognitive therapy strategy, but it works well.
    d. a fine example of intermittent reinforcement.

(a) **Continuous reinforcement—recommended at the beginning of treatment—occurs when you reinforce each desired behavior, such as completing a math problem.**

114. At first, you give Almeda a piece of candy after she completes each math problem. You do this for the first five problems. Then you decide to give her a piece of candy after every other problem. This is

    a. known as cognitive restructuring.
    b. known as thinning.
    c. an old gestalt therapy technique recommended by Fritz Perls.
    d. an old reality therapy technique recommended by psychiatrist William Glasser.

(b) **Thinning occurs when you stop reinforcing each and every desirable behavior. The term is also used to show that you're reinforcing less than you did at first. So, if you gave the client a stick of gum after each math problem and then lowered it to a stick of gum for every two problems completed, you're using thinning.**

115. You give Almeda a piece of candy after each problem. When you reach problem number 27, she says, "Yuck, I hate that candy, I'm sick of it." This is most likely

    a. psychoanalytic resistance.
    b. an unusual situation and virtually never happens when using behavior modification.
    c. an indication that satiation or habituation is an issue.
    d. due to childhood sexual abuse.

(c) **When you give a reinforcer too often, habituation or satiation sets in. When this occurs, the individual is no longer reinforced and might not even want the reinforcer.** A funny little story. A fellow who was taking one of my classes told me he didn't believe this principle was correct. His favorite food was fried chicken, so I asked if his wife would be willing to make fried chicken (or go out and purchase some) for a full 2 weeks. He was going to eat it for every meal. By the seventh day, he was begging his wife to make or buy something else!

116. A schedule of reinforcement tells the worker

    a. quite a bit about the client's personality.
    b. whether the client is a morning or an afternoon person.

    c.   something about the client's IQ or intelligence level.

    d.   when a reinforcer should be given.

(d) Your schedule for school tells you when you should be in a certain class. Along these same lines, **a schedule of reinforcement tells the human services practitioner when to use the reinforcement.**

117. An addiction treatment center for adolescents gives the clients play money that can be turned in for real goods and services, such as a baseball glove or trip to the park. In this case, the fake play money is

    a.   used to create a token economy.

    b.   a secondary reinforcer.

    c.   choices a and b.

    d.   a primary reinforcer.

(c) **In a token economy, a secondary reinforcer (something that represents the real primary reinforcer) is used, such as fake money, plastic chips, or a gold star. When you get enough fake money, gold stars, or tokens, these can be turned in for the reward.**

118. Almeda is given her favorite candy after every two math problems she completes. This is

    a.   an interval schedule.

    b.   a ratio schedule. _— based off of performance_

    c.   a continuous reinforcement schedule.

    d.   choices a and b.

(b) **Ratio schedules are based on performance or work output. After every two problems, you'll receive a piece of candy, or after every three problems, you get a toy, etc. In a ratio schedule, we don't care about time. Maybe she completed the problems in 10 seconds and maybe it took her 10 minutes. It doesn't matter: she still gets the candy.**

119. Almeda is given a piece of her favorite candy after each 5 minutes she works on her math. This is

    a.   an interval schedule.

    b.   a ratio schedule.

    c.   thinning.

    d.   an example of using a secondary reinforcer.

(a) **Interval schedules are based on time. After each 5 minutes, you get a toy or maybe a stick of gum. A super memory device is simply that in everyday conversation when we say the word "interval," it usually means time. In an interval schedule, we don't care about work output—we only care about time. Maybe Almeda did one problem in 5 minutes or perhaps she knocked out 60 problems. The reinforcement procedure remains the same.**

120. Almeda is given a piece of her favorite candy after each 5 minutes she works on her math. This

    a.   is a fixed schedule.

    b.   is a variable schedule.

    c.   could be a variable or a fixed schedule. More information is necessary.

    d.   is not an acceptable form of behavior modification.

(a) **In a fixed schedule, the reinforcement is always given at the same interval—say, 5 minutes. If we were talking about a ratio schedule, then the work output would remain the same; so, we would provide the reinforcement after each two problems are completed.**

121. Almeda is given a piece of her favorite candy after she worked on her math for 5 minutes. Then she gets another piece after she worked on the math problems for just 4 minutes. This is

    a.   a gross misuse of the behavior modification model.
    b.   an example of a variable schedule of reinforcement.
    c.   an example of a fixed schedule of reinforcement.
    d.   an example of paradoxical intention.

(b) **In a variable schedule, you vary when the reinforcement is given. You might give the reinforcement after the client completes three problems, then after she completes five more problems, then after she completes an additional two problems.**

122. You work for a non-for-profit agency. All non-for-profit agencies have a board. Your board has decided that all paid employees will get paid once a month. This is an example

    a.   of ratio reinforcement, which is based on work output or performance.
    b.   of a pay schedule that is not based on reinforcement.
    c.   that is based on behavioral techniques, but it is not based on reinforcement.
    d.   of a pay scale that is based on interval reinforcement.   *-time*

(d) **Since the employees are paid by the time they work (and not the number of clients served), this is an interval scale. Again, remember your memory device! When we say the word interval, we generally mean time.**

123. A fixed scale of reinforcement is designated by

    a.   F.
    b.   V.
    c.   R.
    d.   I.

(a) Is it really that easy? It is! You're learning a lot of great information and I know you're going to do fine on the exam. Onward!

124. **A fixed scale is designated by the letter F. A variable ratio scale is designated by**

    a.   V.
    b.   I.
    c.   R.
    d.   F.

(a) Is this great or what? For a change, something in our field just requires common sense. Is your confidence beginning to soar yet?

125. Lillie gets a piece of her favorite candy after she completes five math problems. Next, the human services practitioner gives her another piece after she completes three

additional problems. Finally, the worker gives her another piece after she completes a dozen more problems. This is an example of

a.   fixed reinforcement.
b.   F reinforcement.
c.   a variable reinforcement scale.
d.   none of the above.

(c) **In a variable scale, the point when the reinforcer is given changes. In a fixed scale, it stays the same.**

126. FI stands for

a.   a fixed interval scale.
b.   a variable ratio scale.
c.   a variable interval scale.
d.   a fixed intention model.

(a) **In the FI, or fixed interval scale, the time interval when you provide the client with the reinforcer remains constant, such as every 5 or 10 minutes.**

127. I is to time as R is to

a.   psychoanalysis.
b.   Medicare.
c.   performance/work output.
d.   all of the above.

(c) **This is an analogy question. An analogy describes two things that are similar in one way, but different in another. Light is to day as dark is to night is an example of an analogy. So I, or interval scales, are based on time and R, or ratio scales, are concerned with performance/work output.**

128. Clint must complete 10 problems before he gets a token. This is obviously

a.   a ratio schedule of reinforcement.
b.   an interval schedule of reinforcement.
c.   More information is needed.
d.   a VI schedule.

(a) **Since this has nothing to do with time and everything to do with work output, it's a ratio scale.**

129. Human services workers

a.   believe FI is the strongest or best schedule of reinforcement.
b.   believe FR is the strongest or best schedule of reinforcement.
c.   believe VR is the strongest or best schedule of reinforcement.
d.   are split on whether the best schedule of reinforcement is FI or FR.

(c) **I have a personal memory device for this one. I use: Vocational Rehabilitation is a great agency and they call themselves VR, so VR must be the greatest schedule of reinforcement. If mine doesn't work for you, come up with your own. Memory devices can be personal thoughts and pictures in your mind that only need to make sense to you!**

130. Human services professionals believe

    a. FI is the weakest schedule of reinforcement.
    b. VR is the weakest schedule of reinforcement.
    c. VI is the weakest schedule of reinforcement.
    d. FR is the weakest schedule of reinforcement.

(a) Weakest in this context means it has the least impact in terms of changing the behavior.

131. Lillie gets paid based on the number of clients she sees. The first week, her supervisor made her see 10 clients. During the second week, her supervisor felt she could do even more and made her see 12 clients to secure her paycheck. This is an example of

    a. VI.
    b. VR. *variable reinforcement*
    c. FR.
    d. FI.

(b) Comprehensive exams are fond of paycheck reinforcement questions, so you'll be armed to the teeth if you come face-to-face with one of them on your exam. Here, the number of clients Lillie needed to see to get her hands on her check changed, so it's a variable reinforcement scale (VR) based on her work output. If she always needed to see 10 clients to get paid, then it would be a FR, or fixed ratio scale or schedule.

132. Rolf ignores his client when she curses. This is an example of

    a. VR.
    b. FI.
    c. FR.
    d. extinction.

(d) Ignoring a behavior is a form of extinction. Extinction is intended to reduce, lower, or totally eliminate a behavior.

133. The best example of an extinction burst would be

    a. Rolf's client (mentioned in question 132) will curse even more at first when Rolf ignores her, but then her tendency to curse will go down.
    b. Rolf's client (mentioned in question 132) will begin cursing less as soon as Rolf ignores her.
    c. none of these, since ignoring a client is against ethical guidelines.
    d. none of these because ignoring a client is against state statutes that supersede ethical guidelines.

(a) When you first begin to ignore or extinguish a behavior, it will go up before it goes down. This is known as a response burst or extinction burst. Choice d, although incorrect, introduces you to the fact that if a law is different than an ethic, the law is the stronger of the two.

134. Time out is a form of

    a. positive reinforcement.
    b. the Premack Principle.

   c.   an FI reinforcement schedule.
   d.   extinction.

(d) **Time out is a form of extinction that reduces an unwanted, inappropriate, or dysfunctional behavior. Extinction is a lack of reinforcement.** News flash: Sending a child to his room where he has a ton of video games, a 60-inch big screen television, his cell phone, and a monster-sized cheese pizza paired with a 64-ounce cup of a sugary energy drink isn't extinction! Heaven? Maybe to him! Reinforcing? Yeah! To make time out effective, the situation in the room or time out area must *not* be reinforcing, such as a room with no windows and nothing in it except possibly a chair.

135. Pick the most accurate statement. Most experts agree that

   a.   positive reinforcement and punishment are equally effective in terms of changing behavior.
   b.   positive reinforcement and punishment are equally effective in terms of changing behavior, but since punishment hurts the client, it should not be used as often.
   c.   positive reinforcement is superior to punishment in terms of changing behavior.
   d.   positive reinforcement and punishment are ideally used together to change behavior in most instances.

(c) **B. F. Skinner, one of the key pioneers in behavior modification, was adamant that reinforcement was superior to punishment.**

136. Negative reinforcement

   a.   lowers behavior.
   b.   does not raise or lower behavior.
   c.   raises behavior.
   d.   is the same thing as time out.

(c) **Say this out loud at least three times because it's so important: All reinforcers, both positive and negative, raise behavior.**

137. Choose the correct statement:

   a.   Punishment lowers behavior. Reinforcement is used to raise or strengthen it.
   b.   Negative punishment is spanking your child lightly and telling him you love him.
   c.   Punishment never works, so don't use it.
   d.   Negative punishment is spanking your child lightly, but not telling him you love him.

(a) **Reinforcement (positive or negative) raises behavior—punishment lowers behavior.** This ought to be easy enough to commit to memory if you think back to your childhood. When your mom, dad, or caretaker said, "If you talk back again, I'll punish you," it certainly didn't mean you were going to be rewarded or reinforced. Well, did it? Choice b is, without a doubt, the most common definition I get from my students when I ask them what positive punishment is. Unfortunately, it's wrong! "You've been watching too many therapists on television," I tell them.

138. Positive and negative punishment

    a.   raise behavior.
    b.   do not impact the rate or frequency of behavior.
    c.   lower behavior.
    d.   are never recommended in the same treatment program for a single client.

(c) **Come on, your vocal cords are warmed up. This time, say, "All punishment—both positive and negative—lowers behavior." Say it again, and again. Okay, you're good to go.**

139. You instruct Max to take his daughter's video game system away if she doesn't stop cursing. Her cursing continued and Max took the video game system away, as you suggested.

    a.   If the cursing stops, negative punishment has taken place.
    b.   If the cursing stops, positive punishment has taken place.
    c.   If the cursing stops, extinction has taken place.
    d.   If the cursing stops, positive reinforcement has taken place.

(a) **A cool memory trick: Think back to your third grade arithmetic lessons. When you saw the positive sign (+), it meant you should add. When you viewed a negative sign (–), it meant you should subtract, or take something away. In this situation, Max has taken something away (negative sign), so it's negative punishment. If a client gives a child a light swat on the butt to keep her from running in the street, that's adding something, so positive punishment has occurred. Just for the record, I worked in child abuse for over 10 years, so I want to share something important. A client can swat their child without it being child abuse. Once you leave marks, then it's the province of the state who might say it** *is* **abuse.**

140. Maranda decided to lightly swat her 4-year-old daughter on her posterior because she crossed the busy street herself. Maranda tells you that the technique was effective and her daughter has not been trying to cross the street. This is

    a.   an act of child abuse and needs to be reported in a timely manner, even though Maranda meant well.
    b.   positive punishment.
    c.   negative punishment.
    d.   cognitive restructuring.

(b) **To repeat: In positive punishment, you add something to the behavior to lower it. See the previous question for more detail.** Cognitive restructuring, featured in choice d, is a fancy way of saying you're teaching the client to think in a more effective manner about his or her life. This is the basis for treatments such as cognitive behavioral therapy (CBT), or rational emotive behavior therapy (REBT), pioneered by psychologist Albert Ellis.

141. **Dr. William Glasser, a psychiatrist, created reality therapy.** When using reality therapy,

    a.   make friends with the client.
    b.   accept no excuses.
    c.   never give up on the client.
    d.   all of the above.

(d) Glasser's model is one of the few that actually suggests you make friends with the client. Keep in mind that he's talking about the way you treat the client during a session, not going to dinner and a movie with them!

142. **Reality therapy was created by William Glasser, a psychiatrist. Rational emotive behavior therapy (REBT) was created by Dr. Albert Ellis, a psychologist.** REBT uses the

    a. VR theory of personality.
    b. eight concrete steps for treatment.
    c. the ABA design.
    d. ABC theory of personality/ABCDE theory of treatment.

(d) **A** is the a̲ctivating event. This could be anything in your life. **B** is the b̲elief system, which, for most folks, is irrational, illogical, and unscientific. **C** is the emotional c̲onsequence. **D** occurs when the therapist d̲isputes B. When B (the belief) is replaced with a rational, logical, scientific thought, then **E**, a new, healthier e̲motional consequence, is the result.

143. REBT, or rational emotive behavior therapy, focuses on

    a. irrational beliefs (also abbreviated as IRBs), and works well for depressed clients and those with anxiety issues.
    b. dream analysis.
    c. radical behaviorism.
    d. insight from childhood.

(a) **Ellis believes that humans have a genetic propensity to think in a crooked, irrational manner that leads to emotional problems. The goal of REBT is to help the client think in a rational manner. In REBT, the therapist is very didactic, meaning he or she functions somewhat like a teacher to instruct the client how to think in a new, healthy fashion.**

144. **Dr. Carl Ransom Rogers, a psychologist, created non-directive therapy. This is a form of humanistic/existential treatment.** It can also be called

    a. Rogerian therapy.
    b. person-centered therapy.
    c. self-theory.
    d. all of the above.

(d) With all those names, you can see why you need a study guide!

145. Carl Rogers popularized the concept of

    a. free association.
    b. dream analysis.
    c. empathy.
    d. the use of psychological testing in the treatment process.

(c) **Empathy—also called accurate empathy—is the ability of the practitioner to understand what it's like to experience the life of the client (feelings, thoughts, behaviors, and even their overall world view). Next, the helper needs to convey this understanding back to the client. This is a very important term in our field, so commit it to memory right now. Some experts feel empathy is the most important component of helping.**

146. Carl Rogers popularized the concept of

    a. genuineness (also called congruence) on the part of the helper.
    b. disputing illogical, unscientific beliefs in therapy.

    c.   unconditional positive regard.

    d.   choices a and c.

(d) Rogers believed that *three components* he called "conditions for change" were necessary for efficacious helping. First, the helper needed to show empathy (see the previous question.) The second condition is genuineness or congruence. Basically, genuineness is the opposite of being a phony. Finally, unconditional positive regard takes place when the practitioner accepts the client exactly as he or she is, regardless of what the person says or does. No conditions are placed on the client that would determine whether the helper would like the client.

147. **Psychoanalysis—which is both a theory of personality and a modality of therapy— was created by Sigmund Freud.** A psychoanalyst would use

    a.   free association.

    b.   dream analysis.

    c.   insight.

    d.   all of the above.

(d) Psychoanalysis is a long form of treatment. It can take three to six sessions a week and can last three to five years, or more. It's considered a historic theory since analysis focuses on the past and the client's childhood. The analytic client (sometimes called an analysand) lies on a couch (just like you see in the movies and cartoons). The analyst tells the analysand to "say whatever comes to mind." This is known as free association. Dream analysis is also important because dreams allow the analyst (a person performing psychoanalysis) to get a glimpse of the client's unconscious mind. When something that was unconscious is brought into the conscious mind, it's known as insight. Psychoanalysts believe insight can be very curative. Behaviorists often disagree with this notion.

148. A client, who is diagnosed as mentally challenged, must learn to write her name in order to fill out a job application for employment. Your supervisor recommends that you use shaping with successive approximations to help your client accomplish this task. She does know how to spell all the letters of the alphabet. Her name is Heidi. You should

    a.   reinforce her for writing the letter H. Next, tell her to write the letters HE and give her a reinforcer when she does this successfully.

    b.   tell her to spell the letters of her name out loud at least 20 times.

    c.   give her instructions to relax her entire body before you begin to teach her how to do this.

    d.   use REBT. It is very successful in situations like this.

(a) Successive approximations, also called shaping or successive approximations with shaping, teaches clients to learn more complex tasks by breaking the big task into small chunks or baby steps, very similar to what I'm doing with the information in this book. I've personally used this technique to train adults who are mentally challenged—and could not write a single letter of the alphabet—to fill out a job application and secure a good job. Oh yes, even I was amazed at the effectiveness of the technique.

149. **Transactional analysis (TA), which was very popular in the 1970s, is still used occasionally today. This approach was created by a psychoanalytically trained psychiatrist, Eric Berne (pronounced like Burn).** TA champions

    a.   Parent, Adult, and Child ego states.
    b.   the PAC, which roughly correspond to Freud's super-ego, ego, and id.
    c.   life scripts (a personal life plan based on childhood decisions which can shape the personality and identity) and games.
    d.   all of the above.

(d) TA took psychoanalytic concepts and made them simple to understand and fun to use. It also took into account transactions between individuals, a dynamic that was not emphasized very much in psychoanalysis. Practitioners of TA often used diagrams to illuminate transactions and communication patterns between individuals.

150. **Narrative therapy, created by Michael White of Australia and David Epston of New Zealand, is a post modern approach.** A practitioner of this method is most likely going to

    a.   use operant conditioning techniques created by B. F. Skinner.
    b.   use behavior therapy techniques based on Ivan Pavlov.
    c.   send the client a letter.
    d.   do none of the above.

(c) **Note, choice a reminds us that B. F. Skinner's behavior modification is often called operant conditioning. Narrative therapy centers on the belief that stories we and others tell about us help create our identity and personality. Stories can create meaning in the client's life. The post modern theory asserts there's no objective truth. Instead, anything which happens to us in life can be interpreted in many different ways. Narrative therapists often send letters to clients between sessions to summarize or give new perspectives on the client's stories.**

151. Which therapy would be the most likely to take six sessions or less?

    a.   Psychoanalysis.
    b.   Person-centered Rogerian therapy by Carl R. Rogers.
    c.   Brief strategic solution-focused therapy based on the work of Gregory Bateson, Jay Haley, and Milton H. Erickson.
    d.   Transactional analysis.

(c) **Brief strategic therapy is famous for asking clients the so-called miracle question.** Basically, it goes something like this: "Say you went to sleep tonight and a miracle took place. You were magically cured of your problem. How would you know this? How would your life change or in what ways would it be different? What would it be like for others who know you?"

152. A client is given antabuse so she will become nauseous if she drinks an alcoholic beverage. The therapist is most likely using

    a.   systematic desensitization.
    b.   reality therapy.
    c.   aversive conditioning.
    d.   Not enough information is given.

(c) **Aversive conditioning takes place when an unpleasant/aversive consequence follows an undesirable behavior.** Antabuse is a drug (disulfiram) that causes a client to get sick if he or she ingests alcohol. Truth be told, I use this technique with my dog Katie almost daily!

Katie is pretty wild (make that really wild) despite having experienced every obedience school, training program, and trainer known to man and woman kind. Therefore, she has a collar that grips her tightly if she pulls or tries to go after another dog on a walk. I wouldn't say it's 100% effective—she's still a wild child—but it certainly seems to help.

153. Lisa has a wonderful performance rating at work but can't muster up the courage to ask her boss for a raise. The best treatment would be

    a. assertiveness training in a group or individual setting.
    b. sensate focus.
    c. brief strategic therapy based on Jay Haley's work from the study of Milton H. Erickson.
    d. William Glasser's reality therapy.

(a) **Assertiveness training is a behavioral procedure used in group and individual treatment to help nonassertive individuals—as well as aggressive—become assertive to better meet their needs. Assertive behavior takes place when a person stands up for his or her rights without violating the rights of others. Modeling and role playing is often used.**

154. You are pleased that your client is now attending a community college program. Unfortunately, she is procrastinating and is not working on a term paper that is due in three weeks. To help her, you assign her a homework assignment using the behavior modification Premack Principle, named after David Premack, who created it.

    a. You would reinforce an LPB (writing a page for her term paper) with an HPB (enjoying her favorite dinner at her favorite restaurant).
    b. You would reinforce an HPB with an LPB.
    c. You would have her write the entire 10-page paper (the LPB) and then reinforce it by having her eat her favorite dinner at her favorite restaurant (the HPB).
    d. You would discuss her self-talk, also known as internal verbalizations.

(a) Homework in human services is rather similar to homework given in college and graduate classes. You're given an assignment to complete between sessions. LPB stands for low probability behavior (wanting to clean your basement, writing a term paper, or enduring a root canal). Basically, the LPB isn't something you'd do or engage in unless you absolutely must. HPB, however, stands for high probability behavior. Let's say I said, "Stop reading this book and go do something you really love to do." Some of you might go shopping. Others might watch television. Still others would surf a favorite social media site, or visit a friend. These are examples of HPB behaviors. To use the Preamack Principle, you reinforce the LPB with the HPB. **Super important reminder: You can't reverse the order of the LPB and HPB. If you engage in the HPB first (for example, buying a new outfit), you won't clean the basement, the LPB. The HPB should come very soon after the LPB.** Using good old-fashioned common sense, choice c can be rejected because writing the entire 10-page paper is just too long. When using this approach, keep the LPB at a very low level.

155. Instead of using the Premack Principle for your client's issue in the previous question, a counselor who believes in Albert Ellis' REBT, or rational emotive behavior therapy, would most likely

    a. discuss her self-talk centering around her irrational beliefs.
    b. focus strictly on the real problem—the client's childhood.

    c.   focus strictly on the real problem—the client's dreams.

    d.   focus strictly on the real problem—the client's life script.

(a) REBT is a type of CBT, or cognitive behavior therapy. Cognitive methods focus on thinking and belief systems. A lot of helpers just say cognitive therapy helps change "stinking thinking."

156. The statement, "The behavior will most likely get temporarily worse before it gets better," most likely applies to

    a.   a worker who is using extinction and notices response bursting or an extinction burst.

    b.   a counselor using REBT, which is a cognitive behavior therapy (CBT).

    c.   a counselor using reality therapy.

    d.   a counselor using a non-directive model.

(a) Just testing you to see if you're still paying attention! In a response burst, the behavior will get worse before it gets better. Another popular form of CBT therapy was created by Aaron T. Beck. He has been called the father of CBT.

157. Meg has been a longtime client of yours. She often spends lots of time during the day thinking negative thoughts about herself. You teach her to use the behavioral technique of thought stopping. This would entail

    a.   trying to get Meg to relax as soon as the thoughts manifest themselves.

    b.   clenching each major muscle group and then relaxing them when the thoughts are present.

    c.   yelling the word stop in her mind as loudly as possible.

    d.   taking three long, slow, deep breaths.

(c) This is a covert technique. Another version might be placing a rubber band on her wrist and snapping it to disrupt the pattern. **Overt techniques are behaviors you can see and hear, like smacking that rubber band. Covert techniques are private, or in the person's mind. We can't actually see them.**

158. Your client has taken a meditation course and still can't relax. Psychiatric medication hasn't worked either. The most logical referral would be

    a.   REBT.

    b.   brief strategic solution/resolution-focused therapy.

    c.   biofeedback.

    d.   psychodynamic psychotherapy.

(c) Biofeedback uses sensitive electronic equipment to monitor relaxation or tension. *The meters and equipment don't do anything to you! They merely tell you what your body is doing.* For example, a person might look at a screen or perhaps listen to a tone. When the tone gets lower, the biofeedback device is indicating the client is relaxing.

159. The client's record indicates that he seems to do best with a therapist who talks a lot and gives homework assignments. The best referral would be

    a.   a strict Freudian analyst.

    b.   a psychodynamic psychotherapist.

    c.   a therapist who practices REBT, since this is an active-directive model.

    d.   a person-centered (nondirective) Rogerian counselor.

(c) REBT and CBT are considered active-directive models because the therapist talks a lot, is active, and often is very directive, telling the client what to do or how to think in a different manner.

160. Rhonda hated her last therapist because he talked too much and gave her too much advice. The best referral could be

    a.   the REBT therapist who uses the principles set forth by Albert Ellis.

    b.   a Rogerian person-centered therapist who uses the principles set forth by Carl R. Rogers.

    c.   a behavior therapist who uses principles set forth by Ivan Pavlov and John B. Watson.

    d.   a behavior modification expert who uses principles set forth by B. F. Skinner.

(b) In most situations, the Rogerian would be best since, typically, he or she would not give a lot of advice and, in most instances, would talk less.

161. A person who is having family problems

    a.   could benefit from family therapy.

    b.   should only participate in individual therapy because change starts with the individual.

    c.   should be placed in group counseling.

    d.   should be in individual therapy for 6 months and then transfer to family therapy.

(a) Family therapy assumes that the entire family system is relevant.

162. You are going to run a psychoeducational group for adult substance abusers in an addiction treatment center. Most experts would agree

    a.   eight members is the perfect size.

    b.   15 members is ideal.

    c.   you can have as many as 25 clients if you have a leader who is very perceptive.

    d.   four members is the number of people that would be best.

(a) If you have a co-leader, the number can be bumped up, but no more than 75% higher. If you're seeing extremely disturbed people or kids, even the figure of eight is generally too high. Unfortunately, in the real world, students often work or serve practicum experiences at agencies where a group in an addiction treatment center might have 30 plus clients. Yipes!

163. You are leading a group composed of poverty-stricken individuals in your caseload. The drop out/termination rate will be

    a.   almost nonexistent. People in lower socioeconomic classes stick to their commitments.

    b.   the same as any other population.

    c.   higher or lower; it depends on the type of group.

    d.   higher than normal.

(d) Some research indicates that prematurely dropping out of a group (also known as early termination) can be related to low socioeconomic status, a below normal IQ score, and lack of motivation. Hint: A poor leader can also have something to do with it!

164. **Behavior modification, based on operant conditioning,** is often performed by human services practitioners. **Behavior therapy, based on classical conditioning,** is only practiced by licensed therapists. In classical conditioning,

   a. a dog sees meat and salivates. A tone is presented before the meat several times. Eventually, the dog salivates to the tone without the presentation of the meat.
   b. a form of punishment is always used.
   c. a dog sees meat and salivates. The meat and a tone are presented together (at exactly the same instant) several times and the dog salivates.
   d. a dog sees meat and salivates. A tone is presented before the meat several times. Eventually, the dog salivates to the meat, but it is much stronger than the original response to the meat.

(a) A tone or a bell is used in this experimental model made famous by **Ivan Pavlov.** Experts often refer to this as **Pavlovian conditioning. Conditioning in this case means learning.**

165. **The meat is an underlined stimulus, or US. It is sometimes written or called a UCS because, once again, it stands for unconditioned stimulus.** The US/UCS causes the dog to salivate or, as my students say, slobber! The response when the dog salivates is called

   a. a CR, or conditioned response.
   b. a UR, or unconditioned response.
   c. a CS, or conditioned stimulus.
   d. choices a and b.

(b) **A US/UCS, or unconditioned stimulus, causes a UR, or unconditioned response. Unconditioned simply means it's unlearned or automatic.** The everyday man or woman's translation: The dog doesn't need an AAS degree in human services or a PhD from Harvard in clinical psychology to respond. And if you think you're any different than Pavlov's dogs, try sticking a lemon (a US or UCS) up to your mouth and nose. What happens? In fact, it might be happening right this very moment by just thinking about it—you're salivating, or is it slobbering? This occurs even if you don't know the technical reasons why it's occurring. The great behaviorist Andrew Salter once quipped that a dog will salivate even if it doesn't know the principles of classical conditioning. So true, and so will you.

166. In Pavlov's famous experiment, the meat is the

   a. CR, or conditioned response.
   b. CS, or conditioned stimulus.
   c. US or UCS, or unconditioned stimulus.
   d. UR, or unconditioned response.

(c) Repetition is wonderful for learning. Repeat after me: In the US, we eat a lot of meat. Okay, I know it sounds silly, but let's say it again a little louder: In the US, we eat a lot of meat. When you see the US or UCS in a Pavlovian experiment, you'll know it's the meat. In fact, I doubt you'll ever forget it.

167. In the Pavlovian experiment, the CS (the tone or ringing of the bell) must

   a.   come before the US, the meat.
   b.   come after the US, the meat.
   c.   occur at exactly the same time as the US, the meat, is displayed.
   d.   be loud enough to scare the dog.

(a) Repeat out loud: C comes before U in the alphabet. Once again: C comes before U in the alphabet. This goes a long way to helping you remember that the CS comes before the US or UCS in the experiment. Nice, right? Memory devices—you've got to love them.

168. A question asks you to state whether the procedure is classical conditioning or oper-ant conditioning.

   a.   If it occurs in nearly every member of a species, it is operant.
   b.   If it occurs in nearly every member of a species, it is classical conditioning.
   c.   If you are using a token economy, then you are using classical conditioning.
   d.   If you are using plastic tokens, then you are using classical conditioning.

(b) Ask yourself this: Would nearly every human salivate if I put a lemon in their mouth? Answer: Yes! Would nearly every dog salivate if I shoved a piece of meat in their face? Answer: Sure! I know my dog does—I've tried it! But would nearly every single kid do her math homework to get baseball tickets? Answer: Not really, because some kids don't like baseball games! **So, if nearly every person responds in the same way, it's classical Pavlovian conditioning and not operant conditioning.** Tokens are used in behavior modification or operant conditioning, rather than the classical conditioning model.

169. You are meeting with Carson and his mother because Carson is staying out almost all night. He is 16 years of age. You create a behavioral contract. Find the *incorrect* statement.

   a.   Have his mother reinforce him for coming in at a reasonable hour as set forth in the contract.
   b.   Have Carson and his mom sign the contract.
   c.   Allow Carson's mom (but not Carson) to have input into the time he must be home, which will be stipulated on the contract.
   d.   Give Carson and his mom a copy of the contract.

(c) **Ideally, all parties should sign a behavioral contract**. Why? Hey, great question! If Carson doesn't sign it, then he will say, "I never signed that stupid contract, so I didn't agree to come home early."

170. Family therapists often rely on circular rather than linear causality. The best example of circular causality would be:

   a.   You line up 100 dominos and push the first domino on the left. The first domino hits the second domino next to it on the right, which hits the third domino, until they all topple over with a single push.
   b.   You give a child his favorite candy after he finishes a math problem and then he does his math more frequently.
   c.   A client ignores her son's behavior and the behavior increases.

d.   A lab rat was given a piece of food every time it pressed a lever. After it pressed the lever, the researcher spent more time with this experiment than any other experiment he was working on at the time.

(d) Linear causality proposes that causation occurs in one direction; like in the situation with the dominos. Circular causality—again, very popular in family therapy—postulates that you affect others, and they, in turn, affect you. Or, in the case of our rat runner, he affects the rat's behavior; but let us never forget that, according to circular causality, the rat is influencing him, as well.

171.   Uma is a 29-year-old client with three children. She would like to secure a job and get off public assistance, but she is agoraphobic and thus cannot leave her home to look for gainful employment. _____ would be the best treatment.

a.   REBT, or reality therapy with choice theory,
b.   Psychodynamic therapy
c.   The research clearly shows that family therapy
d.   Systematic desensitization

(d) Yes, all of the aforementioned choices might be helpful; however, a **procedure based on classical conditioning, known as systematic desensitization, is extremely effective for curbing or eliminating fears. A phobia (such as agoraphobia, which manifests itself as a fear of being outside or being in public places, or claustrophobia, which is a fear of small, closed places or rooms) is an extreme, irrational fear which generally causes the person to avoid the thing he or she fears.** In this case, Uma will remain in the house and not look for gainful employment if she doesn't overcome her phobia. **Public assistance, mentioned in the question, consists of payments administered by the state, such as _TANF_ (or _T_emporary _A_ssistance for _N_eedy _F_amilies, formerly known as welfare payments or _AFDC_, _A_id to _F_amilies of _D_ependent _C_hildren), and food stamps (now called SNAP, or the _S_upplemental _N_utrition _A_ssistance _P_rogram), which are given to needy families who have no other way to support themselves.** There are two other popular public assistance programs, but these are administered by the Social Security Administration (SSA): _**Supplemental Security Income (SSI)**_ for older adults, those who are blind, or people with a disability; and _**Old-Age, Survivors, Disability, and Health Insurance (OASDHI)**_, more commonly known as Social Security.

172.   Mr. Salmon is a 51-year-old parent who has been _emotionally_ abusive to his children. His 16-year-old daughter, Tyra, has run away numerous times and is verbally abusive to her dad. His 14-year-old son, Clint, is using drugs and alcohol on a regular basis. You refer the family to see a family therapist. _____ will most likely be the IP.

a.   Clint (since he has a substance abuse problem)
b.   Mr. Salmon (since he is emotionally abusive)
c.   Tyra (since she might be pulled out of school and placed due to truancy)
d.   The family

(d) IP is an old human services abbreviation that stands for identified patient, or the person in the family who has a problem. In family therapy, however, the assumption is generally that the family system, rather than a single individual, is the client or IP.

173. The family therapist chosen to help the Salmon family in the previous question believes that an extended family model might work best. _____ might be included in the family sessions.

    a. A boarder living in the home
    b. Mr. Salmon's father
    c. Mr. Salmon's girlfriend
    d. All of the above persons

(d) Don't worry how many a, b, c, or d answers are in a row. A lot of folks taking the test will say something like, "It can't be choice d since a majority of the questions seem to have an answer of choice d." Well, guess what? The answer is choice d. Since a boarder (such as an exchange student) is living with the family, this person is often included in the family counseling and therapy.

174. The family therapist who is treating the Salmon family, mentioned in the previous two questions, is using a **multigenerational model**. If this is the case, _____ would most likely be included in the family therapy sessions.

    a. Mr. Salmon's father, who has a record of shoplifting,
    b. Mr. Salmon's home health worker
    c. Mr. Salmon's food stamp caseworker
    d. Tyra's history teacher

(a) **Multigenerational means including family members from other generations**; in this case, Mr. Salmon's dad.

175. Tyra, who has run away on several occasions, admits that sometimes when she leaves it is *not* because her father is abusive. Instead, she has a morbid fear of giving a speech in front of her high school class. You have referred her to an individual counselor, in addition to the family therapy the family is receiving. The individual counselor is using **paradoxical intention** with Tyra. She will most likely

    a. tell Tyra to take three deep breaths before beginning her speech to calm down.
    b. refer Tyra to a psychiatrist for some prescription medicine to relax her.
    c. ask Tyra to purposely try to shake as much as she possibly can in front of the class.
    d. analyze Tyra's thought process because she is definitely a victim of stinking thinking.

(c) Paradoxical intention strategies are a bit like what the average person calls reverse psychology. The client is told to purposely engage in the behavior she wants to eliminate and then exaggerate it.

176. Mrs. Clarkson, a 79-year-old client, is so depressed she actually runs out of a session with you and climbs on a ledge outside her kitchen window and is threatening to jump. The client lives on the 10th floor of her housing project. Which approach would be totally <u>inappropriate</u>?

    a. Tell her that you really care for her and don't want her to do it.
    b. Remind her that if she commits suicide, there will be nobody to teach her grand-children how to sew.

    c.   Use paradoxical intention, such as commenting, "Well, if you want me to help push you, I'll be glad to help."

    d.   Yell out, "Let's examine what you are thinking right now that is causing this behavior."

(c) **Older adults (those 65 years of age and older) have a much higher rate of suicide than the general population.** To be sure, there are no perfect words when a person's life is on the line. Having said that, choice b is typically considered a very good approach, since it reminds her of her value to others. On the other hand, the question is asking you for basically the worst strategy. That honor clearly goes to choice c. I know you've seen this approach used successfully in the movies, but in real life, **never, ever, ever use paradox when a client is suicidal, homicidal, or both**. The consequences are just too high if it fails and it's ethically incorrect.

177. After Mrs. Clarkson is over her suicidal crisis, you refer her to a gestalt therapy group. Which statement is she most likely to hear in this treatment setting?

    a.   "Tell me the dream as if it is happening right this minute."

    b.   "What is your foot doing right now?"

    c.   Both choices a and b are very good possibilities.

    d.   "Umhm. I hear you saying that it seems hopeless and I can feel your pain."

(c) Gestalt therapy stresses the importance of dreams. Unlike most practitioners, gestalt therapists believe the *client must tell the dream as if it's happening in the present moment.* This approach also focuses in on nonverbals such as, "What is your foot doing right now?" or, "What is going on with your left hand?"

178. You are meeting with Trish for the first time at a domestic violence shelter where you are the intake coordinator. Trish has been married for just six weeks and her husband beat her severely. From a theoretical standpoint,

    a.   the husband will never beat her again.

    b.   she will never go back to her husband.

    c.   she will go back to her husband and he could beat her again.

    d.   she will go back to her husband, but he will be fearful she will leave again and, thankfully, will never beat her again.

(c) The average battered woman leaves seven or eight times before she leaves for good. **Domestic violence is very often referred to as Intimate Partner Violence (IPV) or Intimate Partner Abuse (IPA). Intimate partner violence and battering does occur in same-sex relationships, as well.**

179. Jean's firstborn child looks exactly like Austin, his dad. Jean's husband was a batterer and beat Jean on numerous occasions. He was verbally abusive to her on a daily basis. Three years ago, he left the country and has never been seen. From a theoretical standpoint,

    a.   Austin could become the whipping boy and could suffer physical abuse.

    b.   because Austin reminds Jean of his father, Jean could be extremely verbally abusive to Austin.

    c.   both choices a and b are realistic possibilities.

    d.   none of the above choices are realistic.

(c) Because Austin looks like her husband, who was the batterer, it's possible Jean might be abusive to this child. The term **whipping boy** has been used in literature.

180. Bella was horrified when she discovered that her live-in boyfriend (often referred to in this client's chart as her paramour) sexually abused her 5-year-old daughter. In terms of planning the treatment, you should consider the fact that

    a. he could abuse the 5-year-old again.
    b. he will most likely not abuse the 5-year-old again.
    c. he will abuse the child again, but not until she hits puberty.
    d. he will most likely sexually abuse her in the future, but will not threaten her to keep it a secret.

(a) Although sexual abuse can only be a single incident, in most situations, it transpires more than once. A quick quip regarding choice d. Perpetrators often *do* threaten the victim, insisting that if he or she doesn't keep the abuse a secret, this could result in physical harm or death. The threat is sometimes made toward the victim or to another family member (say, for example, the child's mother). For example, "I'll kill your mother if you tell anybody about this."

181. You discover during a home visit that Tess was physically abused by her husband for the first time. Based on the cycle of violence theory, you would expect that

    a. he will never abuse her again.
    b. he will give her the silent treatment for approximately 7 days.
    c. he will buy her flowers because he is in the honeymoon cycle.
    d. he will leave the home and spend several weeks with his parents.

(c) Batterers generally abuse their spouses more than once.

182. In the previous question, it was established that Tess was physically abused. According to the cycle of violence theory,

    a. the honeymoon periods will get shorter and eventually may not exist.
    b. the honeymoon periods will get longer and Tess will falsely believe the relationship is improving.
    c. the physical abuse will change into emotional and verbal abuse only.
    d. it depends on the age of the perpetrator what will occur next.

(a) A theory dubbed the **cycle of violence** predicts that after an abusive episode, there will be a **honeymoon period during which the batterer swears he or she will never do it again.** The batterer may buy flowers or shower the person he or she abused with gifts. The bad news is that the honeymoon periods will dwindle in length and frequency. Ultimately, the honeymoon period could vanish and the abuse becomes more frequent.

183. A therapist who puts a lot of emphasis on dreams is most likely

    a. a Rogerian.
    b. a helper who used REBT.
    c. a psychodynamic or gestalt practitioner.
    d. choices b or c.

(d) A little review won't hurt you! Psychoanalytic (psychodynamic) helpers and those practicing gestalt emphasize the value of dreams.

184. Mr. Jefferies informs you that he wants to really do his treatment the right way and focus on his childhood. A good match for him would be

    a. a person-centered Rogerian helper.
    b. a counselor who uses rational emotive behavior therapy, also known as REBT.
    c. a gestalt practitioner.
    d. a psychodynamic helper.

(d) Psychodynamic approaches are based on psychoanalysis, which emphasizes the importance of the client's childhood in terms of the formation of the personality. Rogerian, REBT, and gestalt therapies focus much more on the present than the past.

185. Disputation is used primarily in

    a. REBT, which is a form of cognitive therapy.
    b. group psychotherapy.
    c. family therapy.
    d. couples therapy.

(a) In REBT, the therapist disputes the client's irrational beliefs and shows the client that the beliefs are illogical and not scientifically sound.

186. Edna blames her problems on her circumstances and on everybody else. She has an _____ locus of control.

    a. external
    b. internal
    c. IO or I-O
    d. None of the answers would be technically correct.

(a) Julian B. Rotter popularized the idea of internal or external locus of control in the mid 1950s. Internal—living by your own behaviors, thoughts, and feelings—is viewed as healthy, because you feel you have control over your life. External locus of control implies that your life is controlled by outside environmental factors and, therefore, you're not the captain of your own ship. Choice c isn't correct because there's *no* IO or I-O locus of control. In our field, IO or I-O stands for industrial organizational psychology. IO psychologists apply the principles of psychology to the workplace. They often do research and give tests to help select employees and make certain workers are happy and can perform their jobs in a productive manner.

187. You are working in gerontology (also known in the field as gero). It is accurate to say that

    a. older adults are rarely suicidal because they have accepted their life circumstances.
    b. older adults have a higher rate of suicide than the general population.
    c. older adults are depressed, but strangely enough, rarely take their own lives.
    d. older adults are depressed, but eager to seek out treatment, and thus don't kill themselves very often.

(b) Depending on the age bracket you examine, older adults have a high incidence of depression, and post double, if not triple, the suicide rate for the general population. They're also less likely than younger people to call a suicide prevention center and seek out counseling or therapy.

188. The notion of psychopharmacology suggests that

    a. the client or patient with an emotional disorder could benefit from a prescription medicine.
    b. the client or patient with an emotional disorder could benefit from a natural remedy.
    c. the client or patient should receive a natural remedy and a prescription medicine.
    d. the client or patient should *always* receive a prescription medicine and psychotherapy.

(a) **Psychopharmacology makes the assumption that a chemical imbalance (usually in the brain) is responsible for mental and emotional disorders and this is best treated by a prescription medicine.** In essence, drugs prescribed by a psychiatrist or other physician—rather than talk therapy—is emphasized.

189. SSRI and SNRI medications work well for

    a. xenophobia (a fear of strangers).
    b. schizophrenia (a psychotic condition where the client has a tough time telling what is reality and what is not).
    c. clinical depression.
    d. ADHD (Attention Deficit Hyperactivity Disorder).

(c) You need not be an expert in psychiatric drugs to pass this exam; however, you should know that SSRI and SNRI medications are used to treat clinical depression. SSRI stands for Selective Serotonin Reuptake Inhibitors. These medicines keep a chemical called serotonin at higher levels in the brain to improve mood. Serotonin Norepinephrine Reuptake Inhibitors, or SNRIs, regulate serotonin and norepinephrine in the levels in the brain, once again to improve the client's mood. Now I can hear some of you clamoring: He's wrong. Choice c isn't the answer. I know somebody who has ADHD and is on one of those SSRI or SNRI drugs, as well as some of my schizophrenic clients. Well, I'll tell you a little secret. So do I! Plenty of them. Remember that the test is looking for the best answer, and here you'd pick clinical depression because that's the primary use for SSRI and SNRI prescription medications.

190. Tardive dyskinesia (a neurological difficulty of the face and jaw) is caused by

    a. psychiatric medicine.
    b. non-psychiatric medicine, such as those given for blood pressure or high cholesterol.
    c. incompetent psychotherapy and counseling.
    d. heredity, and it is considered a congenital condition.

(a) Tardive dyskinesia is a disorder where the client has involuntary movements he or she can't control. The movements, such as repeatedly sticking out one's tongue, rapidly blinking their eyes, or smacking their lips, doesn't really serve a purpose. Unfortunately, in a high percentage of cases, this problem is caused by taking antipsychotic medication for disorders such as schizophrenia. **When a doctor or a therapist causes an illness that the client or patient didn't have before treatment (such as tardive dyskinesia), we call it an iatrogenic illness.**

191. The public health model emphasizes

    a. prevention, and the fact that clients are linked to social issues.
    b. psychoanalytic concepts.
    c. the medical model advocating prescription drugs for psychiatric disorders.
    d. the biomedical or psychotropic model advocating prescription drugs for psychiatric disorders.

(a) **Any state, federal, or local program or policy which attempts to prevent disease, improve health, and enhance longevity could be considered part of the public health model.** Government health centers using physicians and nurses to diagnose or stop communicable diseases would be included into this category. Personal hygiene classes and literature are also frequently utilized.

192. Depending on the agency, hospital, or treatment center, clients can be called

    a. patients.
    b. clients.
    c. consumers.
    d. all of the above.

(d) Perhaps you have worked at various agencies or organizations and have used all of the terminology to describe the people you were (or are presently) serving.

193. Abraham Maslow suggested that

    a. dreams were the royal road to the unconscious mind.
    b. the I/E locus of control was the central issue in terms of the personality.
    c. basic physiological needs and safety needs must be met before you can meet higher needs, such as self-actualization.
    d. none of the above statements are accurate.

(c) **Maslow created the hierarchy of needs. The theory postulates that lower needs must be met before you can reach higher growth needs.** At the bottom of the hierarchy, Maslow lists lower **physiological needs,** such as food, water, air, nutrition, sex, and sleep. Next, he mentions **safety needs:** protection for your family, law, and order. Beyond safety, he lists **relationship needs** such as love, friendship, affection, belonging, and the family. Moving up the hierarchy, we have **esteem needs,** such as self-esteem, mastery, achievement, and confidence. Finally, **at the top of the hierarchy, is self-actualization.** Self-actualization is reaching your full potential; a creative state of no prejudice, peak experiences, and the search for personal growth.

194. Pick out the involuntary client.

    a. Mrs. Smith went to family court and was told she must attend six sessions of counseling in order to keep her children and not go to jail.
    b. Mrs. Smith wants counseling for her adolescent son who is very depressed.
    c. Mrs. Smith is homeless. She called the homeless hotline and is now in a shelter.

    d. Mrs. Smith is in an AA group suggested by her caseworker and Mrs. Smith felt it would be beneficial.

(a) **An involuntary client (also called a mandated client) is told by an outside authority, usually the court, that they must use a social or mental health service. Mandated clients can be difficult because they don't necessarily want the service.**

195. Most theories believe you should use direct eye contact when interviewing a client.

    a. Caucasians are generally the exception.
    b. Female Caucasians are the exception because they will see it as flirtatious from either a male or female helper.
    c. Native Americans or Latinos would be the exception.
    d. Males under the age of 16 are the exception.

(c) In the case of Asians, they may or may not prefer eye contact. Hopefully, your clinical experience will help you decide which would be beneficial in such instances.

196. You are working at an organization that prefers interventions based on behavior modification. Your client explains that she never sticks up for her own rights. You should recommend

    a. relaxation training.
    b. a 12-step group, such as Alcoholics Anonymous or Overeaters Anonymous.
    c. negative punishment.
    d. an assertiveness training group.

(d) Again, reviewing the material or simply seeing it in different ways is beneficial to your preparation. The assertiveness training group is ideal for persons who are nonassertive (never stick up for their own rights), or those who are aggressive.

197. CBT, or cognitive behavioral therapy, is to self-talk as

    a. Rogers is to positive reinforcement.
    b. Freud is to insight.
    c. Ellis is to dreams.
    d. gestalt therapy is to accurate empathy.

(b) The folks who create comprehensive exams always seem to throw in an analogy question, such as this. It might be difficult since your exam is based on vignettes, but I still wouldn't bet totally against it. Here, CBT relies on self-talk or cognitive restructuring, while Freud relied on insight.

198. According to most experts in human services,

    a. approximately half of the people who work their way out of poverty will fall back into it within about 5 years.
    b. most people are in poverty for just a few months.
    c. more African Americans are poverty stricken than whites.
    d. almost nobody working full-time lives in poverty.

(a) **Choice d is totally false! Forty percent of the folks who live in poverty actually work full-time.**

199. Martin E. P. Seligman's theory of learned helplessness syndrome

    a. applies to psychotic clients.
    b. applies to clinical unipolar depression and poverty.
    c. applies to ADHD.
    d. has never been accepted in the field of positive psychology.

(b) **Depression or major depressive disorders are more common in people living in poverty;** hence, choice b stands out as the best of the bunch.

200. According to Seligman's theory of learned helplessness syndrome (originally based on dog studies), the cure or *best* way to fight depression is

    a. learned optimism.
    b. insight psychotherapy.
    c. experiential psychotherapy, such as psychodrama.
    d. empathy, warmth, and positive regard.

(a) My students often assert that their grandparents or caretakers taught them to be optimistic and, indeed, these well-meaning folks were right on target. Optimistic people are healthier. Optimistic sports teams bounce back from a slump more effectively, and politicians who give optimistic speeches win more elections. The key word here is "learned," generally using cognitive therapy strategies. **People can be taught to be more optimistic.**

Chapter 4

Case Management, Professional Practice, and Ethics

201. Liz is going out to houses after a storm to make certain clients are receiving the services they need. Liz is acting as

    a. an outreach worker.
    b. a broker.
    c. a teacher/educator.
    d. a mobilizer.

(a) An *outreach worker* will make home visits and provide services in the client's neighborhood or environment.

202. Reggie is collecting statistics and data to give to his organization's statistician. The statistician will use this to evaluate his program's new policy to help the homeless. Reggie is acting as

    a. a broker.
    b. an evaluator.
    c. a data manager.
    d. an advocate.

(c) Though b isn't a bad answer.

203. Louise is running a group to inform middle-school students about the dangers of drugs and alcohol. Louise is *most likely* acting as

    a. a teacher/educator.
    b. an advocate.
    c. a mobilizer.
    d. a consultant.

(a) We often refer to preventive groups as primary groups, and they fall into a larger category called psycho-educational groups. Yes, there's a lot of terminology in our field of choice!

204. Armand's client has a host of problems. He has referred her to the lead poisoning clinic, an audiology (hearing) clinic, a speech therapist, a clinical psychologist for testing, and the local public assistance office. Armand is acting as

    a. an advocate.
    b. a broker.

    c.   an administrator, since he is not doing the work himself.
    d.   an assistant to a specialist.

(b) **In the *broker role*, the practitioner assesses the situation and then finds and links the client up with the appropriate organizations.**

205. Margo sent her client, Tao, to an agency that could help with her heating bills. Tao is in a wheelchair. The agency told Tao they could not be of help as the agency is not wheelchair accessible. Margo contacted the program director of the agency and recommended that wheelchair accessibility be instituted as soon as possible. Margo is acting as

    a.   a broker.
    b.   a caregiver who truly cares and feels for her disabled client's needs.
    c.   a community planner who is helping to mobilize community agencies.
    d.   an advocate.

(d) **The *advocate* stands up for and champions the rights of clients and community members. Some experts merely define advocacy as speaking up for yourself or your clients.**

206. Beth refuses to do her homework assignments. Because of this, she is almost flunking out of her high school. Tim creates a behavior modification plan using positive reinforcement to personally help her accomplish this task. Tim is acting as

    a.   a teacher/educator.
    b.   a consultant.
    c.   a behavior changer.
    d.   a caregiver.

(c) Okay dudes and dudettes, just use a little good old common sense here. Wouldn't the most logical answer be that a person who performs behavior modification be a behavior changer?

207. A tragic school shooting took the lives of several high school students. A human services practitioner from the local crisis center was brought in to help the guidance counselors create grief groups and offer bereavement services. This human services employee is acting as

    a.   a behavior changer.
    b.   an assistant to the specialist.
    c.   a teacher/educator, since this is a school setting.
    d.   a consultant.

(d) **When a human services practitioner uses his or her expertise and knowledge to assist another professional or organization, then he or she is acting as a *consultant*. An agency or practitioner will often request a consultant when they feel they can't handle the situation on their own.** When I served as the program director for a crisis center, I performed consultation services similar to the one described in this question on many occasions.

208. The Southern Regional Education Board (SREB) identified 13 roles for human services workers. Pick the role which was *not* set forth by the board.

    a.   A mobilizer who organizes client and community support to provide needed services.

    b.   A community organizer who designs, implements, and organizes new programs. This person works with boards and communities.

    c.   An intake worker who will interview the client in person or over the phone and provide a complete psychosocial assessment.

    d.   An evaluator who assesses programs to ensure agency accountability.

(c) Clearly, intake worker isn't one of the 13 roles delineated by the SREB. Note that at many agencies (such as a hotline or helpline), the intake could be conducted using the telephone rather than face-to-face.

209. Millie has been diagnosed with cancer. She lives alone and is in need of support and encouragement. Based on this limited information, her human services practitioner would be the most help to her by operating out of the _____ role.

    a.   assistant to the specialist

    b.   caregiver

    c.   teacher/educator

    d.   behavior modifier

(b) The *caregiver* provides encouragement, direct support, and hope, and can perform tasks the person often can't perform for him or herself. In many cases, the term applies to helping an older parent or family member.

210. Dr. Menendez is a D.O. psychiatrist. Some psychiatrists have the M.D. degree. He wants to hire a human services worker to help him find referral sources for clients who have social service needs that go beyond just providing medication management. Dr. Menendez would be best served by a human services worker who is experienced in the _____ role.

    a.   assistant to the specialist

    b.   behavior changer

    c.   broker

    d.   administrator

(a) The *assistant to the specialist* works as an aide or helper to a professional.

211. You are a supervisor at a large agency. You need to hire a human services practitioner to oversee three exciting new programs with large budgets. Your best bet would be to hire

    a.   a human services practitioner with years of experience as an administrator.

    b.   a human services practitioner with years of experience as a consultant.

    c.   a human services practitioner with years of experience as a data manager because he or she could collect valuable statistical data.

    d.   a human services practitioner who was very experienced in the evaluator role, since he or she could assess each program and analyze accountability issues.

(a) *Administrators* manage entire programs and many (if not most) don't engage in direct client contact.

212. Ethical guidelines (also called ethical codes or codes of ethics) are

    a.   not the same as laws, but laws are generally neutral or supportive of ethical guidelines.

    b.   virtually the same as laws because they are always state statutes.
    c.   always the same for psychologists, counselors, social workers, and human ser-
          vices workers.
    d.   always the same for psychologists, counselors, social workers, and helpers who
          have HS-BCP.

(a) Here I must interject my famous "caseworker who likes the client story." I created
this little saga for my students so they would never forget the difference between ethics
and laws. Imagine that a caseworker interviews his client for the first time. He likes her
so much he asks her out to dinner and a movie. *Clearly, this is totally unethical.* But, let's
assume the client calls the police on her worker. She's offended and wants him arrested.
I tell my students that not only won't the cop arrest the caseworker when he arrives, it's
conceivable if the officer is unethical, he might ask the client to go out on a date, as well!
The take home message: Ethics are not always equal to laws.

213. Ethical procedures, standards, and guidelines

    a.   are static within a given profession (e.g., human services).
    b.   stay the same within a given profession (e.g., human services).
    c.   are updated from time to time and do change.
    d.   only apply to licensed practitioners (e.g., licensed clinical social workers) and
          thus are not applicable to those who have snared HS-BCP status.

(c) Why are choices a and b incorrect? Well, thanks for asking! **Different ethical organizations within the same profession can differ.** For example, NOHS and HS-BCP both sport
different ethical codes, at least at this point in time. Or take me: I'm a member of the
American Counseling Association (ACA) and the National Board for Certified Counselors
(NBCC). Here again, their ethical codes—although the two organizations represent the
same profession—are not identical. Just for the record, an ethical code only applies or is
binding to members of the organization. For example, a psychologist who's a member of
the American Psychological Association (APA) would be expected to adhere to APA ethics, while a counselor who's a member of the American Counseling Association (ACA)
would be bound by ACA's ethical policies. **Ethical guidelines do differ by profession. Thus,
a social worker, counselor, psychologist, and human services practitioner working in the
same job would be bound by different ethics.**

214. A client tells you during an individual session that she had a very violent childhood.
      She is also working with a master's level psychotherapist. The therapist contacts you
      and wants to know what information you have gathered to better help this client.
      You agree with the psychotherapist that sharing the information would be a good
      thing to do. You should

    a.   tell no one under any circumstances—even the psychotherapist—because confi-
          dentiality is an entrusted secret.
    b.   tell the psychotherapist what you believe he or she needs to know if, and only if,
          your client has completed a signed release of information form, allowing you to
          do so.
    c.   not tell the psychotherapist anything under any circumstances because you
          would be in violation of a state law.
    d.   do whatever you wish on a case by case basis because workers who hold the HS-
          BCP are exempt from ethical guidelines because of their expertise.

(b) **Except in rare legal and dangerous or emergency situations, you'll never give out information on a client without a signed release of information form.** As far as choice d, let's not let the HS-BCP credential go to your head!

215. Your 28-year-old client, Tina, has threatened suicide. Her plan involves using a firearm and taking action next week. Based on the famous Tarasoff ruling in 1976,

   a. you could call her 30-year-old sister who lives in the home and ask the sister to watch her closely and remove the firearm from the household.
   b. this is a clear example of absolute confidentiality. You would not be permitted to call Tina's 30-year-old sister.
   c. you should immediately call the police and ask them to break down the door.
   d. you should immediately call the suicide prevention hotline and let them take over from here.

(a) **A worker who doesn't follow the duty to warn/protect policies set forth by Tarasoff and ethical guidelines can be legally charged (think sued!) for professional negligence.** (Quick side bar: If the question had said, "Tina called you and was actively threatening to kill herself right at that moment with a firearm," then choice c, calling the police, would be in compliance with Tarasoff.) **Again, an excellent tactic for doing well on comprehensive exams is not reading into things that aren't there.**

216. You are working with Matt who is a 46-year-old construction worker. Matt confidentially reveals that he plans to kill himself and three of his co-workers at the construction site. Based on the Tarasoff case, you should

   a. keep it confidential because Tarasoff only dealt with suicide; not homicide or murder.
   b. realize that, statistically, the behavior he is describing, rarely, if ever, occurs, and you should be very active-directive. Confront him immediately and tell him you won't put up with this type of pathological talk from any client.
   c. break confidentiality using minimal disclosure in an attempt to stop this tragedy. This is a situation where the principle of relative confidentiality would be relevant.
   d. make a referral to a board certified psychiatrist. You are in no position to handle a tough case like this.

(c) **The key point here is if a client is endangering his own life or somebody else's life (or both), you'll break confidentiality if necessary. This trend was put in place by famous Tarasoff legal decisions.** You need not remember the names of very many legal judgments, but because this one changed the way mental health and social service workers practice, this is one I *would* commit to memory. Prior to Tarasoff, workers had **absolute confidentiality,** in the sense that confidential was confidential. Period. If a client told you something, it was a secret. End of discussion. After the famous Tarasoff case, ethical bodies basically switched to **relative confidentiality,** meaning *there are rare times when a practitioner must break/breach confidentiality.* To make a very long legal battle short, the rules changed when a college student, Tatiana Tarasoff, was killed by a young man named Porsenjit Poddar (they were both students at the University of California at Berkley). Poddar had kissed Tarasoff at a New Year's dance and was convinced they had a serious relationship. Basically, Tarasoff told Poddar she wasn't seriously interested in him and, in fact, wanted to date other guys. Poddar became very depressed and saw a psychologist, Dr. Lawrence

Moore, for therapy, and told Dr. Moore he planned to kill Tarasoff as soon as she returned from her summer break. He did, in fact, take her life on October 27, 1969. The parents later asserted that if they had known their daughter was in danger, they could have protected her and she would still be alive. The parents took legal action against the school and lost, but then appealed the decision to the California Supreme Court, which overturned the lower court's decision and, quite frankly, that changed everything. **Now most experts agree therapists and helpers have a duty to warn/protect an intended victim.** It was the ultimate argument for relative confidentiality (i.e., there are times when you should breach or break confidentiality). P.S. Don't count on ethical codes to have statements that cover every situation you'll encounter. To put it bluntly, they don't! All codes of ethics have limitations.

217. You have the HS-BCP credential. You have been assigned as Ms. Patterson's TANF worker. During your initial session with Ms. Patterson (intended to assess her eligibility for TANF), she casually mentions her interest in airplanes. You instantly realize you have a lot in common because this is your overwhelming interest in life, as well. You are also physically attracted to her. You ask her out on a date to lunch and then take her to the aeronautical museum. If you follow through with the date,

    a. this is an example of a dual relationship and ethical guidelines frown on this behavior.
    b. this would be permissible because the date has nothing to do with her eligibility for public assistance.
    c. it is a multiple relationship, so it is perfectly fine.
    d. you could immediately be arrested on a sexual harassment charge.

(a) **Super exam hint: Ethical bodies frown on dual relationships (also called multiple relationships) because they get in the way of the human services worker's objectivity.** A dual or multiple relationship occurs when you have a professional relationship with a client (say you're her public assistance worker) and you have another significant relationship with the client (she's dating you, she's your cousin, or she's doing construction on your home). As mentioned earlier in this book, imagine how you'd react when Ms. Patterson decides she's going to date somebody else. Can you really, truly still be objective? Not on this planet!

218. Pick the correct statement based on the last question regarding Ms. Patterson.

    a. If you have sex with her, it would still be ethical if she likes you.
    b. Any romantic or sexual relationship with a current client is unethical.
    c. It would indeed be ethical, but since it is risky, most experts would recommend against it.
    d. Human services ethical guidelines fail to take a position on this issue.

(b) **Repeat this loud and clear: It's unethical to have a romantic or sexual relationship with any—yes, any—current client. No exceptions, no way!**

219. You see Ms. Patterson at a party 10 years after you served as her TANF worker. She likes you a lot. You decide to date her and have sexual relations with her. She wants the relations, as well.

    a. This is still a serious ethical violation and you could lose your HS-BCP status.
    b. This is still a serious legal violation and, yes, you could do jail time.

    c.   Since you are no longer her human services worker, ethics are not relevant.

    d.   Believe it or not, if you are not exploiting her, it might well be totally ethical.

(d) The HS-BCP ethics stipulate that 2 years must pass after your last professional contact with the client (i.e., the final date you terminated her for services) before you can enter into a sexual relationship. So yes, it would be ethical.

220. Nellie beat her 4-year-old 2 weeks before you held a session with her, and left marks on her child. You should

    a.   keep it a secret because ethical guidelines are very strict on this issue.

    b.   report it to the child abuse hotline.

    c.   report it if, and only if, you feel the Children's Division who handles this in your state will code the case as "substantiated" or "reason to suspect" and open a case on Nellie.

    d.   make a child abuse report if, and only if, you feel it will not harm your relationship with the client. As Carl Rogers emphasized, the relationship with the client is the basis for the treatment.

(b) **Reporting child abuse goes beyond merely following an ethical code; it's a federal law in every state. If you don't report an incident, you could end up doing jail time and/or pay a fine. It doesn't matter where you practice in the US, since all states have had reporting laws since 1967.** In reference to choice c, the decision to open the case or not rests with the Child Protective Services (CPS) worker, not with you! Your job is simply to make the report.

221. You run into Nellie, mentioned in the previous question, while shopping at the local grocery store. You should

    a.   acknowledge her immediately and say, "Well, it looks like we are both doing a little grocery shopping today."

    b.   ignore her. If she speaks to you, you could politely walk away or say, "I'm sorry, I don't believe I know you. You must have me confused with somebody else."

    c.   speak back to her very briefly if, and only if, she acknowledges you first.

    d.   say, "Human services practitioners are not allowed to speak with their clients outside of the agency or a home visit."

(c) The rule of thumb, according to most experts, is to be polite and respond to the client briefly if she talks *to you first*.

222. Teria wants to continue taking her children to your day care center. However, she tells you she cannot afford the fee any longer. She worked for years as a house painter and offers to paint your apartment free of charge if you will allow her to bring her kids to your child care center for another month.

    a.   This is an example of bartering and the American spirit was built on it. Even the pioneers and the American Indians (often called Native Americans) engaged in this practice. "I'll let you have this land if you give me your horse." Feel free to let Teria, your client, paint your apartment, if it truly needs this service.

    b.   This is an example of bartering and it generally impairs objectivity and thus is frowned upon.

    c.   This is not mentioned in any ethical guidelines, so use your best judgment.

d.   Since painting your apartment is not a romantic or sexual activity, ask your supervisor. He or she might tell you it is perfectly ethical.

(b) Bartering is actually a type of dual/multiple relationship and could get in the way of your judgment related to human services activities. You best bet is to avoid situations of this ilk like the plague!

223.   You are working with Mr. K and his family. He is also working with a licensed private practice psychologist. The psychologist would like Mr. K's chart because the file has some previous psychological test write-ups conducted by the local university psychology center, which could be helpful in terms of planning his treatment. Mr. K agrees to sign a release of information so his psychologist can get a copy of his university tests from your record.

a.   You should simply send a copy of the entire record.
b.   You could send a copy of the record, but could *not* include the previous psychological testing from the university psychology center, even though the current psychologist feels he needs this report.
c.   You could only send a one page summary of the chart, even if it is hundreds of pages.
d.   You cannot release the client's record under any circumstances because that would be a blatant ethical violation.

(b) You should release only information in the chart that you or others at your agency acquired. Thus, you couldn't release a chiropractor's report, a report you received from the homeless shelter, the university psychological center's assessment, the lead poisoning clinic's report, or anything else you amassed from other sources. In essence, if you or your agency didn't secure the information, don't even think about giving it out. Now, that said, the private psychologist could easily get his hands on the information by having Mr. K sign a release for the university psychological center. In other words, go directly to the source.

224.   Norton tells you during a confidential session that he is having an affair with his neighbor. You receive a subpoena to testify in court over a custody battle. Norton's wife's attorney asks you on the witness stand if Mr. Norton has told you he is having an affair.

a.   You do not have to tell the attorney a thing. Human services workers are protected by privileged communication.
b.   You would not need to tell the attorney a thing if, and only if, you have snared the HS-BSP credential, because without it, you do not have privileged communication.
c.   Simply tell the attorney that HS-BCP ethics will not allow you to answer the question.
d.   None of the above answers are correct.

(d) Although privileged communication appears in virtually all textbooks in the chapter on ethics, it's actually a legal term. Privileged communication asserts that it's the client's privilege—not the worker—whether to release the information to a court of law. However, keep reading, my friend. There's another piece—and I mean a very important piece—to the puzzle.

225. After you testify (see the previous question), Norton's licensed clinical psychologist is now placed on the stand and asked the exact same question ("Did Norton tell you in a confidential session he was having an affair?").

    a. The ethical behavior for the licensed psychologist would be identical as the answer for the human services worker.

    b. Since the licensed psychologist could rely on privileged communication, he or she would not necessarily need to reveal that Norman is having an affair.

    c. More information is definitely needed to answer this question.

    d. The licensed psychologist would point out that he or she is not a psychiatrist and thus could not accurately answer the question.

(b) **Sorry to be the one to lay this on you, but human services professionals, HS-BCP or not, do not have privileged communication with their clients.** I know I'm using a lot of **bold phrases,** but this is important stuff and I need to have your full attention. Generally, only ordained ministers and licensed practitioners, such as licensed clinical social workers, licensed professional counselors, licensed psychiatrists, and licensed psychologists, would be covered by the privilege in our field. Because privileged communication is a legal concept, it can vary by state. Hence, a state might say that psychologists have the privilege, but not social workers. **However, a human services professional—unless he or she is licensed in one of the aforementioned professions—would never be protected by privileged communication. Sorry, but that's the truth, the whole truth, and nothing but the truth. This has actually led some practitioners to say to their clients, "You might not want to tell me that because I'd have to reveal it, if asked about it in court."**

226. Documentation is considered an important competency for human services practitioners. *Documentation could also be called recording, charting, dictating, case write-ups, or even writing a narrative on your exam.* Today, you called a local church to see if they have shoes and clothes for your client. In terms of your documentation,

    a. you do *not* need to put this in the record because it is considered collateral information.

    b. you do need to put this in the record because it is considered collateral information.

    c. this is not collateral information; so, yes, it needs to be in the record.

    d. in most situations, whether to place this information in the record would be totally based on the policy of your particular agency.

(b) **All contacts, whether they're direct (say, interviewing the client) or collateral (calling a church for shoes and clothes or contacting somebody to verify eligibility for a program), should be included in the record. Always put the date of the contact.**

227. Once you have snared the HS-BCP credential,

    a. you will need CEUs to keep your credential.

    b. you have the credential for life; no CEUs are necessary.

    c. since it is not a state license, there is no reason to secure CEUs.

    d. CEUs are not required, but highly recommended.

(a) **CEU stands for continuing education unit,** and virtually all professional credentials require them so you can update yourself and remain current in regard to what's going on in your field. As it currently stands, the HS-BCP credential requires 60 contact (clock) hours in a 5 year period. Six hours must be specific to ethics.

228. Loraine is a 17-year-old high school student. You perform a lethality assessment and determine that she is highly suicidal and lives at home with her mother and father. You thus follow your ethical code and breech confidentiality by calling her parents. Ethical guidelines

    a.   are intended to protect you as well as Loraine.
    b.   only protect you.
    c.   only protect Loraine in this instance.
    d.   will not protect you or Loraine.

(a) **Ethics protect *you as well as the client*, since when you behave in an ethical manner, you're following the guidelines set forth by the profession.** By the way, most children commit suicide at home.

229. Mindy is binging and purging and has been diagnosed as having bulimia. You have no training in eating disorders. The client clearly needs treatment. You should

    a.   talk to your supervisor about reading some informative books on the subject.
    b.   talk to your supervisor about reading some informative, refereed journals on the subject.
    c.   act as a broker and refer her to a treatment facility that specializes in eating disorders.
    d.   use informed consent and tell the client you will find a consultant to help you treat her.

(c) This is referred to in the trade as a *boundaries of competence issue.* **Never treat a client for something you have not been trained to treat.**

230. A well-known athlete is admitted to your addiction treatment center. You say bad things about him and it leaks and ends up in the newspaper. This is

    a.   an example of defamation known as slander.
    b.   an example of defamation known as libel.
    c.   not enough information to determine if it is libel or slander.
    d.   not necessarily unethical if what you are saying is actually true.

(a) **Libel occurs when you put something in writing that could damage an individual's reputation. Slander is similar, but here you're making a false verbal statement about the person, rather than publishing it.** Slander begins with an "s" and so does speaking. Hmm, nice memory device.

231. You hold HS-BCP credentials *and* you are a licensed clinical social worker. You move to another state and the state does <u>not</u> accept your social work license. It is safe to say

    a.   the new state has reciprocity.
    b.   the new state does not have reciprocity.
    c.   the new state has portability.
    d.   the new state does not license social workers.

(b) It's time for another must-know term! **Reciprocity occurs when one state accepts another state's credentials.** Do all states have reciprocity? Um, dream on! I once had a licensed counselor tell me that when she moved to another state, the new state wanted her to snare 34 more graduate hours to license her. Ouch! The professions are working to achieve portability. Portability means that once you receive a credential, it would be good in any other location (at least in the US).

232. Gwen dislikes her client and does something harmful to her. Ethically, this is an example of

    a.   nonmaleficence.
    b.   maleficence.
    c.   privileged communication.
    d.   pro bono services.

(b) Maleficence merely means to do harm, while nonmaleficence literally means do no harm. Pro bono, choice d, simply indicates the service was provided for free.

233. Art's human services worker helped him secure the money to pay his heating bill. Ethically, Art's worker has acted on the principle of

    a.   didactic helping.
    b.   maleficence.
    c.   beneficence.
    d.   non-directive helping.

(c) **Beneficence literally means to do good to others or in the client's best interest.** In our field, it refers to promoting the welfare of the client, or helping the client meet his or her needs and goals. **Another key term is nonmaleficence, which means to do no harm to your clients or even protect them from harm.**

234. Art's human services worker promised to call the utility company to ensure that his electric would not be turned off. Unfortunately, his worker did not follow through. Ethically, his human services worker did not practice

    a.   fidelity.
    b.   EBP.
    c.   EBT.
    d.   ECT.

(a) **Fidelity is the act of being loyal, trustworthy, and following through on promises and commitments.** All the other alphabet soup answers could appear on exam questions, so let's touch on them briefly. Choice b, EBP, stands for evidence based practice. Don't be surprised if you see it as EBT, or evidence based treatment, on some exam questions. In a nutshell, this approach says that a practitioner should look toward the finest research for guidance when performing assessments and treatment interventions. Choice c, EBT, is an electronic benefit transfer card that allows you to spend food stamp allowances or cash benefits. It's kind of like a debit card for public assistance (often dubbed as cash benefits or Temporary Assistance for Needy Families, otherwise known as TANF) and food stamps, now referred to as SNAP, or the Supplemental Nutrition Assistance Program. For you young upstarts, a while back, food stamps really were actual stamps. ECT is electroconvulsive shock therapy, used in cases of extreme depression. Years ago, it was simply referred to as EST, or electro shock therapy.

235. Art's helper didn't have time to call the utility company about his electric bill because he was spending too much time helping another client named Sharon. His worker felt Sharon was very attractive and he liked her personality. His worker lied and told Art he did not have time to contact the electric company because his agency made him attend a workshop on ethics. Art's worker

    a. was practicing justice.
    b. was practicing beneficence.
    c. was practicing choices a and b.
    d. was not practicing justice and veracity.

(d) **Justice suggests that you treat all your clients fairly and provide equal access to resources, if possible. In this case, the worker was not practicing veracity (which is simply a big 25-cent word ethical experts throw around that means honesty).**

236. Ella wants to see her sixth-grade child's record. She attends a public elementary school. You should tell her that

    a. because of confidentiality laws, she cannot do it.
    b. since it is a public school, it is really up to the school superintendent.
    c. according to FERPA, the Family Educational Rights and Privacy Act of 1974 (also known as the Buckley Amendment), she can view the record.
    d. since it is a public school, it is really up to the school principal.

(c) **Must know concept: FERPA stipulates that if a school is receiving federal funding, then parents can see their children's records, if the child is under 18. The act also grants students over 18 the right to view their own school records. Finally, if the student is under 18, his or her school records can't be released to another party without written consent of the parents, or by the written consent of the student, if he or she is over 18. The school** isn't permitted to charge a fee for this service. In most cases, foster parents are afforded the same rights under FERPA as natural parents.

237. Ella (mentioned in the previous question) is attending a public community college program in human services. The college receives federal funds. Ella would like to see her own college record. She is 41 years old. You should tell her that

    a. colleges are markedly different than K-12 institutions and she will need to talk to the college president.
    b. according to FERPA, she can do it.
    c. FERPA does not apply to adult clients.
    d. colleges simply do not allow students to see their records; however, they will provide official transcripts if necessary.

(b) Review the previous question if you're still confused. Since Ella is well over 18, there's no problem with her seeing her own record.

238. Ella's daughter saw the guidance counselor because she was angry at Ella a few months ago. Ella is anxious to read the counseling record to see what her daughter said about her as a parent to the guidance counselor. You should tell her that

    a. FERPA does not apply to the counselor's case notes. She cannot see the notes or reports from the guidance counselor.

b. according to FERPA, she has a right to review and inspect the counseling record and see what her daughter actually said about her.

c. it is up to the guidance counselor who saw her daughter.

d. in this situation, the school board will make the call whether to allow it or not.

(a) **According to FERPA guidelines, counseling records are exempt.**

239. Human services practitioners must have cultural competence. Examples of this would be

a. to develop a tolerance for philosophies and worldviews different than your own.

b. to alter interventions to meet the needs of other cultures.

c. to amass knowledge of cultures different than your own.

d. all of the above.

(d) Expand your comfort zone and develop a mindset of openness and respect for cultural differences.

240. Mickey's 12-year-old daughter refuses to go to school. You believe that giving her daughter a dollar each day she attends will improve her attendance. You, as the worker, realize that if this works, it will be a form of behavior modification known as positive reinforcement. Mickey asks why you want her to do this. According to the notion of informed consent,

a. you should explain the purpose of the assignment.

b. you should not explain the purpose of the assignment, since research shows the behavior modification will work better if there is some degree of mystery involved.

c. as a competent human services worker, you can make the call whether to explain it to Mickey or keep it a secret.

d. most clients will simply comply with your directives and they won't ask for additional information.

(a) Informed consent is a *huge topic* in ethical circles. **You must give the client the information to consent or reject a procedure, treatment, program, assessment, etc. In essence, informed consent answers the question, "Why are you recommending such and such?" Virtually all ethical bodies support informed consent.**

241. Sarah is a human services practitioner for a local non-for-profit agency. She will be running a shyness group. In order to conform to the ethical principle of informed consent, her supervisor told her to create a professional disclosure brochure to give to all her clients before the group begins. She must include all of the following information *except*

a. her name and contact information.

b. a statement about her education and training.

c. a statement about the fact that she overcame her own shyness using these strategies.

d. the cost of the group, time it will meet, meeting dates, and location where the actual group will meet.

(c) The key word here is "must." She could include something about her personal road to recovery, but it's not required by informed consent guidelines.

242. Ron refuses to talk about his abusive childhood. You feel it is imperative to know about this part of his life to help him.

   a.   Do not pressure him to talk about it because, ethically, clients have a right to privacy.
   b.   Put direct verbal pressure on him to reveal this because it could be life changing.
   c.   Keep bringing the subject up until he caves and talks about it.
   d.   Refer him to a hypnotist who will hypnotize him and get it out of him. It is for his own good.

(a) **A client has the right to withhold whatever he or she doesn't wish to share.** Experts generally assert that Asian Americans, Hispanics, and American Indians (Native Americans) are typically less likely to embrace self-disclosure as a valuable treatment modality when compared to Europeans and Americans.

243. Bill physically abused his two sons and his neighbor reported this to the state child abuse and neglect hotline. You are working as a child abuse/neglect (CAN) intake worker for the state's children's division, which performs protective services. Bill does not want you to come out for the investigation and says this is a private family matter.

   a.   You should still go out and do an assessment, although Bill is an involuntary client.
   b.   You should not go out to do an assessment. You can only assess and treat voluntary clients.
   c.   Clients have rights. If Bill doesn't want you there, do not go. He has a right to refuse services.
   d.   As with any involuntary client, you should call the police for immediate assistance.

(a) Child abuse, neglect, exploitation, and sexual abuse go beyond the privacy issues in the previous question.

244. Case management occurs when a human services practitioner assesses the needs of a client (or entire family, if necessary) and arranges for multiple services to meet their needs. The human services practitioner will monitor, coordinate, advocate, and evaluate what transpires to ensure the client receives the bundle of services. The first step in case management is

   a.   assessment, or gathering relevant information regarding the client's situation, strengths, weaknesses, needs, and goals.
   b.   planning.
   c.   service implementation.
   d.   service coordination.

(a) Hopefully, the question itself led you to the proper answer. To put it another way, **case management is a type of service delivery approach where clients and families who have multiple problems receive all the necessary services. The emphasis is on linking, in the sense that the case manager hooks the client/family up with the necessary services and can** provide some of the services personally. The case manager is accountable for making sure the services are provided in a timely manner. The case management movement was popularized in the 1960s due to the growth of human services agencies and the deinstitutionalization in the fields of developmental disabilities and mental health. Deinstitutionalization (a big word that simply means less people reside in psychiatric hospitals) was partially spawned by the psychotropic drug movement that espoused the notion that clients could live on their own if they were just properly medicated. Most experts now feel it wasn't such a great idea.

245. When several agencies are involved in the case management assessment, a

    a.   licensed social worker is required to help plan the strategies.
    b.   a licensed psychologist is required to help plan the strategies.
    c.   a licensed social worker or counselor is required to help plan the strategies.
    d.   a case manager coordinates a multidisciplinary/multi-agency team which might be needed to help plan the strategies.

(d) The case manager has been dubbed as the only member of the team who has the responsibility of being aware of the whole client.

246. The first step in case management is virtually always assessment. The second step could be

    a.   service implementation.
    b.   planning and creating a complete case plan for each client or family.
    c.   service coordination.
    d.   evaluation.

(b) **Planning is simply the act of identifying who will do what for the client and focusing in on what services will help the client (or the client's family) meet their goals. Again, step one is assessment, and step two is planning.**

247. Which aspect of case management would be impacted the *most* if the worker displays accurate empathy?

    a.   Service coordination.
    b.   Involvement.
    c.   Planning.
    d.   All are equally impacted since empathy is a very important skill.

(b) Involvement suggests that you're building a relationship with a client, and thus this would be the best answer. **Exam hint:** Building a relationship with a client can also be termed engaging the client.

248. Monitoring is another key aspect of case management. In order to do a good job in this area, you will need to

    a.   refer the client for psychological tests.
    b.   visit the client or contact her on a regular basis. This is known as ongoing contact.
    c.   visit the client at least once every 3 days.
    d.   perform a new initial assessment each week.

(b) The frequent contact (often in the form of face-to-face meetings with the client) allows you to reassess the client's predicament and change the plan if it's necessary. As far as choices c and d, many agencies might find every 3 days or each week a little over the top (translation: too much or impossible). **Case managers coordinate and monitor the success of multiple service providers.**

249. In the brokerage model of case management,

    a. the case manager need not provide the direct services to the client.
    b. the case manager does not need advanced clinical training skills.
    c. it is popular with workers in the TANF and social welfare system.
    d. all of the above statements are true.

(d) When a case manager is acting as a broker, he or she is **linking** the client with appropriate services and social programs. Take, as an example, choice c. Although you're the TANF worker, you wouldn't personally provide the client with personality testing or child care services for her children.

250. In the clinical model of case management,

    a. the case manager *is* expected to provide direct services to the client.
    b. the case manager *would* need training in clinical issues.
    c. it has been a popular model for dealing with clients who suffer from mental illnesses.
    d. all of the above statements are true.

(d) Here, the worker goes a step beyond merely acting as a broker or linking clients with services. He or she will also provide some of the direct services and would need special training to handle this role.

251. The rehabilitation model of case management

    a. does not focus on the goals of the overall human services system (e.g., keeping people out of inpatient facilities).
    b. focuses on building social skills, such as helping clients learn to clean their living quarters.
    c. can focus on building social skills to help with social situations or even dating.
    d. includes all of the above.

(d) This model is associated with the ideas of psychiatrist William Anthony and his associates at the Boston University Center for Psychiatric Rehabilitation.

252. Marco is in seventh grade, but can barely read. He is so embarrassed by this fact, he is skipping school and, thus, the family court is threatening to remove him from the home. His mother has not been able to effectively deal with this situation and is out of ideas how to help Marco. On your first home visit to the household, you discover that Marco loves working with engines. He has lawnmower engines in the yard and has even worked on automobiles in the neighborhood, even though he is too young to have a driver's license. You decide to bring an auto parts catalog on the next home visit. You point to an ignition coil and ask, "What's that?" Marco says, "Duh, anybody knows that is a coil." You respond with, "Whenever you see those two words in writing, you will know they mean ignition coil." Next, you assign a reading

specialist to the family. You will have the reading specialist bring her son's motor bike with her to the session to have Marco take a look at it because it is not running properly. Once Marco diagnoses the problem, the reading specialist will attempt to teach him to read the words associated with the engine's issues. The case manager is

a. using the rehabilitation model.
b. relying on the strength based model.
c. is not truly performing case management since he is involved in the treatment process himself.
d. using a psychodynamic approach to casework.

(b) If this sounds realistic, that's because I had a client just like this once. No, his name wasn't Marco (remember to disguise any identifying information when your speak or write about current or past clients), and I successfully used some of these very techniques! The whole idea of strength based treatment/case management is that helpers often spend too much time dwelling on the client's problems. If, on the other hand, the worker would concentrate on the client's strengths, it would be easier for the person to reach his or her goals.

253. Linda is working as an addiction treatment specialist. She believes she is falling in love with Jerry, who is an inpatient in the center. She thinks about dating him nearly every waking moment of the day. This is getting in the way of her work. Linda is a victim of

a. counter transference.
b. transference.
c. projection.
d. displacement.

(a) These are all important terms for an exam, so let's review them. Counter transference— the correct answer—occurs when the helper has feelings that get in the way of the treatment process. **Again, counter transference takes place when the helper (namely you!) has an issue that will hinder the treatment process.** Transference, on the other hand, is when a client responds to you the way he or she did to a significant other growing up, say a parent or caretaker. This usually only takes place during long-term treatment. Now jump down to choice c and you see the ego defense mechanism, projection. Here, a person sees something in somebody else that he finds too distasteful to notice in himself. For example, a man who unconsciously wants a divorce might accuse his wife of being distant. Displacement, another popular ego defense mechanism, takes place when somebody is scared to show anger toward the true target, so it's directed elsewhere (say you're a teacher and you're miffed at your principal, so you take it out on a child who's a student in your third grade class).

254. Jerry is a client in an inpatient addiction treatment center. He has been in the center for an extended period of time. He believes he is falling in love with Linda, who is working there as an addiction treatment specialist. According to psychoanalytic theory, Jerry is experiencing

a   counter transference.
b. transference.
c. reaction formation.
d. suppression.

(b) If you missed this one, have a gander at question 253. Since the other answer choices could help you tackle questions on the real exam, let's have a brief look at them, as well. According to psychoanalytic/psychodynamic theory, **reaction formation** transpires when you have an unconscious impulse that's psychologically threatening, so **you act in the opposite manner**. A client who fears he or she is homosexual might make fun of gays or talk about how much he or she dislikes them. In choice d, we're reacquainted with our old friend **suppression.** The most common question professors and exams like to ask is, **"How is suppression different than repression?"** Answer: Repression is automatic and unconscious. You can't remember a trauma from your childhood because it was too painful to examine at the time. Suppression, however, is conscious. How many times have you said, "My credit card bill really isn't that high," when it was way beyond your limit? **Therefore, repression is automatic while suppression/denial is a choice.**

255. Linda (mentioned in the previous two questions) is running a psycho-educational group for opiate abusers. During the group, she tells a client named Carlos that he is "engaging in stinking thinking." From a theoretical standpoint, Linda is operating out of

    a. the humanistic model.
    b. an applied behavioral analysis paradigm.
    c. gestalt therapy.
    d. CBT.

(d) CBT, or cognitive behavioral therapy, revolves around the fact that cognitive distortions, such as "I'll never be happy, all bosses are jerks," or "If I don't get this job, nobody will ever respect me," cause emotional issues. A lot of folks avoid the fancy terminology by just referring to this as stinking thinking.

256. During the final session prior to termination, Millie's treatment worker, Saul, suggests that her depressed mood will reappear in a few months. Nevertheless, he suggests the future depressed mood will not last as long as the blue mood that brought her to treatment. He is using

    a. a paradoxical intervention.
    b. accurate empathic reflection championed by Carl Rogers and other non-directive practitioners.
    c. open posture.
    d. synthesizing.

(a) A paradox is a statement which seems to be contradictory. Why would you tell a client who's experiencing a depressed mood that it might come back? Well, friends, life is strange and paradoxical interventions, such as telling the client she will experience the symptom again, often work to eliminate the symptom. Paradoxical strategies defy common sense. Unless you have a graduate degree and are a licensed helper, I'd confer with your supervisor before using paradox. It doesn't always work and should *never* be used with clients who harbor suicidal or homicidal impulses.

257. Lucy is visiting the methadone clinic. Her drug of choice would be

    a. heroin (an opiate drug synthesized from morphine).
    b. alcohol.

    c.   barbiturates which cause drowsiness and, in higher dosages, can even induce a coma or death.

    d.   steroids for improved athletic performance.

(a) **Methadone is a prescription drug used to treat heroin and opiate addiction.** Opiates (or opiods) sedate the person and can be used for pain relief.

258. You are working at the campus life office in a community college setting. Cliff comes in and reports he is grinding his teeth (bruxism) and quite jittery. Chances are

    a.   he is intoxicated from drinking too much alcohol.

    b.   he is using anabolic steroids to enhance his physique.

    c.   he is huffing gasoline. This is known as inhalant abuse.

    d.   he is using or abusing amphetamines.

(d) Grinding one's teeth can even be caused by amphetamines which are legally prescribed, such as Ritalin and Adderall. Amphetamines (aka uppers) can also cause brittle fingernails, ulcers, and weight loss; hence the other nickname, "diet pills." Faking symptoms to get Ritalin and Adderall is a major form of drug abuse on college campuses.

259. A client is obviously intoxicated from drinking too much alcohol prior to the session held at your agency. Your agency serves clients on an outpatient basis only. You should

    a.   continue the session as usual. The idea is to eliminate her tendency to drink.

    b.   scold the client and tell her you will never see her again if she comes in drunk.

    c.   send her home in a safe manner such as calling a taxi or having a friend or relative transport her home.

    d.   have the police escort her home.

(c) This is the answer espoused by most experts and textbook authors in the field.

260. At the end of the session, you summarize what has been covered and ask Mia, your client, if she feels the session was valuable. She smiles and politely tells you it was very helpful. Later that day, your secretary tells you that when Mia was leaving, she kicked a chair over in the agency waiting room and yelled, "God, I hate my human services worker." This client is most likely

    a.   a substance abuser who will need a 12-step recovery group.

    b.   a psychotic client who has obviously lost touch with reality.

    c.   displaying passive-aggressive behavior.

    d.   behaving this way from a head injury.

(c) Another typical example of passive-aggressive behavior: Child abusers (and clients who neglect their children) often display compassion regarding their child's situation and then virtually ignore the child after the worker leaves. Other examples of passive-aggressive behavior might be pouting or putting off a task. We use the term *passive* because no direct aggression is ever shown to the person the individual actually feels anger towards.

261. Madison is a 12-year-old girl who has been sexually abused. You are a child protective services (CPS) intake worker. As you begin your investigation, you know that, statistically speaking,

    a.   the perpetrator is a male who knows Madison, such as her biological dad.
    b.   the perpetrator is most likely Madison's mom.
    c.   the perpetrator is a stranger who never met Madison prior to the abuse.
    d.   the perpetrator is probably a 17-year-old neighbor boy who is huffing.

(a) Okay, granted, this sounds more like a "who done it" mystery novel than an exam prep guide. Strictly speaking, any of the above persons *could* have been the abuser. Nevertheless, in child abuse cases, about 50% of the time, the perpetrator will be a male, and approximately half of the time, the perpetrator will also be the biological father. In general, perpetrators have low self-confidence/self-esteem, unmet childhood needs, and they often lead isolated lives fearing others won't like them (i.e., they harbor a fear of rejection). When we look *specifically* at sexual abuse, the most common perpetrator is a father or stepfather. Sexual abuse of girls is higher than in boys. When the perpetrator is related to the child via marriage or genetic linkage, we use the term **incest** to describe the situation. Choice d, although it's the wrong answer, is a must-know concept. **Huffing, the street name for inhalant abuse, occurs when the client sniffs the vapors of a substance to get high.** In some cases, the substance is heated or burned. Gasoline, propane, glue, paint, toluene (street name, tuleo), amyl nitrite (aka poppers), non-stick cooking sprays, and nail polish removers are often the inhalants of choice. Huffing the aforementioned substances can cause immediate health problems and even death. Other individuals in close proximity can get a contact high, which is damaging as well.

262. Noah is 18 years old and living with his family. His mothers suspects he is "on drugs." When you ask for more information, Noah's mom mentions that her son has numerous bottles of one drop room deodorizer, leather cleaners, and VCR head cleaners in his room. She also reports he is attending raves. The chances are good

    a.   Noah is using crack, the so-called fast food version of cocaine.
    b.   Noah is addicted to pain killers.
    c.   Noah is addicted to Xanax.
    d.   Noah is huffing.

(d) The substances in the question are all commonly used for huffing. Compounds that contain amyl nitrite are often called poppers. They're common at raves and reputed to increase sexual pleasure. Nasal cavity burns are sometimes the result of usage. And, just in case you didn't know, a rave is a dance party that generally sports electronic music or a DJ that lasts all night. These parties often attract drug users.

263. The CPS worker substantiated that Humberto was physically abused by his mother. Which of these goals would be helpful for you to work toward with Humberto's mother?

    a.   Better impulse control.
    b.   Improved problem-solving skills.
    c.   Knowledge about parenting and child development.
    d.   All of the above.

(d) Stress management, nurturing, and impulse control are other goals which would be appropriate to focus on.

264. Human services practitioners want to empower the elderly. At this point in time, adults over 85 years of age (known as oldest old) are the fastest growing population

in America. You are in a micro-practice setting and have been assigned to help a client who is 86 years old. He has mobility problems because of his health and cannot travel outside his current facility. He wants to attend a mutual support group for persons with Alzheimer's disease at another facility, as he was recently diagnosed with this affliction himself.

   a. The best practice with older adults is total honesty. You need to be firm. Simply tell him this is not a possibility.
   b. Tell him that although it sounds like a good idea, you totally don't recommend it based on your experience.
   c. Show the client video footage from an Alzheimer's support group, as well as videos where elderly people talk about how they are coping with the disease.
   d. None of the above ideas are helpful.

(c) You could also connect your client with other individuals who are attempting to cope with similar issues by phone or e-mail. Sharing appropriate newspaper articles, stories on the web, and informational pamphlets would also be useful. When working with older adults, helping them to look at ways they coped with issues in the past is also a valuable technique.

265. Older adults often feel better when they use their own competencies to help others. This could include

   a. volunteering to transport other seniors who can no longer drive to appointments and shopping.
   b. volunteering to read to other seniors who have poor vision and cannot see well enough to read themselves.
   c. volunteering to oversee and organize the activities in choices a and b.
   d. all of the above, which are excellent examples of using strengths to help others while generally feeling better about yourself.

(d) Indeed choice d says it best: All of the above are superb examples of elderly persons helping others while helping themselves.

266. Your supervisor has lowered your performance evaluation based on the fact that you have done virtually nothing related to macro practice with the elderly. The best strategy to raise your rating would be to

   a. perform more family therapy with your elderly clients' families.
   b. help your clients form a group to protest legislation that will raise the age your clients can receive Social Security benefits.
   c. perform more one-on-one sessions with your elderly clients.
   d. form a support group for the elderly clients at your site.

(b). Choices a and d fall into the mezzo practice category, while choice c is clearly a micro practice activity. **Remember that macro means big or on a very large scale** Thus, by process of elimination, you're trying to change Social Security, which isn't just trying to change a big system—it's enormous! Now that's seriously macro.

267. Ethan is a 26-year-old veteran who fought in the Middle East. He is suffering from post traumatic stress disorder (PTSD). His symptoms are somewhat typical: flashbacks to battle scenes, recurrent nightmares, feelings of detachment, attempts to

avoid situations that might remind him of the traumatic situations, outbursts of anger, an exaggerated startle response, hyper-vigilance, and an inability to sleep. The best treatment of choice would be

a.   EMDR.
b.   client-centered counseling.
c.   psychodynamic psychotherapy.
d.   assertiveness training.

(a) EMDR stands for Eye Movement Desensitization and Reprocessing, created by Francine Shapiro, PhD. I purposely didn't tell you what the letters stood for in the question answer choices, since the writers of the actual exam might not be that generous, either. This form of intervention is highly desirable because it often produces dramatic results with PTSD and other forms of trauma very rapidly; say, 3 to 12 sessions.

268. You are unable to set Ethan (see the previous question) up with a qualified EMDR licensed practitioner. _____ might prove to be just as effective to help him with his PTSD condition.

a.   Anti-depressants and cognitive behavioral therapy (CBT)
b.   Gestalt therapy
c.   Adler's individual psychology
d.   Jung's analytic psychology

(a) In addition to the description in choice a, systematic desensitization can also be used with PTSD. **You'll recall that systematic desensitization is very effective for helping clients deal with phobias.**

269. Isabella's home was completely shattered by Superstorm Sandy. Your agency was providing crisis intervention to her in the aftermath of the tragedy. Your goal is

a.   to help Isabella return to her pre-crisis level of functioning.
b.   to help Isabella attain a larger home. Human services is all about progress.
c.   total personality reorganization.
d.   all of the above.

(a) Crisis intervention specialists believe that the goal of crisis intervention services is to *help the client return to a level of functioning that was present before the crisis took place.* Crisis intervention is a short-term intervention in which the practitioner uses active-directive strategies. Now, as far as choice b is concerned, hey, a bigger house might be nice, but it's beyond the scope of crisis intervention.

270. Chloe is dying of a terminal disease. She begins crying during a session.

a.   Tell her not to cry. It might suppress her immune system.
b.   Tell her not to cry. It is not a necessary part of grief.
c.   Encourage her to cry if she feels the need to do so. It can help relieve tension that is part of the grief process.
d.   Strangely enough, the best thing might be to lie to her and tell her she is not dying to stop the crying.

(c) Remember to encourage, but do not <u>force</u> clients to share feelings during a grief reaction. Also, nearly every expert *would not advise you to lie to the client* even though it's difficult to tell the person the truth in cases such as this.

271. Mrs. Suarez tells you that her teenage daughter, Savana, is threatening to run away. She notes that Savana told her she was a lesbian. You should

   a.   recommend that Savana be placed in a residential facility at once because it will greatly lower the probability that she will become a runaway statistic.
   b.   recommend to Mrs. Suarez that you want to work with the family immediately because most runaway children never return to their natural family and, thus, prevention is the only way to handle the situation.
   c.   recommend to Mrs. Suarez that you want to work with her family to discover what factors in the family are causing Savana to want to leave. Family problems and sexual orientation issues are often cited as situations that cause teens to run.
   d.   tell Mrs. Suarez that the stories about runaway juveniles are totally exaggerated. It is highly unlikely that her daughter, Savana, would get involved with drugs, prostitution, or other dangerous activities. The runaway experience might actually prove therapeutic. Moreover, if her daughter is a lesbian, that has virtually nothing to do with the situation. Do not intervene.

(c) Juveniles usually leave because of problems in the family. If a child is in a foster care or residential facility (**often referred to as substitute care on exams**), the likelihood of leaving is actually much higher! The reason: less ties to the child's caretaker. Also, kids in substitute care run away for longer periods of time and they go farther. Choice b is totally false, as only 1% of the kids that run never return. Unfortunately, choice d is misleading. A very high percentage of kids do use drugs, engage in prostitution or pornography, and other risky behaviors. Some statistics indicate that gay and transgender youth are more likely to run away.

272. Unfortunately, despite your best efforts, Savana, cited in the previous question, did run away. The police found her and brought her back to the home.

   a.   Explain to Mrs. Suarez, her daughter should be severely punished and harsh restrictions must be put into place.
   b.   Prosecute any person who harmed the child or contributed to her delinquency.
   c.   Listen to her reasons for leaving and seek counseling and medical care (if necessary).
   d.   Both choices b and c are correct.

(d) Advise Mrs. Suarez, it's certainly appropriate to set realistic rules and behavioral standards for the child. Also, try to get her back into school ASAP or in a GED program.

273. Benjamin has been clean and sober from alcohol for several years. Now he has a relapse. Which strategy would *not* be appropriate?

   a.   Role-play alcohol-seductive situations during your sessions with him.
   b.   Scold the client. This is a very serious situation.
   c.   Teach the client to handle the stressors that might have led to drinking in the past.
   d.   Emphasize what the client has learned from the situation rather than making the relapse sound like a major catastrophe.

(b) Alcoholics (or any addicts for that matter!) need "new playmates and new playpens." Imagine a recovering cocaine addict driving by the building where he purchased his coke from his dealer. Or try this one on for size: A recovering alcoholic goes to the bar where he reconnects with all his old drinking buddies. Bad idea—really, truly a bad idea!

274. Geraldo was tested during today's session at your agency and has a blood alcohol level (BAC) of .09. He is

    a. legally intoxicated and should not drive home.
    b. legally intoxicated, but it is not impairing his manual dexterity, so he can drive home.
    c. still way below the legal limit, so he can drive home.
    d. barely below the legal limit, so you should advise him not to drive home, but he can defy you legally if he wishes.

(a) At this point in time, virtually all states are setting the legal limit at .08. Some experts believe this limit is still too high. Many countries other than the US set the limit at .05. As far as choice b is concerned, it makes no difference. He can still receive a ticket for a DWI, or driving while intoxicated, or a DUI, known as driving under the influence. **This is the kind of statistic that can vary over time, so check reliable sources before taking your exam.**

275. Mrs. Gibson was repeatedly abusive to her daughter. The child was removed on several occasions and placed back in the home. Each time, Mrs. Gibson would physically beat her daughter again. Now the court has ruled in favor of a "termination of parental rights." The best plan of action would be

    a. to prepare Mrs. Gibson for the fact that she will still see her daughter, but the court will set the dates.
    b. to help Mrs. Gibson secure intensive counseling so she can handle her daughter without being violent.
    c. have Mrs. Gibson take a battery of tests to secure an accurate personality diagnosis and then help her secure intensive counseling so she can handle her daughter without being violent.
    d. to inform Mrs. Gibson that the legal parent-child relationship has ended and the child can legally be placed in a permanent home via adoption.

(d) Just for the record, it's possible for one parent to have termination of parental rights while the other doesn't.

276. Hong is a teenage male in your caseload. He has informed you he is seriously thinking of joining a street gang.

    a. He is probably contemplating this because he likes to party and take drugs.
    b. He sees it as a way of connecting with girls his own age.
    c. He likes the power and prestige of being in a gang.
    d. All of the above are very good possibilities.

(d) Very often, the gang is actually like a substitute family. Another interesting fact is there are currently nearly as many females in gangs as males. Generally speaking, the more males there are in the gang, the higher the rate of delinquency. Hence, an all-female gang is less likely to commit delinquent acts.

277. Pick the correct statement.

    a. Social Security is an entitlement program.
    b. SNAP is an entitlement program.
    c. The food stamp program is an entitlement program.
    d. TANF is an entitlement program.

(a) Well, if choices b, c, and d aren't entitlement programs, what in the world are they? Simple, we categorize them as means-tested programs. What's the difference? In a means-tested program, you must qualify for the services. Although the word *entitlement has been criticized* in human services, an entitlement program allows you to receive the service or benefit because of your position or status. An extremely wealthy person who has paid into Social Security could still receive benefits.

278. ____ is/are to micro, as ____ is/are to mezzo, as ____ is/are to macro.

   a. individuals and families, group, community
   b. community, individuals and families, group
   c. group, individuals and families, group
   d. group, community, individuals and families

(a) Repetition never hurts!

279. Your co-worker is in clear violation of the *HS-BCP Code of Ethics*. She has applied for the HS-BCP credential. You should

   a. do nothing. Your job is human services and not to police other workers.
   b. report it only if the violation relates to sexual harassment.
   c. report it using reasonable and clear facts according to the ethical code.
   d. do nothing because the *HS-BCP Code of Ethics* does not cover this situation.

(c) **An easily missed point:** Interestingly enough, the code specifies that you should report ethical violations whether the individual is a certificant (i.e., he or she already has the HS-BCP credential) or is an applicant (i.e., he or she has applied for the HS-BCP credential).

280. At the end of a confidential session, your client reveals he is planning to bomb the local post office. You should

   a. disclose this to the proper governmental agencies, since the client appears to be a danger and is unable to act safely.
   b. keep it a secret. As noted earlier, confidentiality is an entrusted secret.
   c. use your own clinical judgment. In most cases of this ilk, the client is merely blowing off steam to get his anger out and virtually nothing is going to happen.
   d. write a letter to the appropriate court and let the court take action.

(a) Please indulge me while I quote the *HS-BCP Code of Ethics* verbatim. **Section A titled, "Compliance with legal requirements and conduct standards number 7,"** states, "Make appropriate disclosures and referrals to government agencies and employers when a client appears to be a danger or is otherwise unable to act safely concerning him/herself or others. Such disclosures and referrals shall be consistent with legal and occupational requirements."

281. You are running a group and two members are having a power struggle. You remember seeing a technique in an old psychology book which suggested that you have the two clients arm wrestle to work through their issues. Today this practice would

   a. still be appropriate. Recommend it to the two group members.
   b. possibly be harmful to the clients. Do not use it.
   c. be totally appropriate in some therapeutic groups, but clearly inappropriate in others.
   d. be appropriate if the clients in question agree and the group votes on it.

(b) Times have changed! Many of the activities we (yes, me too!) used in groups could now be considered unethical in today's world. See *HS-BCP Code of Ethics* **Section C, titled, "Performance of services and other Occupational Activities number 5."** Also, keep in mind that you should inform clients about the purpose, application, and results of the techniques, assessments, or strategies. **The group leader is responsible for the safety of the group members.**

282. The state has custody of your client's 14-year-old son. You are conducting a home visit/home study to determine if the client's child will be allowed to come back to the home. This client knows you are a hockey fan and gives you front row tickets to an upcoming game. You should

    a.   take the tickets if you really want them and thank your client.

    b.   tell the client you really want the tickets, but want to discuss how this gift will impact your professional relationship if she doesn't get her son back before you will accept them.

    c.   do not take the tickets because it could influence your judgment.

    d.   call your supervisor before you take them. Lots of factors would enter into this decision.

(c) Read **number 5 in Section D, titled, "Avoidance of Interest and the Appearance of Impropriety"** in the *HS-BCP Code of Ethics*. Let's look at the facts. The key word in the ethical code here is "significant." If the client gave you a refrigerator magnet with the professional hockey team's logo, worth a buck, then it might not influence your occupational judgment. (However, you still might wish to turn it down or call your supervisor just to be sure.) But front row hockey tickets <u>are</u> significant in terms of their monetary value.

283. You run into a former client and are very attracted to him. Your last visit was 4 years ago. According to **Section D** of the *HS-BCP Code of Ethics*,

    a.   you cannot date this client.

    b.   you can have a romantic relationship with the client, but not a sexual one.

    c.   you could have a romantic and a sexual relationship with this client.

    d.   you can be friends, but you absolutely cannot date this client.

(c) I know I've touched on this issue before, but it's an important one that students ask me about repeatedly, so I want to be 101% sure you know the correct answer. The code says you must not engage in sexual or romantic interactions with a former client for 2 years. Since this question stipulates that 4 years have passed, it would be ethical, assuming you were *not exploiting the client.*

284. Lance overheard his new client tell another client in the waiting room that, since she has a master's degree in psychology, she was hoping to be placed with a human services worker who has at least a master's degree. Thus, when Lance introduced himself to his client, he erroneously told her he had a master's degree in psychology. In reality, although Lance does possess the HS-BCP credential, his sole degree is an Associate of Applied Science in Human Services from a community college.

    a.   Lance has committed an ethical violation known as a dual relationship.

    b.   Lance has committed an ethical violation known as a multiple relationship.

    c.   Lance has committed an ethical violation known as misrepresentation.

    d.   Lance is an impaired professional.

(c) **Misrepresentation occurs when you say you're something you're not.**

285. Because of medical issues, Mollie cannot have a baby. She does want a child and she wants the same legal rights as natural parents. You could explain to her that

    a. she can adopt a child.
    b. she can be a foster parent.
    c. she can provide respite care.
    d. there is no solution to this dilemma.

(a) **Foster parents do not possess parental legal rights; however, parents of adopted children have the same legal rights as parents have for their own birth children.**

286. After speaking with you, Mollie decides she wants to adopt a child. Your next step would be

    a. to conduct an initial psychosocial assessment with her, just like you would with any other client.
    b. to conduct a home study.
    c. to refer her to a doctoral-level clinical psychologist for psychological testing.
    d. to refer her to a psychiatrist who is a medical doctor to perform a mental status exam.

(b) **No matter where you reside in the US, a *home study* is required if you wish to become adoptive parents. The process educates and prepares the parents for the experience. It assesses the family and the home environment, and helps connect the family with an appropriate child. Keep in mind, the family could be screened out and not accepted, since the idea is to promote the welfare of the child.**

287. You are a social worker who is a member of the National Association for Social Workers (NASW). You also hold the HS-BCP credential. You are very attracted to your former client and have a sexual relationship with him 4 years after you terminate him as a client. Here is the problem. NASW ethics state, "Social Workers should not engage in sexual activities or sexual conduct with former clients because of the potential for harm to the client." The HS-BCP rule is that sexual or romantic interactions with former clients should not occur for a minimum of 2 years following the last HS-BCP contact. Unfortunately, you and your former client are not getting along well, and he threatens to sue you for having sex with him.

    a. You have nothing to worry about. HS-BCP stipulated that you will wait 2 years before engaging in a sexual relationship, and you waited twice that long.
    b. It might depend on your job title.
    c. It might depend whether you were acting in a social worker role or a human services practitioner role.
    d. Choices b and c.

(d) It might surprise you that nobody can give you a perfect answer to this question at this time, but, as you may have guessed, that doesn't stop comprehensive exams from asking similar questions! You have probably heard the old line, "You can't serve two masters." In this case, the two masters are the two ethical bodies. You have a true ethical dilemma on your hands. In this situation, if you went to court, the court might investigate your job title. Are you working as a social worker, or are you functioning more in a human services position? Also, what were you doing at the time? Was it more geared toward social work or human services? Sometimes courts would take the position that you should be adhering to the more stringent ethical stance (in this instance, NASW's guideline stating you should never have sex with a former client.) So, to get to the point, choices b and c aren't perfect answer stems, but they're the best ones listed. If you're a member of the American Counseling Association (ACA), you'd need to wait 5 years after the last professional contact, and the National Association for Drug and Alcohol Abuse Counselors (NAADAC) takes a position that coincides with NASW. Hmm. Make that trying to obey **more** than two masters for many of you!

288. You have the HS-BCP status and you are a licensed professional counselor who is a member of the American Counseling Association. You are running a psychoanalytic group for persons with severe anxiety disorders. A client is unhappy with your services and decides to take legal action against you. You will most likely be judged by

   a.   the ethics set forth via the American Counseling Association.
   b.   the HS-BCP code, of course.
   c.   the NASW code.
   d.   choices b and c.

(a) Psychoanalytic therapy is depth psychotherapy that would be conducted by a trained therapist. Thus, counseling is more closely related to the job skill than human services.

289. You have a client who is receiving assistance. Many experts are worried that after 2030, this program will be bankrupt. Your client is most likely receiving

   a.   food stamps (assistance from the SNAP Program).
   b.   TANF, also known as Temporary Assistance for Needy Families. Participants who are able-bodied must secure work or job training/job seeking within the first 2 years of receiving benefits.
   c.   Medicaid.
   d.   Social Security benefits.

(d) Most experts concur that after 2030—give or take a few years—the Social Security program won't have the necessary funding to provide the current level of benefits for individuals over the age of 65, or those under 65 who are disabled. The age to receive Social Security benefits has already climbed. The idea of this policy change is to lower the number of people who would otherwise receive benefits and, needless to say, this will cut costs.

290. Your client has been receiving benefits for nearly 60 months, or 5 years. You are worried because her benefits will be ending soon. Your client is receiving

   a.   TANF, or Temporary Assistance for Needy Families, which provides financial assistance to eligible families with children under 18 years of age.
   b.   Medicaid, a healthcare coverage program for some eligible persons who receive SSD, TANF, or Supplemental Security Income (SSI).
   c.   Medicare, a national social insurance program that provides health insurance for older adults, as well as younger individuals who are disabled.
   d.   Social Security Disability (SSD) benefits, a program intended to assist persons who are diagnosed as unable to work for at least 1 year because of a mental or physical disability to due to drug or alcohol addiction.

(a) TANF—which replaced AFDC, or Aid to Families With Dependent Children, in 1996—has a lifetime limit of cash benefits for 60 months (also known as a 5-year lifetime cap) for clients who are not disabled. *Test tip: Some exams refer to TANF as welfare-to-work.* The verdict? Many social welfare pundits often say that welfare-to-work is a positive thing. However, practitioners often counter with the fact that during a tough economy, even those who are working are living below the poverty level.

291. Which client would best be served by a significant-other group, rather than a mutual aid group or a health group?

   a.   Marty, who just discovered her daughter is bisexual and is very upset.
   b.   Jill, who has just been diagnosed as having AIDS.
   c.   Len, who has a serious gambling addiction.
   d.   Regis, who is newly divorced.

(a) For several years, I ran a survivors-of-suicide group, where significant others came to deal with their feelings related to a friend, relative, or loved one's suicide. By definition, significant-other groups—like the survivors-of-suicide group I ran—help a person's family or friends who are experiencing (or have experienced) a powerful life event. Choice b isn't a bad answer, so give yourself a friendly pat on the back if you felt it was the proper answer, but a medical/health-condition group would be a better choice. A gambling addiction group (choice c) and a group for individuals who are divorced (choice d) fit better into the mutual aid/support group category. The lines between these groups are blurry at times.

292. Who would best be served by a disease/health-condition group?

   a.   Marty, who just discovered her daughter is bisexual and is very upset.
   b.   Jill, who has just been diagnosed as having AIDS.
   c.   Len, who has a serious gambling addiction.
   d.   Regis, who is newly divorced.

(b) Even if you consider gambling addiction a disease/health condition, b is still the best choice because Len would be better served by an addiction group than a health-condition group. Groups for cancer, strokes, and other maladies are popping up nationwide.

293. Chu, a homeless client, suffers from an addiction to pain medications, and also has a mood disorder (clinical depression). He is therefore considered a dual diagnosis client. On some exams, dual diagnosis clients are said to have co-occurring disorders or conditions. He also has AIDS. As his case manager, you would *most likely*

   a.   create a behavior modification program for him.
   b.   use applied behavior analysis, or ABA, to help him.
   c.   develop, coordinate, and mobilize a variety of health, mental health, and social services for him.
   d.   simply refer him to a private practice psychiatrist.

(c) First things first. ABA stands for applied behavior analysis, which is a paradigm/model that's based on behavior modification; hence, choices a and b mean roughly the same thing. Since Chu has an array of difficulties, you'd *most likely* tackle this situation by using a case management approach rather than try to treat him yourself with a single theory. Choice c is almost a textbook definition of the case management strategy.

294. Joyce has a bachelor's degree in human services and a master's degree in counseling. She is also certified by the department of elementary and secondary education as a K-12 school guidance counselor. She snared a terrific job at a private high school as a guidance counselor. She also has a small private practice she runs after school and on weekends. She gives every student who comes to see her at school a business card for her private practice and instructs each child to give the card to their parents, mentioning that she can help them a lot better if she can give them the extra time.

    a. Ethically, she should not be doing this.
    b. It is fine since she is an employee and not a school board member.
    c. Ethical guidelines set forth by all agencies and organizations shy away from this topic, so she could counsel these children if she wishes.
    d. Ethically, she can do this, but most ethical bodies and schools frown on this practice.

(a) Some organizations and most agencies/schools have a rule you can't charge for a service outside of the agency/school that the client, patient, or student could receive for free at the agency or school. Bottom line: In many, if not most instances, Joyce could lose her job for this little stunt and, indeed, I personally know of situations where this has occurred. P.S. As previously stated, many exam questions have irrelevant information. In this case, the fact that Joyce has a bachelor's degree in human services and not psychology or education, and the fact that she's employed at a private school and not a public institution is totally irrelevant in terms of answering the question.

295. Mickey suffers from trichotillomania, an affliction where she pulls her hair out and often tries to eat the hair strands. You are using a solution focused approach. You say to her, "What's better since you have been taking the new medicine?"

    a. This would be a totally inappropriate question.
    b. This is a fine example of a scaling question.
    c. This is a fine example of a "What's Better?" question.
    d. This is a fine example of an exception question.

(c) Yep. Good old common sense here might have just landed you the correct answer. Trichotillomania is called "hair pulling disorder" in the new DSM 5. **Scaling questions, exception questions, and what's better questions are used in solution focused therapy.**

296. You say to Mickey (mentioned in the previous question), "On a scale of 1 to 10, how would you rate your level of hair pulling at this point in time?"

    a. This would be a totally inappropriate question.
    b. This is a fine example of a "What's Better?" question.
    c. This is a fine example of a scaling question.
    d. This is a fine example of an exception question.

(c) Let's say Mickey quips that she's at 4. You might use a scaling question once more and ask, "What would it take to get you from 4 to 9?"

297. You ask Mickey (mentioned in the two previous questions), "Was there ever a time when you didn't pull your hair?"

    a. This would be a totally inappropriate question.
    b. This is a fine example of a "What's Better?" question.

c. This is a fine example of a scaling question.
d. This is a fine example of an exception question.

(d) Exception questions are very popular when using brief, strategic, solution focused approaches, and illuminate the fact that when a client protests that the behavior is always present, this isn't necessarily 100% true. An analysis of exceptions can lead to different/healthier ways to handle or cope with the issue.

298. Rosalie has strong urges to murder her boss. In addition, she has severe arthritis and has missed several appointments with her physician. The arthritis is so intense, she can barely move, and it is taking a toll on her ability to work and parent her children. She is also suffering with a low grade of depression known as dysthymia. By definition, dysthymia (called persistent depressive disorder) is not as severe as clinical depression, but it lasts considerably longer. As her human services practitioner, you should

a. refer her to a physician immediately. This is clearly a medical emergency.
b. first deal with her dysthymia, then her homicidal urges, and finally her arthritis.
c. first deal with her homicidal urges, next the dysthymia, and finally the arthritis.
d. first deal with her homicidal urges, next the arthritis, and finally her dysthymic mood disorder.

(d) A great little review here. **When a client is thinking of hurting herself (aka self-harm) or somebody else, or both, then you should deal with that issue first!** No exceptions! Her arthritis would be the second most serious challenge, so you'd deal with it next. Persons with dysthymic disorders are less likely to make suicide attempts than those with severe clinical depression (on many exams, just called depression). *In cases where a client has the urge to harm herself, another person, or both, a safety plan should be created ASAP. Needless to say, this is in the client's best interest, but it will also help cover you from an ethical and legal standpoint. Final hint: Although the new DSM 5 uses the persistent depressive disorder to categorize both forms of depression now, it's possible your exam could still be using the longstanding dysthymia vs. clinical depression distinctions that have been around for years.*

299. Your agency is starting a group for women who have been sexually abused. Leveta was repeatedly sexually abused by her stepfather growing up. Ideally, you should

a. allow Leveta in the group and, ethically, any other woman who wants to join.
b. make Leveta take a complete battery of psychological tests to determine if she is eligible for the group.
c. do an individual *and* a group screening with Leveta to see if she is appropriate for the group.
d. do an individual screening (never a group screening) with Leveta to see if she is appropriate for the group.

(c) This is the ideal answer, though to be sure, it's not *always* possible to conduct an individual and a group screening in real world situations. When a question has several answers that are possibly correct, pick the best answer, *even when the question doesn't say, "pick the best answer."*

300. You are a case manager and you are meeting your client for the first time. You have decided to use a reality therapy approach created by psychiatrist William Glasser.

This is not unusual because on some occasions (but certainly not all), the case manager actually engages in direct practice. You like your client and trust her a lot. She asks you if you would mind giving her your personal cell phone number, and whether you would like to purchase some frozen pizza to help support her daughter's soccer team. You should

a.   give her your personal cell phone number and buy the frozen pizza, assuming it is not a financial strain for you. You like the client and the first step in reality therapy is to "make friends with the client." There is no doubt this will help you accomplish this first step.

b.   not buy the pizza or provide the client with your cell phone number. To do so would cause boundary issues between you and your client.

c.   offer to give her your personal e-mail for emergencies, but do not purchase the pizza or share your private cell phone number.

d.   take five dollars out of your pocket (if you can afford it) and give it to the client for her daughter's soccer team, but do not accept the frozen pizza, as that would be deemed unethical. The decision to give out your cell phone is best left to your own judgment.

(b) Yes, making friends with the client is indeed the first step of psychiatrist William Glasser's reality therapy, but that isn't the point. The term "boundaries" in our field refers to the emotional and physical limits the worker sets with clients (e.g., the client can call after hours, but must call the agency telephone, rather than your personal cell phone). To share the wisdom so many workers now espouse, **"You can be friendly, but don't be the client's friend."** I hate to even bring this topic up and this could change as the years pass, but I know many of you are wondering how to handle the issue of social media. Should you make a client a friend and should you accept the offer to be a friend on your client's page? As it stands now, the answer is no and no!

Chapter 5

Administration, Program Development/Evaluation, and Supervision

301. You have vast experience in the field and wish to start a non-for-profit (also called a nonprofit or voluntary) agency to counsel children who have lived through one or more divorces. This service is necessary because approximately 40 to 50% of all marriages end in divorce. The rate for second marriages is higher, hovering around 60% or more. Your main concern should be

    a.   IRS 501 (3) (c) guidelines.
    b.   IRS 501 (c) (3) guidelines.
    c.   United Way guidelines.
    d.   State Department of Revenue guidelines.

(b) To the surprise of most students, it's the good old Internal Revenue Service—yep, the IRS—that provides the application to become a nonprofit agency. If accepted, it's the IRS that sanctions the agency's tax exempt status. I purposely included choice a because most people have a tendency to answer the question at the speed of light if they glance at it and *think* they know the correct answer. Why is choice a incorrect? Simple: The (3) comes before the (c), which is wrong. The correct way to write this is 501 (c) (3). **Paying attention to details can improve your score.**

302. Which statement is true for your new nonprofit agency?

    a.   A board of directors would be nice, but it certainly is not required.
    b.   A board of directors is required for all non-for-profit agencies.
    c.   A board of directors is nice, but an advisory board is more important.
    d.   State governments recommend a board of directors and, therefore, about 50% of all nonprofits have one.

(b) When I first entered this field, I believed that only giant corporations like General Motors or Microsoft had boards. WRONG! The IRS stipulates that nonprofits have a minimum of three board members. **Again, all nonprofit agencies have a board of directors.**

303. You did, indeed, start the new non-for-profit agency to help children struggling with the issue of divorce. An ideal cast of board members would be

    a.   a clinical psychologist, licensed counselor, and licensed clinical social worker.
    b.   a school psychometrician, high school guidance counselor, and pastoral counselor.
    c.   a sociologist, forensic psychologist, and psychiatrist.
    d.   an attorney, clinical psychologist, and CPA accountant.

(d) A board composed of just human services types might sound ideal, but it's not! Diversity is important on the board and I don't just mean racial and cultural diversity, although that might be an issue, as well. An attorney would help you with legal matters, and a CPA with your budget, accounting, and book keeping.

304. The average salary for non-for-profit board members in the US is approximately

    a. $20,000 per year.
    b. $40,000 per year.
    c. zero.
    d. $65,000 per year.

(c) **Board members for nonprofit agencies do not make a salary—zip, zero, nothing.**

305. The top paid agency position would be

    a. the President of the Board of Directors.
    b. the Clinical Director.
    c. the Program Director.
    d. the Executive Director.

(d) **Agencies with more than one employee have a structure, or hierarchy (who's over whom). This is sometimes called the chain of command. Often, an agency will have an organizational chart, which is simply a pictorial diagram of the positions and their relationship to other positions. The top paid employee is the executive director or president. In our field, the term "executive director" is more common.**

306. You need to write a grant to raise money. As a supervisor, you get to pick the best employee for this task. In most instances, you would pick

    a. the Director of Development.
    b. the Program Director.
    c. a human services practitioner who focuses on case management and truly understands the clients' needs.
    d. the Clinical Director, who truly understands the services the clients receive.

(a) **It's generally the Director of Development (aka the Development Director) who deals with fundraising and writing grants. Granted, some agencies have a dedicated grant writer; however, this question doesn't give you that choice.**

307. You are a supervisor in a drug treatment center. A board member notices that one of your workers is using a confrontational style with a client. After the session, the board member explains to your supervisee that she should ditch the confrontational style and use a motivational interviewing approach. In most cases,

    a. you, as a supervisor, would be happy because the board member is doing her job.
    b. you would be happy because a confrontational style is never appropriate with substance abusers.
    c. choices a and b are both correct.
    d. the board member would be micromanaging, and this is not a desirable thing to do.

(d) **Board members are there to govern the agency and, in general, shouldn't be handling the small day-to-day issues, such as a given worker's treatment style.**

308. As a supervisor, you want to hire a person who can bring in money for your agency by running a sports auction/dinner each year. The best candidate would probably be

    a. a master's level psychotherapist who actually did his internship with a famous therapist.
    b. a director of development who mainly worked as a grant writer.
    c. a young woman just out of school 6 months ago, who has been working as an event planner for a rival agency.
    d. an intake caseworker for the CPS unit.

(c) Some agencies actually have event planners. A fun job, but, yes, it can be stressful trying to please hundreds of folks at a fundraiser so they'll give money. CPS in choice d stands for Child Protective Services. A worker with this title generally works with child abuse, neglect, exploitation, and sexual abuse.

309. After you hire somebody to put together the sports auction/dinner, you discover that one of your former board members helped plan similar sports auction/dinners for a similar agency for years, and the events were very successful. Pick the correct statement.

    a. You might like the former board member to help, but, legally, she cannot assist you because she is no longer a board member.
    b. You could legally bring her back to help, but she would need to be brought back as a paid staff member.
    c. She could come back and help as an ex officio board member.
    d. The executive director would not allow this in most situations.

(c) **Former or ex officio board members may return to help out.**

310. The board of directors is very dissatisfied with the executive director. Pick the most accurate statement.

    a. The board could hold a closed meeting and decide to fire the executive director.
    b. The board would hold an open meeting and decide to fire the executive director.
    c. The board cannot fire the executive director, as she is the top paid employee.
    d. The board would attend a staff meeting and ask the staff to vote on whether they wish to keep their executive director or not. Whatever was decided would determine the plan of action.

(a) Yes, the board can fire an executive director, but they will usually do so in a closed session, rather than airing their dirty laundry for the whole world to see. Here again, you can always find an exception, but the trick on most certification exams is to go with the answer stem that is correct on most occasions.

311. The HS-BCP is

    a. a state license.
    b. a CEU.
    c. a national certification.
    d. a graduate certificate.

(c) The HS-BCP is a national certificate, since it doesn't matter which state you live in if you have the appropriate credentials. Choice a, a state license, is conferred by the state (think of who gives you your driver's license). Choice b is a huge term in this day and age. CEU stands for continuing education unit. Virtually all licenses and certifications have CEU requirements in order for you to keep your credential.

312. You are Abigail's supervisor. You assign her to create an informal test to determine whether your program is actually helping clients. Abigail created the test and gave it to Madison (the first client who would ever take it). She administered the test to Madison 4 times in a 48-hour period. Madison scored 17, 56, 87, and 99. This demonstrates that

   a. the test is highly reliable.
   b. the test has very poor reliability.
   c. Abigail should have purchased a standardized measure. Informal tests are never appropriate.
   d. the measure is valid, but not very reliable.

(b) Reliability answers the question of whether or not a measure gives consistent results. The verdict: This one stinks! Madison's score varied from 17 to 99 in a 2-day period.

313. You want to hire human services practitioners for your adoption agency, but want to be certain that the candidates have a working knowledge of adoption. You create a measure to test the applicants' knowledge. Before you actually use it, you decide to give the test to your finest adoption workers who have the most experience at your agency. Their average score is 33%. Then, just to get even more feedback, you sent the test to some of the finest foster care experts in the country. The experts scored just three percentage points higher: 36%. A perfect score is 100%. You could safely say

   a. the test is not valid.
   b. the test is valid.
   c. the test is reliable, but not valid.
   d. the test is valid, but definitely not reliable.

(a) Sorry, but the test mentioned in this question is just too dang difficult or it isn't testing the right material! Even your top experts in the field could not get a respectable score. Let's use an example from sports, which should make this a lot easier to understand. If you gave a famous baseball slugger (say, Albert Pujols) or a great golfer (for example, Tiger Woods) a test related to their sports performance and they scored lousy, we would need to conclude that the test just wasn't valid. Again, the test isn't testing what it should be testing! *Validity occurs when a test measures what it's supposed to be testing/measuring.*

314. If you create a valid test for your agency,

   a. it still won't always be reliable.
   b. it will always be reliable.
   c. it would not be reliable because it is not a standardized test.
   d. choices b and c are both correct.

(b) This is a very common question in this field. Please repeat after me: A valid test is always reliable. For example, if your scale indicates you weigh 152 lbs and you really do weigh 152, then the scale will always be reliable and give you the same reading of 152 lbs, day, night, holidays—anytime.

315. You are an administrator at a for-profit agency. Your human services workers are rated by their supervisors using an A, B, C, D, and F grading scale that is analogous to the system used in most community colleges and universities. Out of 100 human services workers, 92 workers received a grade of C for their performance rating. This would most likely mean

    a. the supervisors have a central tendency rating bias (also known as the error of central tendency).

    b. the supervisors are doing their jobs! Although human services workers don't like to admit it, nearly all of them are average.

    c. the supervisors have an unconscious need to feel superior to their workers, and this needs to be dealt with in a staff meeting with workers, supervisors, and administrators.

    d. as an administrator, you need to eliminate the A, B, C, D, and F grading scale immediately.

(a) **The central tendency bias occurs when a person rates too many people as average.** Clearly, that's the case in this situation. **According to a notion dubbed the normal curve, approximately 68% of the population (or 68 workers out of 100) will be in the average range, in this case a C. In this example, 92 out of 100 workers fell into that category.**

316. One of your supervisors only gives high ratings to workers who come to work early, prior to regular working hours. Another only gives good ratings to attractive employees. Both of these supervisors are

    a. demonstrating the central tendency bias.

    b. overly strict.

    c. demonstrating the leniency error or bias.

    d. demonstrating the halo effect.

(d) **The halo effect takes place when you generalize about a person based on a single characteristic or trait.** For example, we often think models or movie stars are smarter than they truly are, just because of their good looks. **The leniency error/bias occurs when ratings of individuals are too high or too positive, and not really accurate. Ratings such as this fail to point out shortcomings and areas which need improvement.** (That said, I'm certain if you've ever had a professor who gives straight A's to students, even if the students know next to nothing, then you, my friend have experienced the leniency effect firsthand.)

317. Your supervisor assigns you to create some groups to help the clients. She carefully explains that the agency does <u>not</u> have the money to pay you or any other helper as the leader. You should

    a. form reciprocal groups.

    b. form mutual aid groups.

    c. form support/self-help groups.

    d. All of the above answers are correct, and describe a group with common goals that is allowed to use nonprofessional member leaders. The 12-step Alcoholics Anonymous group is the most popular example of this type of group where members themselves provide the leadership.

(d) The reciprocal, mutual aid, support, or self-help group is very cost effective, since a paid group leader is <u>not</u> utilized.

318. Fritz is working as a human services practitioner in a very large halfway house for clients who have been released from prison. You are his supervisor. Normally, you would

    a. give him a comprehensive formal performance evaluation daily.
    b. review his work periodically.
    c. review his work only when a serious tragedy takes place, such as when a child dies.
    d. meet with Fritz on a daily basis to discuss each client in his caseload.

(b) Periodically literally means "from time-to-time," "at regular intervals," or "on a regular basis." A formal comprehensive performance evaluation (choice a) might be conducted once a year, or perhaps even once a month, but certainly a daily evaluation of this nature would be way over the top. Choice d might sound ideal, but in the real world, consider the fact that at many agencies, the human services practitioner has 200 or 300 clients! (Okay, maybe not in a halfway house, but, indeed, this could occur in some settings such as public assistance agencies.) Fritz would be spending so much time meeting with his supervisor, he'd never get to interact with a client.

319. You are a new practicum student in your agency. Your first activity should be

    a. meeting the board of directors.
    b. asking to see an intake initial evaluation sheet.
    c. meeting with the executive director.
    d. meeting with staff members.

(d) Often, an executive director is busy or oversees several facilities, and could not meet with you immediately. Ditto for members of the board.

320. You want to serve your practicum at the XYZ agency. The agency asks you for a child abuse check, a police check, and a TB test. You should

    a. report this to your instructor in the human services program because it is illegal.
    b. report this to a federal or state agency because the XYZ agency has violated your right to privacy.
    c. kindly explain why this is not ethical. Do not accept this practicum, but call the executive director to inform him or her that this occurred.
    d. comply with the agency. They have every right to ask for this.

(d) Actually, this type of information is becoming the rule rather than the exception. My advice: Get used to it!

321. You are supervising a practicum student from a local college. She is working on an Associate of Applied Science degree in human services. She is placed at a local addiction treatment center. She has been faking drug testing samples, so many of the clients pass when they should have failed. This is clearly unethical and illegal.

    a. The student, her practicum supervisor, the college, and the agency could be responsible/liable for her actions.
    b. Only the student is responsible for her actions.
    c. Only the agency is responsible for her actions.

  d. The student would not be responsible since she is not working on a bachelor's degree.

(a) As far as choice d, I can only quip, you wish! Working on a BA, MA, MSW, or PhD is *never* a license to engage in unethical or illegal behavior. If you're an instructor or professor teaching in a human services program, please be aware that *you, too,* could be held responsible for the actions of your practicum students. You should walk—no, make that run—to your nearest college administrator to ask whether your institution of higher learning has a malpractice policy that covers your students and yourself!

322. Imagine you are the agency employee who is supervising the student depicted in the previous question. After reading the question, you are convinced you should have malpractice liability insurance. All of the following choices would be good places to search for a policy *except*

  a. going to your insurance agent who sold you your auto policy.
  b. contacting professional organizations such as the APA, ACA, or NASW.
  c. looking for advertisements for malpractice policies in newsletters, journals, or magazines produced by professional organizations such as the APA, ACA, or NASW.
  d. searching the Web for malpractice insurance for mental health workers, caseworkers, human services workers, social workers, addictions counselors, etc.

(a) If the person who provides your home, auto, or earthquake insurance is totally honest, he will tell you he either *can't* provide you with malpractice insurance or, if he can, that you could get it a heck of a lot cheaper from the sources (e.g., a professional organization) listed above.

323. You firmly believe that a car wash could be an effective method to raise money for your agency. In most cases,

  a. the clinical director would be the best person to determine if this is true, since he or she runs the entire treatment program.
  b. the volunteer coordinator would be the best person, since he or she could get volunteers to actually wash the vehicles.
  c. the development director would be the best person, since he or she is in charge of bringing in contributions and donations.
  d. the PhD clinical psychologist would be the best person, since he or she has the most education and knowledge of human behavior and could tell you whether people would really come to the event.

(c) The individual in the development position generally handles fundraising events. An employee with a PhD (e.g., choice d) might know virtually nothing about raising money.

324. You are creating a resource guide for your city. The best person to create the guide would be

  a. your resource and referral coordinator.
  b. any member on your board of directors.
  c. the program director.
  d. the executive director.

(a) Sometimes, good old common sense pays off. The problem in the real world is that many agencies don't have a resource and referral coordinator. Generally, only very large organizations or hotlines/helplines that serve as a giant resource bank would have such an individual on staff. Mental health associations sometimes find it worthwhile to have a resource person. **Another exam hint: Some exams call the referral process and/or the person who's coordinating it I&R for Information and Referral Services or Information and Referral Coordinator.**

325. You are supervising Gary. Gary has a Hispanic client named Maria. Maria's native language is Spanish. She has difficulty speaking English. She speaks English slowly and her verbalizations make sense. Gary does not speak any Spanish. You are gearing up to do his rating. It is important to remember that

   a. Gary can still be a culturally competent practitioner even if he doesn't speak Spanish.
   b. Gary can still be a culturally competent practitioner, but he needs to speak fluent Spanish.
   c. Gary can still be a culturally competent practitioner if he knows Spanish street language and can communicate with Maria.
   d. Gary can still be a culturally competent practitioner if the agency has a translator available for all his sessions with Maria.

(a) A culturally competent worker doesn't need to speak the client's native language. Choice d might fit the bill if Maria spoke virtually no English.

326. Gary, mentioned in question 325, is discussing Maria's situation in a case conference.

   a. This is clearly unethical.
   b. This would be ethical only if Maria is in imminent danger.
   c. This would be ethical only if Gary is licensed as a social worker, counselor, or psychologist.
   d. This would be perfectly ethical.

(d) Yes, sir, and yes, ma'am, you may discuss a client's case in a case conference. Case closed—pun intended!

327. Lulu received 80 out of 100 when she took a test regarding agency policy. Her score

   a. indicates she really knows agency policy.
   b. indicates she knows very little about agency policy.
   c. doesn't tell us enough—more information is necessary.
   d. indicates her understanding of agency policy is very average.

(c) In this question, 80 is a raw (unaltered) score that really tells us nothing. A score of 80 could be the highest score ever posted and, indeed, it could be the lowest. More information is clearly needed to discover where this score fits into the scheme of things.

328. Sylvester's score fell into the 98th percentile when he completed an exam focused on agency policy. This score

   a. indicates he really knows agency policy better than most of his colleagues.
   b. indicates he truly knows a lot less about agency policy than his colleagues.

c. doesn't tell us enough—more information is necessary.
d. indicates his knowledge of agency policy is very average.

(a) **Percentile is *not* the same as percentage. Percentile shows your rank compared to others who took the exam or test.** If somebody scored a 98% on a 100 point exam, then he knew the answers to 98 questions out of 100. Percentile, on the other hand, tells you the percentage of people—in this case, a whopping 98%—who scored the same or below Sylvester. It doesn't mean he scored 98% on the exam. Translation: The 98th percentile is a very high score. A score of 40% or 60% out of 100 might be high enough to put somebody in the 98th percentile, depending on the difficulty of the test. **In rare instances, exams substitute the word centile for percentile.**

329. You administered an IQ test to 25 children at your special needs agency. The lowest score was 70 and the highest was 100. What was the range on the IQ test?

a. 30
b. 15
c. 60
d. More data is required to tackle this question.

(a) The range is a statistical term which is determined simply by computing the difference between the highest and lowest scores posted. Hence, 100–70 = 30.

330. An IQ test theoretically measures

a. intelligence.
b. personality.
c. aptitude.
d. vocational choice.

(a) There are tests available for intelligence, personality, aptitude, and vocational choice.

331. Wendy believes her daughter has tremendous potential in music. The best test would be

a. an aptitude test.
b. an achievement test.
c. an IQ test.
d. a vocational or career inventory.

(a) Yes, that's three choice a's in a row. **Key point: Aptitude tests measure potential.** The test is not saying Wendy's daughter can play the piano, violin, or even a toy guitar at this point in time. Instead, the aptitude test examines whether, with practice and training, Wendy's daughter *could* excel in this area.

332. Kurt's son, Lester, is a third grade student in an elementary school. Kurt is worried that his son is not reading as well as he should. The best test would be

a. an IQ test.
b. an aptitude test.
c. an achievement test.
d. a personality test.

(c) When you're told that your son, daughter, or client is reading at the third grade level, you're reaping the benefits of an achievement test. If I told you that your client ran the

60 yard dash in 7 seconds, that, too, would be an achievement test. **Achievement tests measure current performance.**

333. Martin is receiving primarily grades of D and F in high school. Your record indicates that Martin scored 126 on his IQ test.

   a.   Martin's IQ is well below normal and therefore D's and F's would be what we would expect him to receive.
   b.   Martin's IQ is very average.
   c.   An IQ of 126 is very high and Martin has high intelligence. He should be able to have much higher grades, assuming something like an emotional problem is not impacting his grade card.
   d.   The IQ score will not help you determine this.

(c) Since the average IQ is 100, Martin scored extremely high. A human services practitioner working with Martin would want to check for lack of effort, addiction issues, emotional problems at school such as bullying, or difficulties at home. The worker would also want to rule out physical issues and learning disabilities.

334. You are working with adults. The IQ test you will most likely see in your files would be

   a.   the MMPI.
   b.   the Rorschach.
   c.   the TAT.
   d.   the WAIS.

(d) **The Wechsler Adult Intelligence Scale (WAIS) is the most popular intelligence test for persons 16 and over.** Expect to see some Wechsler scores in your records, charts, and files.

335. Your agency takes children under 6 years of age for respite care when their parents or caretakers are experiencing a crisis. The best intelligence tests for these children would be

   a.   the WAIS.
   b.   the WISC.
   c.   the WASI.
   d.   the WPPSI.

(d) **The Wechsler Preschool and Primary Scale of Intelligence (WPPSI, pronounced whip-see) is geared toward kids in the 4- to 6 ½-year-old range.**

336. A funding source has asked you to provide the mean yearly salary at your agency for caseworkers. You have three caseworkers. One is making $5,000 per year. Another is making $10,000 per year, and the final caseworker has an annual salary of $15,000.

   a.   The mean salary is $15,000 per year.
   b.   The mean salary is $10,000 per year.
   c.   The mean salary is $5,000 per year.
   d.   The mean salary is $7,500 per year.

(b) Let me walk you through this one step by step. **The mean is the most popular average used in the social sciences. It's the arithmetic average.** You merely add up the scores: $5,000 + 10,000 + 15,000 = 30,000$. The total is called the **sum**. Once you have the sum (i.e., the grand total), you divide by the number of scores, so 30,000 divided by 3 = 10,000 or, in this case, $10,000 dollars. If you do have to compute any values on this exam, the computations should be very simple. **Key point: The mean is the most useful average. Nevertheless, it's heavily impacted by extreme scores called outliers. Assume in this question that your newest caseworker was Dr. Phil, and he makes about $40 million dollars a year. Add his salary to the mix, and now the mean indicates the average salary of your caseworkers is several million a year! Sounds terrific, but I think you'll agree it's very misleading!**

337. In this distribution of IQ scores, find the mode: 76, 102, 102, 111, 123, and 131.

    a. 131
    b. 76
    c. 111
    d. 102

(d) **The mode is always the most frequently occurring score or category.** In this question, it boils down to the number 102, as it's the only number that appears more than once. Yes, it's really that simple. **If an exam features a graph and tells you to find the mode, it's always the high point on the graph.**

338. Managed care emphasizes

    a. long term psychoanalytic treatment.
    b. short-term behavioral strategies.
    c. the best provider at the highest cost.
    d. clinical intuition over documentation.

(b) Managed care is focused on cost containment (translation: monitoring the treatment to keep the cost down); hence, a short-term behavioral treatment would cost the least. Very few, if any, managed care firms would foot the bill for long term psychoanalytic treatment (choice a). Choice d is incorrect because *case record documentation is required by managed care firms.*

339. You administer an exam at the end of a social awareness group intended to teach community members about school shootings. A perfect score is 100. Your participants scored 47, 66, 79, 88, 89, 94, and 100. The median score is

    a. 79.
    b. 88.
    c. 66.
    d. 94.

(b) **The median is the middle score.** A great little memory device is that the median is the middle of the highway—it cuts the road in half, in a sense. The median score cuts the distribution of scores in half. Because 88 has three scores under it (47, 66, and 79) and three scores over it (89, 94, and 100), it's the median. **Again, nearly every comprehensive exam will expect you to know the differences in the three averages or measures of central tendency: the mean, median, and mode.**

340. A client has filed a law suit against you. You should

    a. immediately contact the client (known as the plaintiff).
    b. contact the agency attorney. By law, all agencies will retain a lawyer.

   c.   remember that you cannot share client specifics with your attorney.
   d.   not contact the client taking legal action against you.

(d) Legal experts agree you should NOT contact the client who has taken legal action against you to discuss the situation. As far as choice b is concerned, unfortunately, a high number of small organizations will *not* have an attorney.

341. You are going to testify in court. All of the following behaviors are appropriate except

   a.   to dress in a professional manner.
   b.   to testify on behalf of your client if you feel it is the proper thing to do.
   c.   to give long, detailed answers when an attorney asks you a question. Do not leave out anything.
   d.   to give short answers when an attorney asks you a question.

(c) Okay, I confess, I love to talk a lot so this is a tough one for me, but this is one time when saying more isn't necessarily better. Just answer the question. Don't add anything extra. **If you receive a subpoena to appear in court, let your supervisor and/or practicum supervisor know this immediately.**

342. You are asked to conduct a study regarding clients at a rape trauma center. How will you pick the participants for your research?

   a.   You are the clinician and can make the choices based on your experience and education.
   b.   Just pick half the clients who received services at the center.
   c.   Use the N = 1 design.
   d.   Use random sampling.

(d) First, let me deal with choice c. An N = 1 design is also called a case study. As you may have guessed, Sigmund Freud popularized this approach. Since the question says "participants," which is plural, and not "participant," then choice c, or N = 1, must be incorrect. Here's why. N = 1 literally means that the number of subjects in the experiment is one person (a single individual). The correct answer is random sampling. Have you ever attended an event and somebody won a prize because their name or number was picked out of a fish bowl, or perhaps a paper bag? You have? Great. That's a crude form of random sampling. In a random sample, every member of the population has the same chance of being picked. **Random sampling helps guard against sampling bias, or picking people you want for the study.** Folks who conduct research don't generally carry around fish bowls or paper bags to conduct a random sample. Instead, they rely on charts included in many statistics books, or random number generators, which can be found in computer programs or on the web.

343. **To conduct a true experiment, you must begin with a hypothesis, which is actually an educated guess or a hunch.** In this case, your hunch is that clients who were sexually assaulted and completed a treatment program at your rape trauma center will have less fear and anxiety than those who do not. *This is called an experimental hypothesis.* To conduct the experiment, you will also need

   a.   a null hypothesis.
   b.   an alternative hypothesis.
   c.   a second researcher.
   d.   a second experimental hypothesis.

(a) **Virtually every true experiment begins with an educated guess and a null hypothesis.** *The null hypothesis states that there will be no difference between the clients who attend the program and those who do not, or that the results are not significant and are the result of chance. Contrast this with the experimental hypothesis, which asserts that the clients who receive your agency's intervention will have less fear and anxiety than those who do not attend the program.* **Please read this question at least two or three times. Nearly all comprehensive exams will ask you to know the difference between an experimental hypothesis (also called an alternative hypothesis) and the null hypothesis. Null means "no thing" or "no difference."**

344. To conduct your rape trauma center study, you will need a **control group** and an **experimental group** in order to perform a true experiment.

    a. The control group will not receive the experimental variable.
    b. The control group could be placed on a waiting list.
    c. A and b could both be correct.
    d. The control group will receive the experimental variable.

(c) Since **the control group <u>does not</u> receive the experimental variable,** choice a is right on target. To make this happen, sometimes a researcher in our field will simply place the persons in the control group on a waiting list, so choice b is also accurate. **In a true experiment, the participants are picked via random sampling, but the choice of whether the participant goes to the control group or the experimental group is also picked by the random sampling procedure.**

345. The persons in the experimental group receive

    a. the DV, also known as the dependent variable.
    b. the IV, also known as the independent variable.
    c. no experimental variable.
    d. choices a and b.

(b) **The experimental group receives the IV, or independent variable (also known as the experimental variable). An easy way to remember this is to think of a person who's receiving medical treatment and has an IV in his or her arm. This image makes the person look like he or she is getting some sort of experimental treatment. Hey, it works for me, but here, again, you may need to create a different image in your mind to use as a memory device.**

346. In an experiment to see whether reality therapy helps depression,

    a. reality therapy is the IV, or experimental variable.
    b. the individuals in the control group all get the IV.
    c. half of the individuals in the control group receive the IV.
    d. a score on a depression inventory would be the IV.

(a) Some other examples: You believe carrots raise IQ scores. In the experiment, carrots are the IV. You believe your group counseling sessions help alcoholics. In this experiment, the group counseling sessions would be the IV, or independent variable. You believe a meditation seminar helps clients learn to relax. Meditation is the IV. (See, you really are getting the hang of this, aren't you?) In these experiments, the persons in the control group would NOT receive the carrots, group counseling sessions, or meditation seminar, respectively.

347. In a true experiment, we always have outcome data (statistics, numbers). We call the outcome data the

    a.   DV, or dependent variable.
    b.   experimental group.
    c.   a random variable.
    d.   the null hypothesis.

(a) Here again, it's not rocket science. You can get this. If you believe carrots raise IQ scores, then IQ scores would be our DV, or dependent variable. If you believe behavior modification can help smokers reduce their smoking, then the number of cigarettes smoked at the end of the study would be the DV. If you believe that GA, or Gamblers Anonymous, helps reduce gambling, then the DV could be the amount spent at the casino each week.

348. Your agency believes that their behavior modification sessions can reduce stealing. An experiment is set up in which 25 clients are placed in a control group and 25 in an experimental group where they receive behavior modification for 6 weeks. In this experiment,

    a.   the number of times the client steals per week at the end of the experiment is the independent variable (IV) and the behavior modification is the dependent variable (DV).
    b.   the behavior modification sessions would be the independent variable (IV) and the number of times the client steals per week at the end of the experiment would be the DV, or dependent variable.
    c.   more information is needed.
    d.   both choices a and b are correct.

(b) **Exams often have questions where you're asked to pick out the IV and the DV.** The clients in the experimental group would get the independent variable (in this situation, the behavior modification sessions). **The DV, or dependent variable, is the outcome data,** so it would be the number of times the client steals per week. **The DV for both groups would be computed at the end of the 6 weeks.**

349. In human services research, the significance level (also dubbed the confidence level and signified by the letter p for probability) should be

    a.   p at the .05 level or lower.
    b.   p at the .05 level or higher.
    c.   p at the .0001 level or lower.
    d.   p at the .1 level or lower.

(a) The p statistic indicates there's a 5% chance that the results of the true experiment are not due to the IV, or experimental variable. Instead, the outcome is the result of chance. Or, to put it in a different way: If you run the experiment 100 times, 5 times out of 100, the results will occur by chance.

350. Your agency is working with depressed clients. According to research, CBT, or cognitive behavioral therapy, might be helpful. Your supervisor has asked you to read four different studies to determine if CBT should be used at your organization. All the studies were nearly identical except for the p level. They all indicate CBT could be helpful. Which study would be the most convincing?

a. The study in which p = .05, the accepted level in human services.
b. The study in which p = .01.
c. The study in which p = .001.
d. The study in which p = .1.

(c) Choice c is very, very, very convincing. P at the .001 level tells us that if you ran the CBT experiment 1,000 times, the results would only be due to chance on a single occasion. Again, although p at the .05 level is acceptable, .001 is even better. Choice b (although not *as convincing as choice c*) still deserves a serious look, as it reveals that 99 times out of 100, the results would not be due to chance. **With significance levels, also called confidence levels or p levels, smaller is better and more convincing. When p is equal to or less than the level of significance, say .05, we reject the null hypothesis. When null is rejected, it indicates that the differences between the control group and the experimental group didn't occur by chance.**

351. You believe many of the clients at your agency have personality issues. You thus institute a new policy stipulating that all new clients take a personality assessment. You should consider administering all of the tests *except*

a. the Binet IQ test.
b. the Rorschach inkblot test, which is considered a projective measure.
c. the MMPI, or Minnesota Multiphasic Personality Inventory.
d. the TAT, or Thematic Apperception Test, which is considered a projective measure.

(a) Although an IQ, or intelligence, test *can and does* provide some insight into the client's personality, it's the *weakest* choice here because all of the other choices are actual personality tests.

352. A study reveals a correlation coefficient (signified by r) of r = .24 for happiness and attendance at the Marijuana Anonymous (MA) mutual aid group. This

a. simply means attendance at MA groups causes you to be happier.
b. shows that a very weak positive relationship or association exists between happiness and attendance at MA groups.
c. shows that a very strong positive relationship or association exists between happiness and attendance at MA groups.
d. statistic indicates there is no relationship between happiness and attendance at MA groups.

(b) Any correlation below .3 would be considered quite low.

353. You have instituted a program at your agency to get the mentally challenged clients to brush their teeth more. Your statistics clearly yield data to show that the number of times clients brush per week is up. At the end of the first year, the correlation between brushing (variable X) and cavities (variable Y) is −.92 (i.e., r = −.92). The take home message here seems to be that

a. the program is working quite well: the more the clients brush (variable X), the lower the level of cavities (variable Y).
b. there is no relationship between brushing their teeth (variable X) and cavities (variable Y). Eliminate the program.

   c.   the association between brushing (variable X) and cavities (variable Y) is a
        positive.
   d.   brushing (variable X) causes cavities (variable Y) to stop forming.

(a) When reading about correlations, one variable is designated as variable X, while the other is said to be variable Y. **Negative correlations, such as −.92, show that when one variable goes up, the other goes down. Some experts call this an inverse correlation or inverse relationship. Correlations over .90 (positive or negative) are considered very strong. Nevertheless, write this on your arm and don't wash it off for a week: Correlation doesn't prove causation—it just indicates an association or lack of it! Choice d is wrong.** Many human services students will be reading this book, but buying this book didn't *cause* you to become a human services worker. If it rains, you may use your umbrella and your windshield wipers, but using them doesn't *cause* it to rain. **While a true experiment searches for causes, a correlation is merely looking at an association.**

354. You are using the Strong Interest Inventory (SII) for career assessment and vocational counseling at your agency. Another testing company wants you to buy its test. The new company tells you its inventory is much lower cost than the Strong. You notice in the literature for the new inventory, when the scores generated by the new inventory are correlated with the results provided by the Strong, the correlation between the scores is .13 (r = .13). You should

   a.   purchase the new measure, as it is just as accurate as the Strong but much more economical.
   b.   continue to use the Strong. A correlation of .13 is extremely low. There is very little association between the scores on the Strong and the scores on the new inventory.
   c.   understand the new measure is not perfect, but is so close to the Strong you should purchase it to save money.
   d.   not switch assessments unless the new inventory has a correlation of 0 with the Strong.

(b) A correlation of zero mentioned in choice d is the worst possible scenario. **A correlation of zero means there's no association or relationship between the Strong results and those of the new career inventory.** However, a correlation of positive .13 isn't much higher! Stick with the Strong. Simply put, we could probably correlate the Strong scores with the price of corn in North America or shoe sizes in your Introduction to Human Services class and get a correlation in that range. A powerful correlation between the results of two tests might be .70, .80, or even higher. So, .13—sorry, but not impressed.

355. Triadic supervision

   a.   is unethical in our field.
   b.   is ethical, but not as effective as one-on-one supervision.
   c.   occurs when you have a single supervisor and two supervisees.
   d.   is used in other fields, but not human services.

(c) **Supervision is merely the process where a human services worker with more experience works with a human services worker with less experience.** Indeed triadic supervision—using one supervisor and two supervisees—is ethical, used in human services, and research shows it's seemingly as effective as making use of a single supervisor with a single supervisee.

356. A good supervisor engages in all of the following behaviors *except*

   a.   monitoring the supervisee's work.
   b.   counseling the supervisee when he or she has severe personal problems.
   c.   evaluating the supervisee's performance.
   d.   stopping an inappropriate supervisee from entering the field.

(b) **Supervisors attempt to raise and improve the level of functioning of the employees, practicum students, or volunteers whom they're supervising.** Supervisors at agencies and practicum sites should <u>not</u> be treating the folks they're supervising, making choice b the wrong answer. Giving the supervisee some referrals for counseling, therapy, or other appropriate treatment would be advised.

357. You are supervising Kayci, who is a new intake worker at your agency. You feel that she should say uh-huh more to keep the conversation with the client moving and to let her client know she was paying attention to what her client was saying. You should speak to her about

   a.   minimal encouragers.
   b.   reflecting feelings with paraphrasing.
   c.   summarization.
   d.   pacing and clarification.

(a) **Minimal encouragers are verbalizations or nonverbals that signal to the client that he or she should continue.** Saying, "uh-huh," "go on," "sure," "yeah," "oh," "I get it," or "yes, I understand;" nodding your head in agreement; or using hand movements to show interest would be examples.

358. Kayci (mentioned in the previous question) was working with her client. Her client remarked, "You probably can't imagine how stupid I feel admitting to you that I didn't pass my American History course this semester in college." Kayci replied, "You might be surprised to know that I struggled terribly with that exact course myself when I attended your college." This is a superb example of

   a.   self-disclosure.
   b.   using a minimal encourager.
   c.   a psychodynamic interpretation.
   d.   summarization.

(a) **Self-disclosure is used with conscious intent (i.e., on purpose) by the worker to enhance the relationship and promote trust. The procedure allows you to let the client know you understand something about the current issue because you have experienced something similar in your own life.** The rule on self-disclosure: While a little is good, a lot is *not* usually better. Or, as I humorously tell my students, "If you went into the addiction field to tell your clients how you spent the '60s high on drugs, you're in the wrong field!"

359. The best example of ad hoc supervision would be:

   a.   Your supervisor meets with you to help you work with the family of a child who is being bullied at school.
   b.   Your supervisor meets with you to help you work with a 72-year-old client who seemingly has Alzheimer's disease.

c. You attend a training session with your superiors to help you understand HS-BCP ethics.
d. An employee for the local suicide prevention hotline is brought in to supervise you for two sessions after a client's son killed himself.

(d) **Ad hoc supervision occurs when a supervisor is brought in or used to provide guidance or consultation for a specific situation, or to meet the demands of a particular client. Ad hoc could *also* refer to an unplanned (impromptu) meeting.** So, let's assume that you always meet with your supervisor each Thursday morning to discuss your caseload. This weekend, however, an earthquake devastated many of your clients' homes. Rather than wait for Thursday, your supervisor would meet with you first thing Monday morning to discuss the situation.

360. As a supervisor, you have been teaching Ronnie how to respond using interpretation. Ronnie feels her client should apply for public assistance. Moreover, Ronnie is convinced her client currently meets the qualifications. Her client remarks, "As a child, my stepmother always taught us that you should never take a handout from the government, so I'm not sure what to do." The *best* interpretation Ronnie could respond with would be

a. "Your loyalty to your mother and her ideas might be getting in the way of accepting what is rightfully yours and can help your family in this time of need."
b. "I sense you are feeling very unsure right now."
c. "Go on, please."
d. "Can you tell me more?"

(a) **An interpretation helps a client gain insight and understanding into their behavior and feelings.** Choice b is a reflection. Choices c and d would fall into the minimal encourager response category.

361. Ronnie (mentioned in the last question) decides to discuss this case at an agency case conference.

a. As her supervisor, you will need to stop her from talking about this in the conference and explain this is unethical.
b. This is perfectly ethical.
c. As her supervisor, you would let her continue, but explain in private after the case conference is complete that she violated an ethical guideline.
d. As her supervisor, you would explain that she would need to tell you in advance precisely what she is going to say in the case conference; otherwise, she could be terminated from the agency.

(b) It's ethical to discuss the client's case and get feedback in a case conference setting.

362. Mary was pulled out of her mother's home and placed in foster care after it was discovered that she was being physically abused. Several years have now passed. Her mother attended numerous psychotherapy sessions and you feel Mary's mom is currently capable of being a good parent. The best forum to discuss this would be

a. a PPRT, or Permanency Planning Review Team.
b. a meeting with the police officer and social service worker present the day the child was removed from the home.
c. an open meeting of the board of directors.
d. a closed meeting of the board of directors.

(a) First, let's explore why choices b, c, and d are incorrect. It's possible that the police officer and the social service worker (another title sometimes given to human services workers focused on child abuse) have not seen the client since the day her child was pulled out of the home. To say that they're totally out of the loop would be an understatement, at best. Choices c and d mention the board of directors. Remember, the board is there to govern the agency and make big decisions (e.g., Should the agency open a new branch, or should the agency have an additional fundraiser this year?). *The board is there to ensure that the nonprofit agency is meeting its legal duty to follow its objectives and goals. Just for the record, there's no ideal size or set number of board members. The size of the board varies from agency to agency and could be determined by the agency's bylaws.* That said, if the board is focusing on this particular client, it's a case of inappropriate micromanaging! Not a good thing! **A foster care PPRT is a team composed of professionals from different agencies, as well as the community, who meet at specified intervals in an attempt to create a stable permanent plan for the child in foster care.**

363. You are supervising a new human services worker and focusing on the area of clarification. A client says, "Work stinks. I'm sick of it." Your worker's *best* response in terms of clarification would be

    a. "Can you tell me, specifically, what you mean when you say, 'work stinks'? Exactly why are you sick of it?"
    b. "I hear you saying that work is really bad right now."
    c. "Oh."
    d. "When you were a child, I bet your parents didn't like their jobs, either."

(a) **Clarification is a strategy that allows the human services worker to better understand what the client is trying to convey (content and feeling), and help the client understand this, as well.**

364. You are running a vocational group to help your clients secure a job. You decide to use summarization at the end of the group. The *best* response would be

    a. "Larry still hates men because, as a child, his father beat him every day after he came home from work. He will have a real problem if a male who reminds him of his dad interviews him."
    b. "I picked up on three key themes today. First, that most of you need to prepare in advance for your job interviews. Second, don't be afraid to send a cover letter with your résumé. And, third, send a thank you card after the interview if you are really serious about the job."
    c. "I hear Kat saying that rejection is really tough for her since she lost her job in retail."
    d. "Next week, we can discuss salary issues."

(b) **Summarization, or summarizing, occurs when the helper shares the key points that came to light during an individual, marriage and family, or group session.** Although summarization generally occurs at the end of a session, it can also take place at the beginning of a session to remind the clients what was important from the previous session.

365. Jordan, a new human services worker, is your newest supervisee. She says, "The way you take notes at this agency is different than my old agency. You also have a totally strange setup for doing intakes, and your referral process is just so complex. I don't

mind telling you, I'm really, really nervous about all of this." In an attempt to para-phrase what Jordon has said, you should respond with

a. "Jordan, look, I've been at the agency a long time. We know what we are doing, trust me."
b. "Jordan, it gets better. I know. I have worked here for 10 years now."
c. "I can refer you to the employee assistance program (EAP) for counseling if you are that nervous."
d. "Our ways of doing things are a lot different than your last agency and it seems to be causing you a lot of stress and anxiety."

(d) **In order to paraphrase, you repeat what the client says using different words in a non-judgmental way. (Some workers use the exact words. Big mistake folks—that's what we call parroting and it often results in a client saying, "Hey, I just said that!")** The EAP—per choice c—is available for very short-term counseling for employees. Clients (i.e., employ-ees) who need long term services are referred to other providers. Needless to say, not every organization contracts with an EAP.

366. You like to write grants. The best position in your nonprofit agency to do this would be

a. the director of development.
b. the intake coordinator.
c. the applied behavior analysis specialist.
d. the case manager supervisor.

(a) The director of development, also referred to as the development director, is generally required to write grants as part of his or her job. Indeed, some agencies have grant writers, but the answer stems here don't give you that possibility as a choice. I've hammered away at this topic in several questions because it's been my experience that many undergraduate students have spent a lot of time on interventions, but not agency structure.

367. Money from a grant

a. is guaranteed for life.
b. is hard money.
c. is soft money.
d. can only be used for diagnosis, assessment, or evaluation, but never for treatment.

(c) **In our field, soft money refers to funds you received from a grant. The grant might only give you money for a year. Hard money is repetitive and you generally have it year after year in your budget. In essence, you can count on hard money.** (These terms may be used in a different fashion in your political science and finance classes.)

368. Which statement regarding grants is *not* true?

a. You must turn your application/proposal for the grant in by the specified date.
b. Grants are often graded, similar to papers you turned in for class.
c. The money always comes from the federal government.
d. The grant can specify what salaries are paid to the workers on the grant project.

(c) The grant source could be a foundation that has *nothing to do with the federal government.*

369. Examples of fundraisers for nonprofit agencies include

    a. sports auctions.
    b. mouse races and bingo.
    c. trivia nights.
    d. all of the above.

(d) All of these are common ideas that are used by literally thousands of nonprofits to make money. Some agencies will have an event planner, rather than or in addition to a director of development, to put together such events. Workers from a large agency once confided in me that they made more revenue from their bingo games than from their clients.

370. The requirements to put together a specific grant are generally included in

    a. the US Constitution.
    b. the Request for Proposal (RFP).
    c. the agency bylaws.
    d. the development committee on your board.

(b) A request for proposal, or RFP, is a document put out by the organization, foundation, or individual who has the grant money. Here's a great way to understand RFPs. Think of any syllabus for your college classes. It tells all the specifics, such as the days and times the class meets, and, most importantly, the requirements to get your grade. The RFP gives the exact specifics to apply for a grant.

371. Your agency wants you to write a press release to announce the opening of your new biofeedback program to help children and adults relax and curb anxiety.

    a. A short press release sent to the local newspaper might be appropriate.
    b. A long press release sent to a national television show would usually be the best.
    c. It has been deemed unethical for agencies to send out press releases.
    d. You could send a press release to the newspaper, but not to a local radio, television, or cable station.

(a) Great news: **An agency can ethically send out a press release for any reason or at any time** to announce a new program, fundraiser, or perhaps even a need for volunteers. It's much easier to get a press release published in a local small paper than in a national publication or television show. By the way, **biofeedback** uses electronic devices and computers to allow clients to scientifically measure and control bodily reactions (e.g., muscle tension). A client sees his anxiety go up or down on a screen or hears it raise or lower via a tone or clicks in a set of headphones. The biofeedback meter is providing biological feedback just like a mirror or a scale. Somehow, when humans see or hear their reactions, they can often learn to control them. Is that cool, or what?

372. You send the local newspaper a press release about a car wash you are holding to raise money to help treat autistic teens. All of these statements are false *except*:

    a. The newspaper must legally run it (i.e., publish it).
    b. The newspaper should ethically tell you the date when the press release will run.
    c. You should write the press release in the third person.
    d. You can send a press release to a newspaper, but not an online source.

(c) **Always write the press release in the third person, as if somebody wrote it about you or your agency.** Okay, here's the cold hard truth, whether you like it or not. A newspaper (or any other source for that matter) need not tell you—and usually won't—if (or when) it's running your press release. Keep in mind they're doing you a favor! Again, they may not run it at all and there's nothing you can do about it. A quick, humorous little quip that illustrates this principle: I once helped my agency create a press release for a radio station. Several years after I created the press release and was working at another agency, I was driving home from a vacation at about 1 o'clock on a Sunday morning and heard the station running my press release! This can be good news, because assuming the press release isn't outdated, I've discovered that many sources will run it more than once. Choice d is incorrect because you can send a press release to *any place* you want, including television, online journals, cable shows, magazines, and websites.

373. You made a referral for your client, Venice, to a private-practice licensed clinical social worker, who has his own office. He runs a cash only practice. Making a referral is a type of **networking or brokering (someone else, not you, will provide the service).** A client might request a referral, or a referral might be appropriate because you, as the human services practitioner, cannot provide the service. In some cases, you might actually refer the client out because you feel that you just aren't making the progress you should with a given client and, quite frankly, another provider could do a superior job. You helped Venice make an appointment, but he has gone for four visits and, each time, the social worker told him he was sorry but needed to cancel.

   a. You should contact the board of directors for the private practice and make a formal complaint.
   b. You or Venice should contact funding sources and make a complaint.
   c. You or Venice should contact the insurance companies who pay the social worker.
   d. You or Venice would need to contact the social worker who provides the treatment.

(d) Please note that the term "cash only practice" means this therapist doesn't accept insurance or managed care funds, so that rules out choice c. Since this is a private-practice therapist, there's no board of directors, so scrap choice a. If you also do a little critical thinking here, you'll come to the conclusion that, since the therapist is private and is a for-profit entity, the only funding sources might be the other clients this therapist sees; and, well, you can't contact them. **The general consensus is that the number of for-profit agencies in the US is increasing. Unlike 501 (c) (3) nonprofits, for-profit agencies are not exempt from paying taxes since they're just like any other business (say, a shoe store).**

374. You are going to purchase a computer for your nonprofit agency.

   a. You should bring your tax exempt letter to the store and show it to the cashier when you check out, so you do not pay sales tax.
   b. You should purchase it just like any other citizen or for-profit agency, so you will pay taxes.
   c. There is no such thing as a tax exempt letter for nonprofits.
   d. You can bring a tax exempt letter, but most retail establishments will not honor it anyway, so you will be paying sales tax.

(a) Oh, the advantage of having nonprofit status!

375. You are supervising a second-year human services student for her first practicum. A practicum is a structured and interactive learning experience. Your supervisee is showing mild anxiety during her first week of work.

    a.   Refer her to a therapist for relaxation therapy.

    b.   Refer her to a psychiatrist. There are many medications to help curb anxiety.

    c.   Practicum related anxiety is normal during the first few weeks, and can even be a positive thing.

    d.   Spend the first supervision session discussing the factors related to anxiety and fear, and teach your supervisee some relaxation techniques.

(c) The supervisor should chill out! Anxiety related to supervision, client interaction, being prepared to handle situations, and safety would be normal in the beginning weeks of the practicum.

376. Your agency wants to begin taking practicum students. You will require a police check, child abuse check, TB test, and drug screening.

    a.   This is very typical. Go ahead and require this.

    b.   This is an invasion of privacy.

    c.   You are violating the student's confidential rights.

    d.   You could require these things, but most colleges and universities will disagree with your organization's position on this and will tell the students to seek another practicum site.

(a) When I first started teaching in human services, some, if not most, agencies required no checks whatsoever. Now, virtually every agency requires some sort of background check. In addition, many sites require a résumé. Often the college career, planning, and placement office will help you write this document. P.S. Don't forget to fill out all the papers and agreements required by your college before you begin a practicum, internship, or work-place learning experience.

377. You are an administrator in a hospital setting and have agreed to take undergraduate human services practicum students.

    a.   You should recommend malpractice insurance as an option.

    b.   You should require malpractice insurance.

    c.   You should speak with your attorney to see if practicum students really need malpractice insurance.

    d.   You should require malpractice for employees, but not practicum students.

(b) Malpractice insurance is a must for practicum students and employees (which is why choice d stands incorrect). But don't run out and purchase it just yet if you're still a student! Many schools pay for malpractice for students who have to do fieldwork, practicum work, or clinicals. Good deal!

378. Your agency decides to allow Alcoholics Anonymous, or AA, groups to meet in your building. The only requirement to be an AA member is a desire to stop drinking. A member need not believe in God or declare that he or she is an alcoholic. All of these statements are true *except*:

    a.   You will need to keep a detailed list of members who attend for your funding sources. Also, members are required to show an official membership card to attend each meeting.

    b.   AA meetings can be designated as open (the general public, students, or people who are not alcoholics may attend) or closed (only AA members and individuals with a drinking problem are present).

    c.   A sponsor, who is an experienced member of the group, could bring the individual to the group, introduce him or her, and provide support and advice.

    d.   All contributions are voluntary. Nobody in the group is required to pay a fee to attend.

(a) **Since the AA group** *is* **anonymous, no membership lists are created and there's no membership card to attend the groups.**

379. You are writing an individual giving campaign letter to raise funds for your agency.

    a.   Putting a P.S. in the letter could raise the amount you take in.
    b.   Putting a P.S. makes the letter look totally unprofessional. Leave it out.
    c.   Putting a P.S. generally lowers the number of people who will send money.
    d.   A P.S. would not be allowed in an individual giving campaign letter.

(a) Surprise, surprise, surprise—a P.S., or post script, at the end of a letter will usually raise the amount of money the agency pulls in and many agencies use this technique. Why? A P.S. is one of the most common parts of a letter people read. Many individual giving campaign letters include a **pledge card** you return with your donation/contribution. The card may specify donation amounts, such as $50, $100, etc. A lot of donors wrongly assume the agency won't accept a donation smaller than the smallest number—in this example, $50. Well, here's a newsflash folks: Of course they will accept your gift! Send a check for $25 and watch how fast they cash your check. Recently, agencies have been accepting contributions online. And, oh yes, gifts-in-kind, such as desks and computers, are also welcomed by organizations.

380. Lester created a wonderful resource and referral guide. It took him months to put it together. His agency is using the guide. Now he is leaving the agency and wants to take it to the new agency.

    a.   It is his, he was paid to write it, and so he should take it to the next agency.
    b.   It is his because he wrote it at night when he was off the clock and not getting paid, so he can take it.
    c.   It is the property of his agency and there is a chance they won't let him take it.
    d.   In cases such as this, the staff generally votes on whether it is appropriate for him to take it to the next agency.

(c) Sorry, but whether he created it on his own time, or not, is irrelevant! If he created it while he was at the agency (even if he did the work at 3 a.m.), it's now the property of the agency. The organization *could allow* him to take it to the next site, but in many cases, they won't. I've personally witnessed several situations of this nature.

381. You wish to donate money to an agency so they can create teen suicide prevention posters. Your *best* strategy would be

    a.   to make a cash donation.
    b.   to pay by credit card.
    c.   either a or b, which are equally effective.
    d.   to pay by check and write, "designated contribution to create teen suicide prevention posters."

(d) **Many contributions go to pay the rent, lights, electric, and gas bills. If you want your money to be targeted for a specific cause or function, then make a designated contribution telling the agency what it should be used for.**

382. You work at a nonprofit agency. The agency sent you out to give a presentation at a middle school regarding gangs. The principal gave you a $50 honorarium.

    a. It is yours, so you could buy some new stereo speakers for your vehicle on the way home.
    b. You would not be allowed to accept the money under any circumstances. Be kind, but explain this to the principal.
    c. You must turn the money into the agency.
    d. In most cases, the executive director will let you keep the money as a salary bonus.

(c) **The honorarium isn't yours! It belongs to the agency.** I remember one time (notice I said "one") I received an honorarium that was less than five dollars and my executive director explained that it would be more expensive to process the contribution, so I was allowed to keep it. That said, it will most likely never happen to you!

383. You take a new job at a child care agency. You did not read the fine print and, it turns out, you signed a non-compete clause. You didn't like your supervisor at the new job and quit.

    a. You could go to work for the organization across the street, which performs the same service.
    b. You most likely could not go to work for the child care agency across street, at least for a few years.
    c. You most likely could not work in any human services job for life.
    d. A lot more information would be necessary to answer this question. Non-compete clauses are very complex.

(b) **A non-compete clause/agreement states you won't compete against your agency if you leave. Often, the clause/agreement will specify a given period of time (say, 5 years) and/or a distance (you can't work for any agency within a 50-mile radius.)**

384. You are the clinical supervisor for a new unit slated to help autistic children. Autism has risen in recent years, and occurs more in boys than in girls. Many autistic children engage in repetitive behaviors called stimming, such as flapping their hands, rocking, or spinning around in circles. Stimming can be any behavior that is self-stimulating. About 10% of autistic kids are savants, with a special talent or intelligence in a specific area. A savant might know thousands of baseball statistics on the tip of his tongue, or she might display advanced musical abilities without ever taking a course in music. The best theoretical approach for your new unit would be

    a. a humanistic approach, such as that espoused by Carl R. Rogers.
    b. REBT, pioneered by Albert Ellis.
    c. brief strategic resolution therapy.
    d. behavior modification called ABA, or applied behavior analysis, based on B. F. Skinner's operant conditioning, with a heavy emphasis on positive reinforcement.

(d) In ABA, which is research (empirical) based, it's assumed that behavior stays the same or is altered by the consequences which occur after the behavior. **ABA is often used with autistic individuals.**

385. Your executive director is engaging in illegal activities.

    a. The board of directors could fire the executive director.
    b. Only a politician would fire the executive director.
    c. Only funding sources can fire the executive director.
    d. Only a commission from the state or federal government can fire an executive director.

(a) **The board of directors can hire and fire an executive director, but the board shouldn't be involved in the day-to-day operations of the agency.**

386. You are working with third graders in an elementary school for children experiencing anxiety issues. Akio is new to the class, having moved to the US from Japan just over a year ago. His English is as good as any of the children born in the US. The school gave him a test related to educational tasks, and he scored very average. Nevertheless, your supervisor accidentally gave you the *wrong results,* indicating he scored higher than any student who ever took the exam. According to the Rosenthal Effect,

    a. he will perform exactly like the real test score indicated: very average.
    b. his performance will go down because this occurs with average kids as they go on in school.
    c. his performance will likely get better and improve.
    d. more statistical information is necessary to answer this question.

(c) The well-known Rosenthal Effect is named after a world renowned psychologist, Robert Rosenthal, not yours truly. We're not related, and I joke with my students that it's his loss. According to the Rosenthal Effect (also dubbed the Pygmalion Effect), the child's performance will get better. Rosenthal did studies using fictitious scores for certain students and this is exactly what occurred. Why? Presumably, reading the very high test scores will cause you to unconsciously treat the student in a slightly different manner, and the student will excel. *There's a very high chance that a comprehensive exam will sport at least one question on the Rosenthal Effect.* I recently received an e-mail from a high school student who needed to write a paper on the Rosenthal Effect, and told me he might as well get his information from the fellow who created it! I told him he had the wrong guy, but I'd explain the principle anyway!

387. You are a supervisor for a mental health agency that does outreach work. A team of sociologists will be tagging along with your outreach workers and observing them for research purposes. Based on the notion of the Hawthorne Effect, you can expect

    a. the outreach workers' production to deteriorate.
    b. the outreach workers' production to remain exactly the same.
    c. the outreach workers' production to increase and improve.
    d. the outreach workers' interventions with clients to increase, but their paperwork/case recording to deteriorate.

(c) *What comes after the Rosenthal Effect question on most comprehensive exams? That's easy, the question pertaining to the good old Hawthorne Effect.* **The Hawthorne**

Effect—based on research related to lighting conditions—clearly predicts that work output will go up when workers are being observed.

388. You are working at an addiction treatment center as a program director. Your executive director wants you to investigate the possibility of adding medical assisted treatment with methadone to help clients addicted to heroin. Your *best* plan of action would be to

    a. look at a minimum of two issues of the annual *Journal of Human Services*, which is distributed to NOHS members, to see if this topic is covered.

    b. review at least five issues of *Social Work*, the journal of the National Association of Social Workers (NASW).

    c. review a minimum of two issues of the American Counseling Association's *Journal of Counseling and Development*.

    d. perform a meta-analysis related to heroin addiction treatment and methadone.

(d) In a meta-analysis, you combine the findings from a number of studies (regardless of which journal or source they appeared in) in an attempt to identify the best answer. In this instance, you'd pool the data for all the studies performed on heroin addiction treatment using methadone. You might have a dozen articles, all from different journals.

389. You have been working with the same client for a year and decide to do an evaluation of your services.

    a. You might decide to redesign your plan and do something totally different.

    b. You might decide to terminate your client and never see her again.

    c. You might decide to continue doing exactly what you are doing now and keep the client's case open.

    d. All of the above are possibilities.

(d) Since all of these strategies are legitimate options and the question provides you with such little information, choice d is the best choice. Continuation (choice c) is often preferred when you notice that the client is making progress toward his or her goals.

390. You are supervising a new practicum student. You ask her to write down her feelings about the practicum on a sheet of paper. She writes things like, "What if my supervisor believes I am not experienced enough to handle the clients?" "What if the other practicum students think I shouldn't be working here because I am only a two-year student and they are working on master's degrees?" "What if I can't keep up with the fast pace of the agency?" and, finally, "What if the clients think I am too young to be their human services practitioner?" As a supervisor, your evaluation of this would be

    a. that it is very normal to have concerns like this in the beginning of a practicum or internship.

    b. that this is not normal at all and the student should be advised to seek help from a college counselor at the school.

    c. that anxiety is generally biochemical and you should refer the student to a psychiatrist for psychiatric medicines.

    d. that, unfortunately, this student has such low self-esteem that she won't make it in this field, despite the fact that she is unusually bright.

(a) According to H. Frederick Sweitzer and Mary A. King, who penned *The Successful Internship: Transformation & Empowerment*, concerns of this ilk do occur in the first (or **anticipation**) stage of the practicum or internship. **When gearing up to take any major comprehensive exams, you should never count on *any study guide, even mine,* as your sole source for preparation. It's imperative that you briefly review the major textbooks in your area of study, especially if a concept I discuss isn't clear or not in-depth enough for you to understand.**

391. After the student mentioned in question 389 spends more time at the agency, she begins to feel disillusioned and disappointed. Your take on this as her practicum supervisor would be

    a. that this, too, is rather normal and often not as intense if the student has successfully dealt with the issues in the anticipation stage.
    b. that this student is thinking in a very irrational manner and REBT might be a good treatment of choice.
    c. that you are her supervisor and not her therapist, so it is not important.
    d. that this attitude will not help the clients, and, therefore, you will need to terminate her. She will be better suited for another agency or organization.

(a) Authors Sweitzer and King list **disillusionment** as the second key stage for internship students, and based on working with hundreds (if not thousands) of students at this point in my career, I'd say they're right on target. The next stage they list is **confrontation**, or facing head-on what's happening to you. This is followed by **competence**, in which you're excited and trust yourself. The final stage is **culmination**. In this stage, you might experience mixed feelings, since goodbyes can be difficult. You may also have guilt or remorse over some of your behaviors during the practicum. And, finally, if this is your last practicum or internship, you must deal with the reality that you need to go out and find a job.

392. You are Kiana's supervisor and are reading write-ups she has placed in her client's charts. All of these statements should be changed *except*:

    a. Ms. B is a cripple.
    b. Ms. B is deaf and dumb.
    c. Ms. B has a disability.
    d. Quite frankly, Ms. B is wacko.

(c) Some terms should be avoided in your charting (also called reporting, recording, write-ups, dictation, and narrative in the record). **Words with dignity should be used. Choice c is fine because the word disabled should be used instead of crippled, handicapped, or invalid.**

393. Kiana had other statements that you felt were inappropriate. The only statement that should *not* be changed is

    a. Ms. B is a victim of cerebral palsy.
    b. Ms. B has cerebral palsy.
    c. Ms. B is afflicted with cerebral palsy.
    d. Ms. B has a birth defect.

(b) In this and the previous question, the correct answers make use of what's known in our trade as **person-first language**, also dubbed **people-first language**. First, you mention the person and then the disability. So you'd say, "Ms. B has cerebral palsy," not "She's one of those disabled people." The latter is often cited as being dehumanizing.

394. Avoid all of these statements *except*:

 a. Ms. B has a psychiatric history and has been diagnosed with emotional disorders.
 b. Ms. B has fits.
 c. Hearing impaired clients are difficult to work with in situations like this.
 d. Retarded adults like Ms. B are difficult to work with in situations like this.

(a) Choice b is person-first language, but it's incorrect because the term "fits" should be replaced with a dignified term, such as epilepsy or seizures. Choice c isn't written in person-first language, nor is answer d. In addition, the term "retarded" should be replaced with a dignified term, such as intellectual disability. Here are some of the most popular word choices human services workers face, and how to handle them:

 Recommended: Uses a wheelchair. **Not recommended:** Confined or restricted to a wheelchair. Wheelchair bound.
 Recommended: The person is non-disabled. **Not recommended:** The person is normal, when referring to a non-disabled individual, since this implies that people with disabilities are not normal.
 Recommended: Deaf or cannot voice for themselves. Non-vocal. **Not recommended:** Deaf and dumb, or deaf mute.

395. You are a supervisor. One of your human services practitioners, Bucky, comes to you and she is extremely upset. She currently has Brand B malpractice liability insurance. An attorney just contacted her to say that one of her clients is taking legal action against her for something that took place 2 years ago. At that time, she had Brand A insurance. She wants to know which company is going to cover her: Brand A or Brand B. You should tell her

 a. neither insurance company will help her, since the client is complaining about something that took place 2 years ago.
 b. both companies will help her, since she paid both of them in good faith.
 c. she need not worry. He cannot take legal action against her now for something that took place 2 years ago. He should have taken action when the incident occurred.
 d. none of the above.

(d) All of the answers are incorrect. You'll discover the reason in a moment.

396. Based on question 394, you should tell your worker

 a. Brand B will cover her.
 b. Brand A will cover her.
 c. Brand A might cover her, depending on the type of policy she purchased.
 d. Brands A and B will cover her.

(c) This is a very important answer that somebody should have taught me in school or in practice, but never did. **In our field, there are two basic types of malpractice insurance policies: claims-based and occurrence-based. Some companies call them claims-made and occurrence-made policies. A claims-based/made policy only covers you while you're** holding it. Thus, if you were covered by Brand A insurance for the year 2014, then, once the calendar says 2015, you're no longer covered. But, if you purchased a more expensive occurrence-based/made policy during 2014, you're covered for virtually anything you did with a client during 2014, even if a client or legal firm contacts you several years later and says you harmed the client at a later date. So, getting back to Bucky: If she purchased an occurrence policy, she would be covered. Typically, if an agency provides free insurance, it's claims-made to keep the cost down. You might want to pay extra to upgrade your own policy if that's the case and the agency will allow you to do so. Some companies selling claims-made policies will allow you to purchase a tail (yes, they really call it a tail) that you pay for to cover you on a year-by-year basis after the time you owned the policy. Tail coverage is sort of a hybrid between purchasing a claims policy or an occurrence policy.

397. You are forming a new treatment program to treat persons who have addictions. Many of your clients are suicidal, as well. Which statement is the most accurate?

    a. You should have an aftercare program. Aftercare programs are often called continuing care programs.
    b. The new treatment program should last at least 6 months long to make sure it is effective.
    c. The majority of treatment center directors agree you should not use medical assisted treatment to supplement the aftercare group because a person will just substitute one drug for another. The Freudians called this symptom substitution.
    d. You should not create an aftercare program, since these programs violate ethical codes.

(a) Let's take the grand tour and examine each answer, since the information here could conceivably help you on several questions on the actual exam. Choice a, **aftercare or continuing care programs, begin after the actual treatment program or hospital program ends.** Since it's been discovered that clients often commit suicide after they finish treatment, these programs just make sense! Choice b might have been the correct answer in the 1970s or early 1980s, but, today, the premium is on short hospital stays to keep the cost down. Good luck finding an insurance company or managed care firm that will cough up the funds for 6 months of treatment. Yes, many Freudians do believe in symptom substitution—choice c. Thus, a person who gives up alcohol (the symptom), but doesn't deal with unconscious impulses, might become addicted to 12-step support groups, or even addicted to drinking coffee while attending 12-step support groups! Nonetheless, medical assisted treatment, which is very popular now, such as using Vivitrol to help alcoholics, clearly puts no stock in the concept of symptom substitution. Maybe we'll wake up one morning and research will show that medical assisted treatment was merely a form of symptom substitution, but it hasn't happened yet. Choice d: Common sense would dictate that since aftercare/continuing care groups serve a viable purpose, the ethical thing to do would be to use them!

398. You are an administrator for a residential treatment center for teens. One of the clients took his own life by jumping out of a fifth floor window. Based on your knowledge of the contagion effect (also called the ripple effect or the copycat effect), all of these would be helpful *except*

    a. closing off the room where the teen jumped for a period of time.
    b. refusing to talk about the suicide because of the contagion effect.

c.   running a survivors of suicide (SOS) bereavement support group.

d.   talking with clients who knew the teen who took his own life to discover if any other clients had pact suicide agreements with him.

(b) **Terminology for the test:** When an individual attempts suicide, he or she may be helped via an *attempter's group*. When someone is grieving/bereaving because a friend or loved one has committed suicide, an *SOS, or survivors of suicide support group,* can help (choice c). Choice a, strangely enough, is appropriate (if it's feasible) because when you have copycat suicides, the persons who take their own lives after the first person suicides often copy the method. If other teens had a suicide pact with the original teen, they may still be at risk, which makes choice d a desirable plan of action. Also, not talking about it won't help those who are grieving. Choice b, refusing to talk about the suicide, may seem like the right thing to do on the surface, but often can be deadly.

399. Your administration has the funds to use co-leaders for the new group mentioned in the previous question. This would

a.   mean you could have a few extra group members.

b.   not impact the perfect size for the group.

c.   mean you should have fewer group members.

d.   not have an impact unless one of the leaders had a PhD.

(a) With two sets of eyes and ears, it's okay to increase the number of members by 50%, or even slightly more.

400. Your agency is not receiving enough radio, television, web, and newspaper coverage to publicize your fundraisers, services, and volunteer needs. Your *best* strategy would be

a.   to try to get free advertising from a local university or community college radio station.

b.   to buy a major radio or television station in your town. These entities really aren't that expensive.

c.   to buy a newspaper. Newspapers are cheaper than radio and television stations.

d.   to form a media board.

(d) Buying a radio or television station won't be cheap; nor would purchasing a newspaper. A media board (which can be separate from your board of directors and your advisory board) is composed of members who have media ties (e.g., an anchorman on the local television station) and can get your agency's message on television, radio, in newspapers, and on the web. Choice a isn't wrong, but most educational radio stations have limited output and, thus, reach less people.

Best wishes on your exam and enjoy the balance of the book!

Chapter 6

Exam Boosters

There are several accepted **definitions of human services:** Human services provides interdisciplinary education and services to clients. These services help clients meet basic needs and can help with remediation of difficulties. The profession advocates for change in systems that impact clients' lives. Human services practitioners organize activities that help people with healthcare issues, mental health conditions (including those who are mentally challenged or disabled), social welfare, childcare, criminal justice, housing and homeless issues, addictions, crisis intervention, and education.

Here's **another good definition:** Human services practitioners meet human needs by using interdisciplinary knowledge and focusing on prevention and remediation of difficulties. Human services workers strive to improve the quality of life of service populations. Improved delivery systems, accessibility, accountability, and coordination of services with other professionals and agencies is promoted.

According to some authors in the field, any service that helps individuals who are experiencing difficulties or stress could be categorized as human services.

In 1969, the **Southern Regional Education Board (SREB)** identified **13 roles for human services practitioners.** All human services workers perform one or more of these functions. The roles include: (1) *Outreach worker,* who might visit the client in his or her home or in the community, rather than in his or her office; (2) *Broker,* who helps find services for clients and makes referrals; (3) *Advocate,* who champions clients' rights and defends causes; (4) *Evaluator,* who assesses programs and helps ensure accountability; (5) *Teacher/ educator,* who's didactic and tutors, mentors, and even models new behavior for the client; (6) *Behavior changer,* who uses behavior modification, counseling, or psychotherapy—if qualified—to assist clients; (7) *Mobilizer,* who organizes client and community support to provide needed services; (8) *Consultant,* who offers support and guidance, and imparts information to help other professionals, as well as agencies and community organizations, meet the needs to help them solve problems; (9) *Community planner,* who designs, implements, and organizes new programs; (10) *Caregiver,* who provides direct encouragement and hope to clients; (11) *Data manager,* who uses data and statistics to create a plan, program, or agency, or to evaluate these entities; (12) *Administrator,* who supervises workers and programs; and (13) *Assistant to specialists,* who works as an aide or an assistant to a specialist.

Historically, the need for human services workers increased after President Lyndon Baines Johnson delivered his **War on Poverty** speech in January, 1964 for the State of the Union address. Programs that evolved from his presentation were later dubbed the **Great Society** programs, such as **Medicaid** (health care for the poor); **Medicare** (health care for the elderly); **WIC,** or Women, Infants, and Children (services for moms with newborns); the **Job Corps** (employment services for young adults); **Head Start** (preschool services); the

Peace Corps (helping the poor throughout the world); and **VISTA,** or Volunteers in Service to America (similar to the Peace Corps, but focused on poverty stricken areas in the US). The programs were coordinated by the Office of Economic Opportunity, or **OEO.**

The **National Organization for Human Services (NOHS)** is the professional organization for human services practitioners. The organization was deemed the National Organization for Human Services Education (NOHSE) until 2005, when the "E" was removed from the name.

Many human services workers are **generalists** or practice the **generalist intervention model (GIM).** These helpers don't specialize in a single area and, thus, could conceivably be involved with any situation or problem. Helpers of this ilk need **eclectic knowledge,** or a broad range of knowledge and skills from a variety of areas. A **specialist** would work with a specific type of client, such as autistic children or persons who are addicted to gambling. A specialist would need knowledge in their specialty area.

Many human services professionals are considered **case managers.** A **case manager** helps a client or family with multiple problems and, thus, he or she coordinates services with other practitioners, agencies, and organizations.

A helper's expertise is known as **competence.**

A **culturally competent helper** can accept attitudes, beliefs, and customs that are different than her own. The culturally competent practitioner has a knowledge of the culture, so he can interview and help a diverse range of clients. In order to be a culturally competent helper, the helper must understand what the client's really saying.

When a group of people doesn't receive the same treatment as another group when necessary, then **disparity** has occurred.

Human services workers abide by the principle of **nonmaleficence,** which means do no harm.

Workers also practice **beneficence,** or doing what's best for the good of society.

Practitioners uphold **fidelity,** which means to maintain trust and **veracity** (truthful and accurate). You're always honest and genuine with your clients.

Ethical codes, ethical guidelines, and ethical standards give workers information about what's good and what's bad in terms of behavior. Noted authors Gerald Corey, Marianne Corey, and Patrick Callahan suggest eight steps for dealing with an **ethical dilemma** in their book, *Issues and Ethics in the Helping Professions.* An **ethical dilemma** is a situation where the human services worker must decide upon a course of action to uphold ethical standards or guidelines.

Step 1: Identify the problem.
Step 2: Identify the potential issues involved.
Step 3: Review relevant ethical guidelines.
Step 4: Know relevant laws and regulations.
Step 5: Obtain consultation. (Note: A colleague or a supervisor can be helpful.)
Step 6: Consider possible and probable courses of action.
Step 7: Enumerate the consequences (positive and negative) of each possible course of action.
Step 8: Decide on what appears to be the best course of action.

In general, **ethics** suggest it's best if human services workers refrain from **dual relationships (also called multiple relationships)** with clients. A **dual relationship** would be any relationship that goes beyond the human services worker/client relationship. A worker who has multiple relationships has **boundary issues with clients.** Thus, going to dinner with your client, paying her to paint your apartment, or dating your client, would not be ethical. Keep your relationship with your client professional and set limits to avoid **boundary issues.** Common examples of retaining professional boundaries include refraining from giving your clients your home phone or personal cell number, and declining to buy cookies to support their children's sports teams or scout troops. Don't give them money or make loans. You want to be friendly, but not their actual friend! **Dual relationships** get in the way of objectivity. Say you're dating your client and she begins to date someone else. Could you really help her without being biased? **Having a sexual or romantic relationship with a current client or his or her family member is always deemed unethical.**

If you know the client from a previous relationship, discuss this with your agency or practicum supervisor to decide how you should proceed.

Informed consent is an important factor in ethical behavior. A client is given the necessary information (including the risks and benefits) to consent to the assessment, treatment, research program, intervention, or follow-up services.

Impaired professionals ethically should refrain from practice. Thus, a practitioner who's using cocaine herself—and is clearly impaired—should <u>not</u> be performing treatment in a cocaine recovery center. The same would apply to a helper who has brain damage and, thus, can't think clearly and has extreme memory loss.

Forensic human services takes place when practitioners work with the legal system in civil (e.g., landlord issues) or criminal matters (e.g., robbery).

Workers who suffer from **burnout** will have a degree of emotional exhaustion and a negative attitude toward clients. It's difficult for these workers to be empathic. They will miss work more, may come late and leave early, and do less for their clients and their jobs. **Secondary** or **vicarious burnout** can be the result of working with another person (or persons) experiencing trauma. Workers may experience burnout and may even consider quitting their jobs. Sharing thoughts and feelings about stress and burnout with your supervisor, mentor, colleagues, or with a professional counselor can help. Some authors suggest that a good sense of humor and cognitive behavioral therapy can be beneficial.

Safety risks can also increase the worker's stress level. Ironically, physical violence directed toward a worker is more apt to occur in the office than in the field or during a home visit. Nevertheless, if you make a **home visit (HV)** and your client is using drugs, alcohol, or has uncontrolled animals, don't stay to conduct your session. Some experts rank **verbal abuse** as the most common type of safety risk. If you're ever threatened (even in your own office), leave and secure help.

Clients sometimes receive a **diagnosis** (or label) based on their symptoms and behaviors from a book called the **DSM**, or the ***Diagnostic and Statistical Manual of Mental Disorders***, which is published by the American Psychiatric Association. Unless a human services practitioner is also licensed as a psychiatrist, psychologist, social worker, or counselor, he or she would generally not be qualified to diagnose clients. A client must sport a diagnosis to receive payments from an insurance or managed care firm. When a client has two or more psychological or medical conditions at the same time, say, alcoholism and post traumatic stress disorder, we refer to the situation as **comorbidity.** If a client has just two conditions, the term **dual diagnosis** can be employed.

Human services practitioners favor **evidence-based practice (EBP)**, also called **evidence-based treatment (EBT),** where the assessment, interventions, and decisions are dictated by the best scientific studies and findings in our field.

Psychiatrists are medical doctors who use **psychopharmacology (medications)** to help clients. They can also hospitalize clients and perform **electroconvulsive shock therapy (ECT). Popular mental health medicines include anti-anxiety drugs** (for anxiety or fear),

antidepressants (for depression and mood disorders), and **antipsychotics** (for psychotic conditions where the client doesn't have a good grasp of reality).

When a team of experts from different fields (say a psychiatrist, pastoral counselor, psychologist, teacher, social worker, and human services practitioner) help to solve a client's problem, we have an **interdisciplinary team**.

When **human services** is provided online or electronically, it can be called **e-treatment, cyber-treatment** or **online human services**.

The science of classifying mental or physical disorders or diseases is called **nosology**. Therefore, the *DSM* is a book of nosology. **Some of the most common mental health disorders are depression (also dubbed a mood disorder or dysphoria/dysphoric condition), anxiety, psychosis (not being in touch with reality), addiction, and eating disorders.** In terms of eating disorders, **anorexia, or anorexia nervosa**, occurs when an individual restricts food intake due to distorted body image issues and a fear of gaining weight. Anorexia is more common in females than males. **Bulimia, or bulimia nervosa**, is expressed by **binging (eating excessive amounts of food) and purging (trying to eliminate the food from the body by using laxatives, vomiting, diuretics, extreme exercise, or other unhealthy practices).** Statistically, most bulimics are female and in the normal weight range.

The old *DSM* included a **Global Assessment of Functioning, or GAF, Scale—the new** ***DSM 5 has dropped this practice.*** The scale rated the client's highest level of functioning in the year prior to the interview. The scale went from 0 (basically highly suicidal or otherwise seriously impaired) to 100 (an absence of symptoms).

FEMA, or the **Federal Emergency Management Agency**, performs crisis and disaster counseling. Unlike many, if not most agencies, FEMA workers don't classify, label, or diagnose individuals. Moreover, no case files or records are kept. FEMA services are done in nontraditional settings and are **outreach** based (performed in the community), rather than being conducted in a human services agency office. FEMA services supplement rather than replace existing services.

Race refers to a client's outward appearance based on genetic factors.

When a person receives inferior treatment or is discriminated against because of his or her age, we refer to it as **ageism**. For example, the head of a job hiring committee might comment, "We can't hire him, he's much too old."

In general, the population of the US is getting older. Longevity is increasing and birthrates are declining. By 2030, older adults will make up 20% of all Americans. **Older adults have a high rate of mental health needs; however, their rate of getting help is lower than desirable.**

The **oldest old**, defined as those persons 85 and over, is the fastest growing segment of the elderly population. According to the Census Bureau, **the senior population is increasing faster than the younger population. Palliative care** (used primarily for older adults, but can be used by individuals of any age) focuses on end of life care, when medical treatment can't cure the patient. Medications are used to reduce pain and provide relief without attempting to fight the disease. **Hospice care** for the terminally ill would be the most common example of **palliative care.**

Alzheimer's disease (AD) is the leading form of **dementia** (loss of brain function) and causes a deterioration in physical (e.g., speech) and emotional skills (e.g., problems related to thinking). **Alzheimer's disease** afflicts 5 1/2 million Americans and is said to be a **progressive degenerative brain disease.** If symptoms occur prior to age 65, the term **early-onset** is often used to describe the condition. The older an individual, the more likely he or she is to have **Alzheimer's disease.** For example, at age 65, 1 in 10 persons has the disease, but after age 85, 50% of the population will have AD.

Another type of **discrimination** is called **ableism**. Here, persons with psychiatric or physical disabilities are seen as inferior to able-bodied or able-minded persons. For example, the director of a hiring committee might comment, "We can't hire her to do telephone because she's visually impaired, and a person with normal vision would do a superior job." Note: Persons who are disabled are often referred to as differently abled.

Approximately 17% or about 55 million Americans have a **disability.** The **Americans with Disabilities Act (ADA)** was signed into a law in 1990 and amended in 2009. It's a civil rights law that attempts to prohibit discrimination related to disabilities. When writing or speaking about an individual with a disability, use **person-first language.** Hence, you wouldn't say or write in a client's chart, "a disabled client," but rather, "the client has a disability."

In 1974, the **Child Abuse Prevention and Treatment Act (CAPTA)** was passed, and nationwide hotlines to report child abuse, neglect, exploitation, and sexual abuse were set up. Helping professionals are said to be **mandated reporters.** That means they must report abuse and neglect, since they're commanded by a higher authority to do so. Mandated reporters are often contrasted with **permissive reporters** (say, the employee at the local market), who has a choice whether to make a report or not.

A **mandated reporter** can be fined and/or imprisoned if he or she doesn't make reports in a timely manner. Services that focus on abuse and neglect are called **child protective services (CPS)**, or merely **protective services.** Hence, a child abuse treatment worker might have the title protective services worker. Methods used to prevent children from being pulled out of the home and put into a placement facility (e.g., foster care or respite care) are part of the **family preservation model.**

A **perpetrator** is someone who abuses others. Perpetrators were often abused themselves as children and the abuser became a role model. Because they could not stop the abuser, they often **displace** their anger as they get older by becoming abusers themselves.

Human services workers should also report elderly abuse. Services to stop or prevent the abuse of the elderly are known as **adult protective services. Older adults** are often afraid to report abuse if the **perpetrator** (i.e., the abuser) is a family member. The individual being abused believes that reporting the situation could result in the perpetrator being removed from the environment; hence, nobody will be present to care for him or her.

Confidentiality can be defined as an entrusted secret. This means that in most situations, a human services provider would not reveal anything that took place during the session to anybody else, except to get guidance from a supervisor. **Supervisors** are legally liable for every case in the human services practitioner's caseload. A supervisor shares the liability with the worker. **Vicarious liability** occurs when one party (the supervisor) is responsible for another party's (the worker's) actions. If a supervisor is observing the session from behind a one-way mirror, the client/clients must consent to this prior to the beginning of the session.

If you wish to communicate with another provider about a client, you'd have the client sign **a release of information or disclosure form.**

When a worker reports child or elderly abuse, we consider this an **exception to confidentiality**. Exceptions to confidentiality are deemed as **relative confidentiality.** Since the worker isn't necessarily present when the abuse occurs, the worker makes his or her report based on a **reason to suspect or suspicion of abuse.** Other exceptions to confidentiality include a person threatening to hurt himself or others; a court order or subpoena; a coroner or medical examiner investigating a death; and the Patriot Act, which allows the FBI to see your records if your client is under investigation as a threat to national security. In the case of the **Patriot Act,** you can't tell the client you've released his or her records.

Here's another exception to confidentiality. When an individual threatens to hurt somebody else, we say that a worker has a **duty to warn** an intended victim and a **duty to protect** the person who's being threatened. Since this policy is based on a famous court case related to a young woman, Tatiana Tarasoff—who likely could have been saved if she or her parents had been warned that she was in danger, professionals in the field often call the duty to warn, or duty to protect, the **Tarasoff duty.** Prior to Tarasoff and the formation of related ethical guidelines, the term **absolute confidentiality** was popular, meaning whatever the client said was confidential and would remain confidential (not discussed with others) under any circumstance or situation. As stated previously, that isn't the case in this day and age.

According to **FERPA, also known as the Family Educational Rights and Privacy Act of 1974** (also called the **Buckley Amendment** on some exams), an adult can see his or her own educational record and the records of his or her minor children. Counseling records are exempt, and this act only applies if the school is getting federal funding. On a similar note, the 1974 **Freedom of Information Act** postulates that individuals have a right to access records kept via federal agencies.

The **Health Insurance Portability and Accountability Act (HIPAA)** restricts what can be shared about a client without his or her consent. Moreover, HIPAA stipulates a client can see his or her record, except for counseling and psychotherapy notes.

Micro practice focuses on the individual.

Mezzo practice focuses on **families** and small **groups.** A **family therapist** working with a family will often construct a map or diagram of several generations of the family; this is called a **genogram.**

A **12-step group,** such as **Alcoholics Anonymous, also called AA,** founded in 1935 by **Bill Wilson (also referred to as Bill W.) and Dr. Robert Smith (known as Dr. Bob),** who was a physician and surgeon, would fall into the mezzo practice category. When a person doesn't "use" or engage in an addiction, we call it **abstinence.** Often, **abstinence** occurs as a result of **medical detox.**

Macro practice takes place when working with communities and organizations.

Triage implies that the worker will prioritize needs and deal with the emergency situation or crisis first.

Several popular types of **treatment settings** include **outpatient (the client comes to the office for assistance), inpatient (the client is staying at the setting day and night), partial hospitalization (sometimes billed as day treatment, since the client may go home at night or on weekends), and residential care (the clients may live at the center for an extended period of time). The term "halfway" house refers to transition facilities that help an individual adjust to society after being in a prison, hospital, or treatment facility.**

When you see a client for the first time, you'll conduct an assessment often called an **initial assessment** or an **initial evaluation.** Your exam could refer to it as a **psychosocial assessment or evaluation.** Agencies often allow you several meetings or visits with the client to complete this task. In the assessment, you'll try to ascertain what problems or difficulties the client has and how you'll intervene to help. You'll also identify strengths and prioritize problems. **Referrals** or brokering services to other agencies and professionals might be necessary. When a referral is necessary, it's acceptable to help the client set up the initial visit with the agency, organization, or provider. You should also determine how you'll ascertain whether the client has improved or been successively treated. A client has a **right to a referral or a second opinion. Referral fees** (I'll give you $10 for every client you refer) are unethical.

Practitioners whose work focuses primarily on initial evaluations and **care plans or treatment plans** are often referred to as **intake workers.** In child abuse settings, these individuals are often called **investigation workers.** These labels help distinguish them from **treatment workers,** who take over *after* the investigation is complete.

Workers often work with their clients to set **goals** (e.g., securing a job or finding housing). The steps taken to reach the goal (e.g., going to an employment office) are called **objectives.** Link goals and objectives to measurable outcomes whenever possible.

During the interview, a practitioner will often conduct a **psychosocial history.** The psychosocial history is conducted by securing information regarding the client's present and past situation. This knowledge is used to determine the best way to help the client. Input from family members and other agencies who have worked with the client can be very helpful.

An assessment can include formal and informal interviews, as well as **psychological and educational testing,** sometimes dubbed **psycho-educational testing.**

Tests that your agency must purchase are called **standardized tests.** A test you or your agency creates is known as an **informal or non-standardized test.**

Some school districts have **psychometricians** who are trained to give students tests. A **school guidance counselor** may also do testing, but psychometricians focus almost exclusively on using tests for assessment and evaluation purposes.

The most important factor for a psycho-educational test is **validity.** A valid test, or test with high validity, tests whatever it is that it should be testing. If a famous major league baseball player who's hitting over 300 takes a batting test and fails, then the test isn't valid!

The second most important factor for a psycho-educational test is **reliability.** A reliable test, or a test with high reliability, gives consistent results. If you step on your scale at home and it says you weigh 163 lbs and then you step on it seconds later and it says you weigh 226 lbs, then we can safely say the scale isn't reliable!

A valid test is always reliable! If you weigh 163 lbs and your scale is valid, it will *always* say 163 lbs.

However, **a reliable test isn't always valid!** If your scale is 10 pounds too high, it will always read 163 lbs, when in reality, you weigh 153 lbs. It's very consistent: You can step on it again and again, and it will say 163, so it's reliable, but since it's *incorrect*, it's not valid!

A good test displays **cross-cultural fairness.** If you need an upper-middle class socioeconomic background to answer the questions, then the test would be biased toward other subgroups.

When a score hasn't been altered, we call it a **raw score.** Just like a food that isn't cooked (altered), the score isn't changed.

When we assess a program while the program is still going on, we call this a **formative or process evaluation.** For example, a caseworker asks a client for feedback on his or her work after every session.

If we wait until a program is finished or completed to conduct an assessment, we call it **summative evaluation or outcome research.** For example, a teacher in a human services program allows the students to evaluate her at the end of the semester.

Schools, treatment centers, and agencies often refer the client for an **IQ test. IQ** stands for **Intelligence Quotient.** The first IQ test was created in France by **Albert Binet and Theodore Simon,** in 1905.

Today, the **Stanford-Binet Intelligence Scales** (named after Alfred Binet, of course) are still very popular, and some experts believe the test is still the best measure for evaluating extremely high or extremely low intelligence.

The most popular IQ tests in the world, however, are the **Wechsler Intelligence Scales,** named after **David Wechsler,** who created the measures.

The **Wechsler Adult Intelligence Scale, or the WAIS,** is used for adults and older adolescents (ages 16 and over). The median **average IQ score is 100.** A number after a Wechsler acronym, such as IV in WAIS-IV, just indicates what version of the test you're using, so in this case, it's the fourth version. The letter "R" signifies a revision in the exam.

The **Wechsler Intelligence Scale for Children, or WISC,** is used for kids from 6 to 16 years old.

The **Wechsler Preschool and Primary Scale of Intelligence (WPPSI)** is intended for kids from 2 years, 6 months to 7 years, 3 months old.

The **Strong Interest Inventory (SII)** is commonly used in career and vocational assessment, and counseling. **Kuder** inventories are also popular for conducting vocational/job counseling, and you may see them in your case records, as well.

A person who's overeducated for a given job, for example, a PhD-level human services practitioner who's sweeping floors, is often said to be **underemployed** or affected by **underemployment.**

Some states have **right-to-work laws** that stipulate it's illegal for a job to require you must be a union member to be employed at the company.

Glass ceiling refers to unwritten policies or barriers that restrict women and minorities from advancing in a job setting. This is a form of **discrimination.** The term **lavender ceiling** is used when this happens to workers because they're not heterosexual.

Human services practitioners rely heavily on the study of data known as **statistics.** When data are represented in a diagram, we call it a **graph.** Bar graphs are referred to as **histograms.**

In the social sciences, when we report testing scores or even program data, we often use **three different measures of central tendency or averages** to report our findings. The most popular measure of central tendency is the **mean,** or what your teachers in high school called the **arithmetic average.** It's often abbreviated by an X with a bar over the X. It's simply calculated by taking **the sum of the scores and dividing the answer by the number of scores.** Thus, if your electric bill for last year was $144 (dream on!) and you divide $144 (i.e., the sum or the total) by 12 months, then your average, or mean, electric bill was $12 per month.

The mean is the most useful average or measure of central tendency, but, unfortunately, it's also impacted by very high or low scores called outliers. Imagine that the average salary in your Introduction to Human Services class is $20,000 per year. Now, a high paid athlete, rock star, or TV celebrity who makes millions joins the class. The average salary in the class might shoot up to $500,000, which is misleading.

The mode is the most frequently occurring score or category. If your professor gave an exam, and the scores were 22, 59, 78, 78, and 100; then 78 would be the mode because it's the only score which appears twice. On a **graph or chart,** the mode will always be the highest point. If there are two high peaks, the distribution of scores is **bimodal or multimodal.**

The median is the middle or theoretical score, when the data are ranked from lowest to highest. Thus, if the exam scores were 55, 80, 92, 97, and 99, then 92 is the median because two scores fall below it and two fall above it. (Memory device: The median of the highway splits it into two.)

The **range** tells you the difference between the highest and lowest score. If the highest score on a test was 98 and the lowest was 48, then the range or spread of scores would be 50.

A **correlation coefficient** is used in statistics to show an **association/relationship, or the lack of an association/relationship, between two variables, say x and y.**

A correlation coefficient is often signified by the letter **r.**

Correlation coefficients range from –1.00 to +1.00 (generally written 1.00).

There are only two possible perfect correlations: –1.00 and +1.00 (usually written 1.00).

A zero correlation means there's no statistical relationship or association between two variables.

A moderate correlation would be .50, while .80 and above is considered high or strong.

In a **positive correlation (e.g., .74), both variables move in the same direction.** So more studying, variable x, is related to a higher GPA, variable y. Or, less studying, variable x, is associated with a lower GPA, variable y.

In a **negative correlation (e.g., –.67)**, one variable goes up while one goes down. This is sometimes called an **inverse correlation.** If you brush your teeth more, variable x, the number of cavities, variable y, should go down.

A negative correlation can be as powerful or even more powerful than a positive correlation. For example, –.67 is just as strong of an association or relationship as +.67 (.67). And –.67 is a stronger correlation than .57, even though .57 is positive.

Correlation doesn't imply causation or causality. There's a high correlation between majoring in human services and carrying a book bag, but carrying a book bag doesn't cause you to be a human services major.

Research can be **quantitative (using numbers/data/statistics)** or **qualitative,** such as observing people. Qualitative research might be necessary when you can't do a numerical analysis of the issues in question.

Historical research occurs when you examine and analyze the past.

Ethnographic research occurs when you examine the members of a given culture.

Naturalistic observation is achieved by observing people in their natural environment/field setting without the researcher interfering.

A **true experiment** begins with an **experimental hypothesis,** such as, "Individual reality therapy sessions will help depressed college students." A hypothesis is a hunch or an educated guess. Another way to define it is that it's a prediction you'll test.

A true experiment will also have a **null hypothesis,** such as, "Individual sessions of reality therapy will have no impact on college students who are depressed."

To pick subjects for a true experiment, we often rely on a procedure called a **random sample.** In a random sample, every member of the population pool has the same chance of getting picked, and the choice of one subject won't impact the choice of another. **An example of random sampling:** We've all been to an event where everybody puts their name in a hat or bag, and somebody picks a name out and that person wins a prize.

True experiments utilize a **control group and an experimental group.** Both groups are picked using a random sample.

If the **researcher didn't randomly pick individuals,** then we call the study a **causal-comparative design,** rather than a true experiment.

A **control group** receives no treatment. (Subjects in the control group might even be on a waiting list.)

The **experimental group** receives the **IV, or independent variable.** The control group won't receive the IV.

The **IV** is the **experimental variable,** which is manipulated. If you believe that group therapy will help shy clients, then group therapy would be the IV in your experiment.

True experiments also yield a **DV, or dependent variable.** The DV is your outcome data. So if you run an experiment to see if a new agency policy raises kids' IQ scores, then the IQ scores at the end of the experiment represent your DV.

True experiments rely on a **level of significance, or level of confidence, of .05 or less.** The level is written with a **p,** such as **p = .05.** This means that if you conduct the experiment

100 times, you'll get the same result 95 out of 100 times. You're 95% sure the results are caused by the independent variable. Some experiments use **p at the .01 level.** This is even more convincing because in 99 out of 100 cases, you'll get the same results. Here, only 1% of the time, the result will be caused by chance factors. **A lower p value gives you stronger evidence.**

The initial assessment will often contain a **prognosis,** which is a **prediction,** or forecast, of whether the client can be helped and, if so, how much.

The **Rorschach inkblot test** and the **Thematic Apperception Test (TAT)** are two popular projective personality tests you may see in a client's chart. In a **projective test,** there's no right or wrong answer. The client looks at an inkblot and tells you what he or she believes it looks like. In the TAT, the client tells you a story about a picture. The client is projecting his or her personality into the card. These tests—which are popular with psychoanalytic or psychodynamic helpers—take a lot of training to administer, but are difficult for the client to fake, as the individual taking the exam doesn't know exactly what to say.

The **Minnesota Multiphasic Personality Inventory (MMPI)** is considered one of the finest personality tests available and is even used for top security clearances by some government agencies, such as the Central Intelligence Agency. Clinicians like the MMPI because it has mechanisms built in to discover whether the client is downplaying or exaggerating symptoms, or otherwise trying to lie on test questions. The MMPI isn't a projective test.

When you write about your clients in their files, it's known as **documentation.** That said, professionals and agencies also use the terms **charting, recording, case notes, narrative, and dictation** to describe the process. The client's file is often referred to as the **case record.**

Practitioners are fond of following the **SOAP** formula for clinical write-ups, record keeping, or notes. The letters in the acronym stand for **Subjective, Objective, Assessment, and Plan. Subjective** simply refers to the client's perception of the situation. **Objective,** on the other hand, is something the human services worker can see, hear, or measure. For example, "The client was crying during the session." **Assessment** is the worker's conclusion after taking the subjective and objective information into consideration. Finally, the helper creates a **plan** to help the client (e.g., specific treatments, medication, referrals, homework, etc.).

When a client talks about his or her problems, it's often curative. With children, play therapy can be used. We call this process **catharsis.**

Human services professionals use **open-ended** and **closed-ended** questions to find out about the client and his or her situation. **Open-ended questions** are generally considered superior or more valuable than **close-ended questions,** since **open-ended questions provide more information.**

A closed-ended question can be answered with yes or no. For example, "Are you still attending school?" or, "Do you have a job?" **An open-ended question can't be appropriately answered with a yes or no;** for example, "What are your feelings about your high school classes?" or, "What is it that you don't like about your current job?"

Interviews and treatment sessions can be **directive** or **nondirective.** In a directive interview, the client is told what he or she should talk about; for example, "Tell me about your difficulties with your teenage daughter." In a nondirective interview, the client can talk about whatever he or she wishes; for example, "Tell me about what brings you here today," or, perhaps, "What would you like to talk about today?"

Interviews can be **structured** or **unstructured.** In a structured interview, you or your agency will decide what you need to ask each client. Thus, by their very nature, **structured interviews** are generally more directive. In the unstructured interview, you can determine what information to obtain from the client. **For research purposes and data collection, the**

structured interview is the way to go. Simply put, it's more scientific, since every client has responded to the exact same questions.

During your assessment, you may decide that several workers are necessary to help a single client, group of clients, or family. This is known as **collaboration.** It can also be dubbed as a **multidisciplinary approach,** since human services workers may represent a number of different fields. You may be working with a day care worker, food stamp worker, child abuse treatment protective worker, and school guidance counselor.

When you contact another individual (say, a psychiatrist, landlord, or neighbor) or agency about your client, it's known as a **collateral source or collateral contact,** and this should be documented in your client's record. Prior to speaking with collateral contacts, you'll need a **signed release of information from the client,** created by your agency. If the client is a **minor,** a parent or legal guardian will need to sign the document.

When a client isn't showing any emotion, we use the term **flat affect, affective flattening, or flat mood** to describe his or her behavior. Affect is just an old word for emotion. Roughly the opposite is **lability,** in which the client's emotions fluctuate and change markedly during the course of the interview. Labile simply means unstable.

When an interview or treatment session is focused on present moment and recent behavior, we call the intervention **ahistoric.** If the treatment is centered on the client's past (say, childhood, as in the case of psychodynamic or psychoanalytic interventions), the approach is said to be **historic.**

Pathology means disease, and **psychopathology** means a **mental disease, disorder,** or **emotional issue.** Psychopathology can also substitute for the term **abnormal psychology. Etiology** refers to the cause or origin of a physical or mental disease.

When a client has a physical condition that needs to be healed or cured, a **therapeutic service** (say, surgery or prescription medicines) might be necessary. If a client has emotional, relationship, or mental health issues, then **psychotherapy or psychotherapeutic services,** such as **Rogerian counseling or rational emotive behavior therapy (REBT),** can be curative. Thus, counseling and therapy are said to be **curative** procedures.

Psychotic clients are not in touch with reality. They have a severe mental disorder that often results in **hallucinations** (seeing and hearing things that are not really present) and **delusions** (such as, the client feels controlled by others or believes others can hear his or her thoughts). Psychotics also display **thought disorder or disorganized thought,** such as switching from one topic to another so rapidly, the human services worker can't understand the client. Confronting the person with the truth won't change his or her beliefs. Psychotics are more apt to harm themselves than clients who are in touch with reality.

Some clients who have been victims of crime, sexual assault, in military battle, or other traumatic situations, need help for **post traumatic stress disorder, or PTSD.** A type of treatment named **EMDR, or Eye Movement Desensitization and Reprocessing,** has been used for PTSD.

A client can receive training or treatment in an **individual session,** sometimes called a **one-on-one session,** or in a **group.**

Some of the best reasons to recommend groups include: The client can't afford individual treatment, or the individual treatment isn't working. You feel the client might benefit from getting **feedback** from others and/or listening to others. The client's issues stem from poor **interpersonal skills.** The client might benefit from the **social support** from the group members.

Groups promote a sense of "**we-ness,**" also called **cohesiveness.**

Groups are generally more **cost effective,** as well as **time efficient,** since a single practitioner is seeing several clients at the same time. In addition, **self-help groups,** including

12-step groups such as AA, are not lead by professional or paid helpers. Self-help groups are also referred to as **mutual help, mutual aid groups, reciprocal groups, recovery groups, or support groups.** These groups (for example, one for fibromyalgia or cancer) are not always based on a 12-step model like AA.

Self-help, 12-step, mutual aid, and reciprocal groups are typically lead by an individual who has the same problem as the members. Hence, a diabetic might be running a group for persons with diabetes.

Many experts believe that groups go through stages. The **pre-group stage,** or screening period, is often called **forming.** The **initial stage** is terming **norming.** This stage can be frightening to new members and, thus, **ice breakers** (non-threatening experiential activities in which new members communicate with each other) are sometimes used to reduce anxiety and tension. Try to create an environment that builds trust. The next stage is called the **transition stage,** or **storming.** In this stage, conflicts occur and the leader may indeed be challenged. Next, the group enters the **working stage,** dubbed **performing.** Here, the group works on the task or gets the job done. And, lastly, the group enters the **final stage,** known as **adjourning.** Here, the group members deal with separation issues and the fact that the group is ending.

Before the group begins, individual and group **screening** procedures are recommended to eliminate persons who aren't appropriate for the group. A client who's totally psychotic would not be a good choice for a group focusing on persons with no psychiatric disorders, and would be screened out prior to the initial session of the group.

When more than one leader is conducting the group, we say the group has **co-leadership, or co-facilitation.** The leaders would generally not sit next to each other in the circle.

Groups promote **universality,** also called **mutuality,** which means the client understands that he or she isn't the only person with his or her problem or life situation.

The ideal size for a counseling or psychotherapy group is **5 to 8 individuals,** with many experts saying most groups shouldn't exceed 9 or 10 members. The perfect size for children's groups is four members.

Very long group sessions are not necessary. For adults, an hour and a half should be the maximum time, while with children, shorter sessions are preferred.

Open groups allow new members after the group begins. **Closed groups** won't allow new participants after the group starts.

Don't confuse open and closed groups with **open and closed meetings.** In an **open meeting,** anybody can attend, such as a student writing a paper on AA or a professional interested in recovery groups. In a **closed meeting,** only specific individuals or members can attend, such as a person who thinks he might want to attend AA or somebody who's an AA member.

Groups and services are often classified as **primary, secondary, or tertiary.** A **primary group,** or **psychoeducational group,** focuses on prevention, such as a group for children intended to keep them from starting to use drugs and alcohol. (Memory device: Primary begins with a "p" and so does prevention.) In a **secondary group,** or **counseling group,** a problem is being treated. In a **tertiary group,** or **psychotherapy group,** a more severe ongoing problem (such as schizophrenia) is being addressed.

Time limited groups (such as a college class) end after a given number of meetings.

When an individual slides back to an illness, behavior, or addiction (such as using drugs again after one has quit), the term **relapse or recidivism** is used to describe the situation.

The most popular **group leadership styles** include the **autocratic (authoritarian) style,** where the leader sets the rules and agenda; the **democratic style,** which favors member interactions; and the **laissez-faire style**, which is basically a hands off approach where the leader interacts very little.

When a leader connects themes, similarities, commonalities, or goals, he or she is using a technique of **linking.** When a leader attempts to stop a member from saying or doing something harmful, it's called **blocking.**

The individual who the group blames for their failures is often referred to as the **scapegoat.**

When a community has several different cultural or ethnic groups, we say that there's **multiculturalism or multicultural diversity. Diversity** conveys the notion that we're all different and unique. Knowing more about a client's culture can help you build **rapport.**

The **melting pot analogy** suggests that the different cultures are assimilating into the general US culture. Many experts believe that this analogy is inaccurate, and prefer the **salad bowl or mosaic analogy.** The salad bowl/mosaic analogy suggests that some melting may be occurring, but for the most part, the cultures (like carrots in a salad or glass tiles used in a mosaic) remain separate or distinct from each other. **Acculturation** is the process by a group or an individual of adopting another culture's practices and traits. **Pluralistic societies** are composed of individuals from a number of different racial, ethnic, religious, and cultural groups. **Ethnocentrism** takes place when we view our own culture or group as superior to all other cultures.

The **etic approach to multicultural diversity** suggests that clients from different cultures can be treated basically the same way, using accepted principles of human services.

The **emic approach to multicultural diversity** suggests roughly the opposite of the **etic approach.** In the **emic approach,** you specifically tailor the interventions to the client's particular culture.

Autoplastic interventions in multiculturalism are based on trying to help the client change to better cope with the dominant culture.

Alloplastic interventions in multiculturalism are roughly the opposite of those used in the **autoplastic philosophy of helping.** In **alloplastic interventions,** the client is counseled to make attempts to change the environment.

Immigration takes place when a person moves (migrates) to a new country. Once the person is residing in the new country, he or she would be an **immigrant.** The label **refugee** is often preferred if the individual moved to the new country to flee danger, including war and persecution. A **consulate** is an official appointed to serve in a foreign country to assist citizens from the consulate's country. Thus, the Chinese Consulate in Chicago could assist persons from the People's Republic of China living in the Chicago area and designated surrounding states.

The **Hispanic** population (also called **Latino or Latina**) is the **largest minority** in the US. The **African American** population is the **second largest minority.** However, **Asians** constitute the **fastest growing minority.**

We **stereotype a person** when we make judgments about them based on race, culture, ethnicity, social class, religion, nationality, or education. For example, the statement, "All Asians are good at math and science," is a stereotype. **Prejudice** occurs when we judge or have a preconceived notion about another person without knowledge or facts. **Prejudice and the act of stereotyping a person** can be favorable, but in most instances, causes hatred.

Anti-Semitism means hatred, discrimination, or prejudicial behavior toward Jewish people.

American Indians are generally referred to as **Native Americans** in literature, even though some survey data show that a high percentage of these individuals prefer the term American Indian, or simply Indian.

The **Arab American** population (which is on the rise in the US) is characterized by common Middle East cultural behaviors and ideas. It's important to note that not all Arab Americans are **Muslim.**

A **transgender** person doesn't identify with his or her gender at birth. The person may or may not use medical procedures, including surgery, to become a different gender than the sexual assignment at birth. (For example, a man might receive surgery and hormonal treatments to be female.)

LGBTQ stands for lesbian, gay, bisexual, transgender, and questioning.

Not having or identifying with a sexual role is called **living in the closet. Coming out** refers to the act of letting others know your sexual identity. For example, a person who's gay shares this with friends and family.

AIDS stands for **Acquired Immunodeficiency Syndrome.** Human services practitioners should be aware that the disease isn't limited to gays, sex workers, and those who are sexually promiscuous.

HIV, or the **Human Immunodeficiency Virus**, kills T cells that keep us healthy and is thought to cause **AIDS. HIV** is also called the **AIDS virus.** A person who has the virus is said to be **HIV positive.** There are different strains of HIV, called **HIV-1** and **HIV-2** (which is more common in Africa).

Condoms help stop the transmission of AIDS; however, it should be noted that some religions don't condone their use. AIDS can also be spread by exchanging bodily fluids, sharing dirty needles used by a person with AIDS (including tattoo needles), pregnancy, and even breast milk.

The ABC model of crisis intervention by Kristi Kanel includes three parts. The worker (**A**) relies on basic attending skills to establish rapport with the client, and maintains contact; (**B**) identifies the difficulty; and (**C**) explores new coping skills with the client (such as attending support groups, exercising, or keeping a journal).

The seven stage model of crisis intervention by Albert R. Roberts and Allen J. Ottens follows these steps. First stage: Plan and then implement a complete bio-psychosocial lethality/imminent danger assessment. Stage two: Establish a collaborative relationship with the client. Stage three: Identify the presenting problems, including what led up to the crisis. Stage four: Use active listening to explore feelings and emotions. Stage five: Explore alternatives, including resources and coping skills. Stage six: Create an action plan. Stage seven: Do follow-up work related to the plan.

A **suicide attempter** is a person who tries to kill himself or herself. A **suicide survivor** is a person who's experiencing grief over a friend, relative, or acquaintance who has suicided.

The **warning signs of suicide include:** The person has made a previous attempt. The person is extremely depressed or the depression is now lifting. Talking, joking, creating artwork, or writing/blogging about death and suicide. Giving away a prized possession (say, your class ring). Displaying a loss of interest or change of behavior for no apparent reason (e.g., a child that loves hockey suddenly totally loses interest in the sport). Turning to drugs and alcohol to self-medicate an undesirable state of mind. Engaging in risk taking behavior.

When a famous person kills himself or herself, or a suicide takes place in your school or treatment facility, the odds go up somebody else will attempt suicide. This is called the **copycat effect, ripple effect, contagion effect, or Werther Effect.**

Suicidal people are **ambivalent.** They waiver back and forth between wanting to live and wanting to die. We use the will to live to motivate them not to take their own lives.

A **suicide assessment** is recommended for every client you see. You'll ask each client if he or she is thinking about suicide, or harming himself or herself. Asking the question will *not* put the idea in the client's mind.

A **lethality assessment** is conducted if the client seems even moderately suicidal. This assessment answers the question, "How likely is it that the person will make an attempt?" The more specific the plan is to commit suicide, the more likely the person will make an attempt.

Low risk for suicide: The client has never attempted suicide and has a strong support system.

Medium/middle risk for suicide: The most common pattern. The client is serious about suicide but those around him are not taking threats seriously. The family should be educated and placed on **suicide watch.**

High risk for suicide: The client has a concrete plan and the means (for example, a firearm). Admission to a hospital is the treatment of choice, even if the client doesn't wish to be hospitalized (known as **involuntary hospitalization**).

Three or four **homicide/suicides** (also referred to as **murder/suicides**) will take place per 100 suicides. For example, a mother kills her children, then herself; telling herself her children won't need to feel the pain of depression she has experienced. An employee might kill other employees who didn't promote him, and then turn the gun on himself.

Females attempt suicide more than males, but males commit suicide more than females.

Always give the suicidal clients the number of the **suicide prevention helpline or hotline,** even if they say they won't call. Always have the client sign a **no-suicide contract/agreement.** Give the client a copy of the agreement. A handshake can enhance the strategy. If you're communicating with a client by phone, a **verbal no-suicide contract/agreement,** while not as powerful as a written document, is still better than no agreement at all. A complete **safety plan** signed by the client, with multiple strategies to keep the client alive, is the most desirable intervention.

Find out **what's keeping the person alive,** and use this to motivate him or her. For example, ask, "Who will go fishing with your kids or teach them how to play baseball?"

At least two referrals should be made for all suicidal clients: **One referral to a psychiatrist (or, at the very least, a medical doctor)** and **one referral for counseling/psychotherapy.**

Act confident when dealing with suicidal clients.

It's actually true that some **anti-depressant medications** can increase the risk of suicide in some clients. This is more common in children and young adults.

Self-mutilation takes place when an individual engages in **self-harm/self-injury,** such as burning, opening a healing wound, or cutting without suicidal intention.

There are many **modalities of psychotherapeutic treatment,** also known as **counseling** or **psychotherapy.**

The model which popularized **talk therapy,** or the so-called **talking cure,** was created by **Sigmund Freud.** Freud created a **theory of personality** and a **treatment model** both called **psychoanalysis.** Sometimes, it's simply referred to as **analysis.**

A professional who performs psychoanalysis is called a **psychoanalyst;** or **analyst,** for short. Technically, the person being analyzed is the **analysand.**

Freud conceptualized the mind as being made up of three basic entities: the **id, ego,** and **super-ego.** This is called **Freud's tripartite model of the personality. Tripartite** just means that there are three parts to the personality. The **id** is present at birth and wants instant gratification. It's been called the **pleasure principle.** The **super-ego** is the morals and the conscience. The **ego** balances **id** and **super-ego** impulses. **The ego** has been called the **executive administrator of the personality.**

Freud also proposed the **topographical model,** where the mind is viewed like an iceberg (that's to say, the bulk of an iceberg is below the water level and the bulk of the mind isn't conscious, or below our awareness). This analogy proposes **three levels of consciousness: the**

conscious (small, like the tip of the iceberg sticking out of the ocean), **preconscious, and unconscious mind.** The conscious is what we're aware of. The preconscious is something we aren't aware of at the moment, but can recall and bring into conscious awareness with effort, such as what you did on your last birthday. It's bigger than the conscious. The unconscious (the largest part of the mind) contains material you're not aware of, which can only be retrieved via psychoanalysis.

The Freudian approach is said to be a form of **depth psychology**, since the unconscious is deep below the conscious. Models based on psychoanalysis are also known as **psychodynamic approaches, and are classified as the first force in counseling and psychotherapy.**

The analyst tells the **analysand** (client) to say whatever comes to mind. This is called the technique of **free association.** A lot of stock is placed in the notion of **transference. Transference** occurs when the client interacts with the analyst as if he or she was actually a parent or caretaker from childhood. This should *not be confused* with **countertransference,** a term that describes a situation where the practitioner's own issues are hindering the treatment process (say, a male practitioner who's getting a divorce and hates his wife, thus, he treats all the women in his caseload badly).

Dream work is used in psychoanalysis. Freud said that, "Dreams are the royal road to the unconscious mind." The **manifest content** is the part of the dream you remember. The **latent content** conveys the hidden meaning of the dream, often revealed by psychoanalysis.

Psychodynamic approaches champion the notion of **insight.** Insight occurs when you understand something about yourself that you didn't know up until this point in time.

In traditional psychoanalysis, the patient (analysand) actually lies on a couch and the analyst is out of sight. The analysis takes place 3 to 5 days a week, for 3 to 5 or so years. Today, when practitioners do therapy, they often use an approach called **psychodynamic therapy or psychoanalytic psychotherapy.** The client is seen face-to-face (no couch) and is only seen once or twice a week.

Psychodynamic or analytic approaches place a lot of stock in **defense mechanisms,** also referred to as **ego defense mechanisms.** All defense mechanisms distort reality to protect our ego. All except one type are automatic, meaning they occur unconsciously.

Repression is considered the most important defense mechanism. Repression takes place when you forget something important (usually traumatic, such as sexual or physical abuse at a young age). This happens automatically.

Suppression or denial is the only defense mechanism that's conscious. It's when you consciously don't think about something negative or scary, such as your high credit card bill or a big paper you should be writing for a college class that's due any day now.

The ego defense mechanism known as **displacement** manifests itself when you're angry at someone, but scared to take it out on the person you're angry at, so you displace the anger on somebody else. (You're mad at your boss, but afraid he will fire you if you tell him, so you take the rage out on your children.)

A popular defense mechanism is **rationalization.** In **sour grapes rationalization,** you underrate a reward. Let's assume you spent your life wanting to get into law school and were rejected. You might say to yourself, "I didn't really want to get into law school. Only nerds, geeks, and eggheads go to law school." In **sweet lemon rationalization,** you overrate a situation. Imagine that you wanted a professional job, but got a job in a factory with machinery that generated tremendous heat. You could assert, "I really love this job. I'm sweating out a lot of my water weight."

Projection is an ego defense mechanism where you can't accept something about yourself, so you accuse others of the impulse or trait. For example, you unconsciously wish to divorce your wife so you accuse her of being distant and wanting to get out of the marriage.

The second force in counseling and therapy is behaviorism. Some books and exams refer to this modality of treatment as ABA, or applied behavior analysis. This approach focuses on behavior generally using techniques tested in research settings using humans or other animals.

B. F. Skinner, Ivan Pavlov, and John B. Watson were famous behaviorists. Behaviorists generally believe in tabula rasa, meaning the mind at birth is like a blank slate, and behaviors are shaped primarily by the environment/experience.

John B. Watson coined the term "behaviorism," and showed that fears could be learned (conditioned) in his famous Little Albert experiment with Rosalie Rayner.

Operant conditioning was popularized by B. F. Skinner. This process usually relies on a stimulus called a reinforcer that raises, increases, or strengthens a given behavior. A child who doesn't want to do his math homework, for example, is given a piece of candy he likes after each problem. When you add something after a behavior (such as in this example), it's called positive reinforcement.

When you add something after a behavior and it lowers the behavior, we call it positive punishment, or punishment. When we take something away and it lowers behavior, it's termed negative punishment. Skinner believed that reinforcement was stronger than punishment. In negative reinforcement, a negative or aversive stimulus is removed, such as when you click your seat belt and it stops the less than desirable bell or tone in your car.

All reinforcers, positive and negative, raise behavior. All punishment, positive and negative, lowers behavior. Behaviorism is based on learning theory.

How often (or when) a worker administers reinforcement or punishment is called a schedule. If you give a reinforcer every time the desired behavior appears, it's considered a continuous reinforcement schedule. When we give the reinforcement based on time, it's known as an interval schedule. For instance, a client receives one dollar for every 5 minutes she does her math problems. A ratio schedule is based on performance or work output. The client received one dollar for every two math problems she completed.

A reinforcement schedule can be fixed, designated by F. In a fixed schedule, the reinforcer is always administered in the same pattern. If we give a client candy for every two math problems she completes, we're using a fixed schedule of reinforcement. A reinforcement schedule can be variable, designated by a V. A schedule is variable when the pattern of giving the reinforcer varies, or doesn't stay the same; say, we give a client candy after she completes one math problem and then wait until she finishes five problems to give her the next piece.

A reinforcement schedule could be fixed interval, or FI. Say, you pay a human services worker his salary for every 40 hours he worked.

A reinforcement schedule could be fixed ratio, or FR. Say, you gave a human services worker her salary for every 40 clients she saw.

A reinforcement schedule could be variable interval, or VI. Here, a human services practitioner collected her paycheck after she worked for 40 hours, and then obtained her next paycheck after she worked for another 80 hours.

A reinforcement schedule could be variable ratio, or VR. Say, you gave a human services practitioner her salary after she saw 40 clients for the first paycheck, and then for the second paycheck, after she saw 80 clients.

Thinning is said to occur when you lower the frequency of reinforcement, such as reinforcing a client after doing one math problem, and then lowering the frequency to reinforcing him or her after two problems.

Partial reinforcement, or intermittent reinforcement, occurs when you don't give a reinforcer each time the behavior occurs. This is often contrasted with continuous reinforcement.

Extinction occurs when there's a lack of reinforcement. Ignoring a behavior or putting a client in a time out would be examples of this. Extinction procedures will produce an **extinction burst, or response burst,** meaning the behavior will get worse and increase before it gets better.

A lot of agencies use the **token economy** model. For example, instead of giving clients actual **primary reinforcers** like candy bars or baseball gloves, the agency gives the clients **secondary reinforcers,** such as plastic tokens, coins, or gold stars that can be traded in for candy or baseball gloves (i.e., the actual primary reinforcers). Clients also experience **satiation** when using primary reinforcers ("Oh no, not another piece of candy. I've already had 10 pieces.").

The first step in **behavior modification** is generally to chart the incidence of the behavior when it's untreated. This is called the **baseline,** and it's signified by **A.** Charting the number of cigarettes a client smokes for 7 days would be an example. The treatment (behavior modification) is signified by the letter **B,** and, thus, this method is frequently called an **AB design.** AB design is also used in research studies for behavior modification.

Behaviorists use **modeling. Your exam might label it observational learning.** A behavior modifier demonstrates something so the client can copy or imitate the behavior. Albert Bandura popularized this strategy, and he originally called it **social learning theory.**

In behavior modification, the term **discrimination** is used to signify that you want a client to respond to one stimulus rather than another. As an example, you could use behavior modification to teach a client that he needs to ride the bus with the number 10, rather than the bus with the number 100 on the back.

The Russian physiologist, **Ivan Pavlov,** popularized what's become known as **classical conditioning.** A **neutral stimulus (NS),** also dubbed a **conditioned stimulus (CS),** such as a bell or tone, is paired with an **unconditioned stimulus (UCS),** such as meat or meat powder. After they're paired together for a period of trials and become associated, the **CS—a bell or tone—**will cause the dog to salivate, and we have a **CR, or conditioned response,** without the meat. **The CS/NS** must come before the **UCS** for this to be effective.

Classical Conditioning Summary:

1. An **unconditioned stimulus, or US,** (meat) causes a dog to salivate, which is an **unconditioned response, or UR.** (Unconditioned simply means unlearned: the dog didn't need to be trained to have this response.)
2. You ring a bell—a **neutral stimulus (NS)/conditioned stimulus (CS)**—and approximately a second later, present the meat, the **unconditioned stimulus.** Do this for a number of trials.
3. The **neutral stimulus (NS), also called a conditioned stimulus (CS)**—the bell alone *without the meat*—will now elicit the salivating, which is referred to as a **conditioned response (CR).** Conditioned means learned, so this is a learned response.
4. **Generalization** can often occur. Here, something similar to the CS/NS, such as a car horn, will cause the dog to salivate. In essence, something other than the original **CS/NS** will cause the **CR,** but the response is generally weaker.

Human services helpers often employ **role playing** to help clients. In **role playing,** the client can act out a skill, rehearse, or practice a skill or behavior. For example, a client who's afraid to ask for a raise might practice asking for a raise with a human services practitioner. If the client doesn't know how to begin, the worker might **model** the behavior first to help the client. The client might even play the role of the boss in the **role play** to help him or her understand the situation.

A very popular modality of counseling or therapy is **CBT, or cognitive behavior therapy.** Cognitive merely means thinking, and the helper tries to change the way the client thinks. This is called changing the **client's self-talk,** also known as **internal verbalizations.**

REBT, or rational emotive behavior therapy, is a type of **CBT** that's very popular. **REBT** was created by Dr. Albert Ellis, who believes humans naturally think in an irrational, illogical, and unscientific manner.

REBT is an active-directive treatment approach, meaning the therapist might talk as much or more than the client. It's also a **didactic method.** Didactic means to teach. With this paradigm, the helper often teaches or lectures the client on how to think rationally.

REBT uses the ABC Theory of Personality and ABCDE counseling approach. A = acti-vating event (anything that happens to you), B = your belief system about what's hap-pened, and C = emotional consequence (you feel hurt, depressed, ashamed, anxious, etc.). In REBT, the helper uses the counseling approach where **D = dispute the irrational belief (IRB), which causes negative emotions and teaches you to replace it with a rational belief (RB),** resulting in **E = a new healthy emotional consequence.**

Albert Ellis lists a number of irrational beliefs (IRBs) that cause emotional problems including:

*   Everybody must love you and approve of your behavior.
*   The past controls the present.
*   It's easier to avoid life's difficulties than face them.
*   That because something was fearful at one time, it will always be fearful.
*   You must be thoroughly competent in all areas of your life or you're worthless.
*   There's a perfect solution to everything and when there's not a solution, it's horrible or catastrophic.
*   You need somebody stronger than yourself to rely on for help.

Ellis believes that **should's, ought's, and must's** in our thinking can cause emotional disturbance. (For example, "I must get a high grade on this exam or my career is over.")

Many treatment approaches rely on **reframing,** in which the client is instructed to think about an existing situation in a different manner or perspective. A common example in everyday life would be: The glass of water is half full, rather than half empty.

Carl Ransom Rogers created **client-centered counseling,** also known as **non-directive counseling, Rogerian counseling, person-centered counseling, or self-theory.** This is a **humanistic approach to helping. Humanistic (also called existential)** models of helping are the **third force in counseling and therapy.** Building a **relationship with the client** is very important in this model. There are **three core conditions** necessary for personality change: **empathy, genuineness, and unconditional positive regard (UPR).**

1. **Empathy:** Understanding the client's feelings, thoughts, ideas, and worldview, and reflecting this back to the client.
2. **Genuineness:** Also called **congruence,** this is the act of being real/authentic with the client to help build trust.
3. **Unconditional positive regard:** The helper is nonjudgmental and displays respect and acceptance.

Reflection is used a lot in non-directive approaches. Here, the helper restates or rephrases the client's feelings and content. **Paraphrasing** is a type of reflection where the worker restates what a client has said in different words. This technique lets the client know you understand his or her viewpoint.

A new theory called **post modern social construction** asserts that reality is socially constructed. Or, to put it another way, there's no absolute truth in the sense that helpers and clients create their own reality. A popular post modern theory is **narrative therapy**, created by Michael White from Australia and David Epston of New Zealand. **Narrative therapy** postulates that our notions of ourselves (our identity) will be shaped and created by **stories** or **narratives** about our lives. The procedure helps clients rewrite their personal stories. Narrative therapy strives to **externalize the problem. Externalizing the problem** means that the person isn't the problem; the problem itself is the problem. The problem is separate from the person. Thus, when the client says, "I suffer from shopping addiction," the therapist could say, "How is your shopping habit affecting your life?"

Some therapies fall into the category of **gender awareness approaches,** such as **feminist therapy** and **men's issues therapy.**

Eclectic/integrative therapy conveys the notion that about one-fourth of all therapists and helpers employ the ideas from several theoretical perspectives when they treat clients. A helper might use relationship building methods from client-centered therapy, behavior modification for habit control, and some psychodynamic principles for working with the individual's dreams.

Reality therapy, also called **reality therapy with choice theory**, was created by psychiatrist William Glasser. Reality therapy advocates eight steps: 1. Make friends with the client; 2. Focus on the present; 3. Help client evaluate current behavior; 4. Create a plan of action; 5. Get client to commit to the plan; 6. Accept no excuses; 7. Use no punishment; 8. Refuse to give up.

Brief strategic solution focused therapy (BSFT) uses the **miracle question, exception questions, and scaling questions.** BSFT is a short-term treatment that keeps focused on the present, what worked, and what's improving.

Systematic desensitization, created by psychiatrist **Joseph Wolpe,** is an excellent behavioral procedure for licensed mental health professionals to use in cases where the client has severe fears or phobias. The paradigm is based on **classical conditioning** and **the Jacobson relaxation method** (basically tensing and relaxing the major muscle groups).

Some new theories are given the label **postmodern** and **constructivist.** This worldview promotes the idea that each client creates his or her reality because there's no single objective reality. **Narrative therapy** that recommends sending letters to clients between sessions is considered a **postmodern/constructivist theory. Narrative therapy** assumes that we construct our identity based on the stories we tell about ourselves and the stories others tell about us.

Developmental psychology is the study of psychological, cognitive, emotional, and perceptual changes over the life span. When a condition is present at birth, it's said to be **congenital.** Relevant **early milestones** include:

3 months: Recognizes a bottle or breast and makes cooing sounds. Turns head in the direction of light.

6 months: Can **reach for objects** and **rolls over.** May try to hold a bottle when fed. Tries to imitate sounds.

1 year: Can **crawl, sit,** or **stand** briefly. Can say short words like "ma-ma." Can wave. **Walking** can first occur from approximately 9 to 18 months. (Note: A **declining death/ mortality rate** is usually attributed to fewer childhood diseases and better treatment, especially with penicillin and later antibiotics.)

Freud's psychosexual stages: Oral, birth to 1 year (mouth); **Anal**, ages 1 to 3 years (anus); **Phallic**, ages 3 to 6 (genitals); **Latency**, ages 6 to puberty (dormant); **Genital**, puberty to death. Each stage is related to an erogenous zone, except the latency stage.

Freud's Oedipus complex is the notion that a boy has sexual feelings for his mother. The most controversial part of Freud's theory, the Oedipus complex occurs in the phallic stage.

Freud's Electra complex occurs in the phallic stage. The girl has sexual feelings for her father, but must give them up.

Freud's development theory is psychosexual, while **Erikson's theory** is **psychosocial and covers the entire lifespan in more depth.**

Erik Erikson's eight psychosocial stages: Stage 1: **Trust versus mistrust**, birth to 12–18 months; Stage 2: **Autonomy versus shame/doubt**, 18 months to 3 years; Stage 3: **Initiative versus guilt**, 3 to 6 years; Stage 4: **Industry versus inferiority**, 6 to 12 years; Stage 5: **Identity versus role confusion**, 12 to 18 years; Stage 6: **Intimacy versus isolation**, 19 to 40 years; Stage 7: **Generativity versus stagnation**, 40 to 65 years; Stage 8: **Integrity versus despair**, 65 to death.

Erikson popularized the term **identity crisis.**

Jean Piaget proposed a **four stage model/theory of cognitive development** in children.

The **sensorimotor stage** (young children's knowledge is sensory from the eyes, hands, and ears) goes from birth to age 2. At the end of the stage, the child has mastered **object permanence.** This means the child knows that an object still exists even when it's hidden.

The **preoperational stage** is from 2 to 7 years (symbolic thinking and behaving, such as pretending a cup is an airplane). **Egocentrism** is present—the child can't see another person's point of view. The child thinks everybody is having the same experience as he or she is having.

The **concrete operational stage** lasts from 7 to 11 years. The child masters the concept of **reversibility** and **conservation.** An example of mastering **conservation:** A child understands that when a small squatty glass of water is poured into a tall skinny glass, the amount of water doesn't change.

The final or **formal operational stage** occurs from age 11 to 16 and beyond. The child can do abstract calculations and reasoning. Some people never master this level.

Piaget calls psychological ways of understanding the environment **schemes or schema.**

Lev Vygotsky, a Russian psychologist, created a **social development theory.** He's well-known for popularizing the **zone of proximal development (ZPD)**, which can be defined as the difference between what children can learn on their own versus what they can learn potentially with the assistance of adults or more advanced peers. **Vygotsky** focused on culture in terms of influencing cognitive development, while **Piagetian theory** doesn't.

A person with **antisocial personality disorder** has no empathy or regard for others' feelings, is unremorseful, and, thus, can commit crimes with no guilt. Nearly 75% of all convicted criminals fall into this category.

Narcissistic personality disorder is present when a person has an inflated sense of self-importance and is preoccupied with himself. These people need constant attention and admiration to feel good about themselves.

Sexual assault victims are usually women; however, the rate for men can be high in prison settings. One in three women will be beaten, or forced to have sex during a lifetime. One in five high school students are physically or sexually abused. Once over the age of 17, 75% of all women will be raped or assaulted. **Leonore E. Walker** believed in the **battered woman syndrome.** The woman believes the violence is her fault, she can't place the responsibility for the violence on someone else, she fears for her own life and that of her children, and she falsely believes the abuser is omniscient and can track every move she will make.

During sexual assaults, 45% of all **rapists** are under the influence of drugs or alcohol at the time of the incident. In a high percentage of the cases (perhaps 75 to 90%), the victim knew the rapist. At one time, women victims were blamed for the rape.

Intimate partner violence (IPV) can also be called **domestic violence.** It refers to violence committed by a spouse, former spouse, or current or past boyfriend or girlfriend. It can occur in homosexual or heterosexual couples.

When a **teen pregnancy** occurs—either in or out of marriage—the mother is more apt to use drugs, alcohol, and abuse her children. Moreover, she's more likely to be abused herself and be unemployed.

Poverty could lead to criminal behavior. A poverty stricken individual could sell drugs, steal, or turn to prostitution in an attempt to lead the life others enjoy. Poor persons are sometimes referred to as **paupers** in literature. The word **indigent** has also been used. The **poverty line, poverty index,** or **poverty threshold,** created in 1964, refers to the minimum amount the government feels is necessary to live at an acceptable level.

In the US, we have approximately 3.5 million people each year who are **homeless.** Over 1 million of the homeless are children. Homelessness can be caused by various factors, including poverty, lack of affordable housing, decline in public assistance, lack of jobs or low paying work, foreclosures, and natural disasters and weather patterns such as earthquakes, floods, hurricanes, or tornados. Domestic violence, issues with addiction, and mental illness are also contributing factors. Temporary residences for the homeless are known as **homeless shelters.**

People often join a **gang** to feel like they belong to a family.

Runaways want to feel autonomy and security. The irony is that runaways can be abused by others, especially pimps. Runaways also use drugs to feel like they have freedom.

A **case manager** uses **case management,** which is assessing, planning, monitoring, and coordinating the treatment process and implementation of services. Sometimes (but not always), the case manager will personally provide some of the services.

A **voluntary client** willingly accepts treatment. An **involuntary client** didn't choose the treatment willingly (for example, a client must attend counseling or is legally required to return to prison).

A **resistant client** attempts to block or oppose the helping process.

A **social program** or **social welfare policy** helps individuals with housing, mental health, hunger, child care, health care, education, criminal justice issues, public assistance, nutrition, or energy programs. Some of the most popular programs include:

TANF, which stands for *Temporary Assistance for Needy Families*, refers to new programs created in 1996 that replaced the **Aid to Families of Dependent Children (AFDC)** welfare payment program. **AFDC** was previously termed **ADC,** or simply **Aid to Dependent Children.** *TANF* stipulates that able-bodied citizens must be engaged in work or work-related activities (e.g., a job search or job readiness program) after 2 years of receiving assistance. There's a 5 year (60 month) lifetime limit on benefits. This is a **means-tested** public assistance program, where you must qualify or meet specific financial guidelines in order to be eligible. In short, if a program is **means-tested,** your income, assets, and possessions must fall below a certain level. For a means-tested program, you must meet the **eligibility requirements** in order to receive the benefits. Other programs totally unrelated to *TANF* and public assistance can have eligibility requirements. For example, an agency might stipulate that you must live in a certain zip code or be a certain age, or be unemployed, to receive benefits.

The **Food Stamp program** is a social welfare program that provides low income individuals benefits to purchase nutritional items. The new name is **Supplemental Nutrition Assistance Program (SNAP). SNAP** is a **means-tested** program, as well.

Medicaid is a **means-tested** program jointly funded by the state and the federal government to provide medical insurance for persons of any age who meet the guidelines (low income and limited assets). The program may reimburse physicians, outpatient prescription medicines, and inpatient and outpatient hospital care. The **Affordable Care Act (ACA)**, signed into law on March 23, 2010 by President Barack Obama, expanded Medicaid coverage, lowered the cost, and is intended to expand coverage to millions of uninsured Americans. The program should cut costs and protect consumers from abusive practices used by insurance companies. The legislation also improved the **Children's Health Insurance Program (CHIP)**.

Medicare is a federal health insurance program for individuals 65 and over, and some persons who are under 65 and disabled. Participants may have co-payments and deductibles. **Part A** covers hospital bills, hospice, a skilled nursing facility, home health care, or a nursing home with no custodial care. **Part B** covers mainly physicians, things like wheelchairs, and lab tests. The **Affordable Care Act** should strengthen the Medicare program. According to the White House, the **Affordable Care Act** aims to improve consumer protection and rights, make coverage more affordable, and increase access to health care.

Social Security is considered an **entitlement or social insurance**, rather than a **means-tested** program. **Social insurance** refers to a government program where the person has earned the right to receive the benefit.

A **practicum** is an interactive learning experience while you're a human services student. You could be placed at a **for-profit** or **nonprofit** agency, hospital, school, treatment facility, or virtually any site where human services are provided. A practicum can also be referred to as an **internship, workplace learning, fieldwork, or clinicals.** Often, your **practicum supervisor** at the site will become a **mentor** to you, just like some of your other human services instructors. **Mentors** can be helpful, even after a practicum or school ends.

If a human services practicum student engages in **unethical** or **illegal** behavior, the student, agency supervisor, college/university, and the agency/organization could be held responsible.

Public agencies include county, city, state, regional, and federal government organizations.

For-profit agencies attempt to produce a profit for the agency, as well as stakeholders. **Nonprofit agencies** are also dubbed **not-for-profit agencies**. These agencies meet guidelines set by the **Internal Revenue Service (IRS)** and IRS **501 (c) (3) guidelines**, and are exempt from paying certain federal taxes, and contributors to the agency can receive a tax deduction. **Nonprofits** are governed by a **board of directors**. Some agencies also have an **advisory board** (to provide feedback about existing programs, future programs, and changes that might prove beneficial) and a **media board** (to help advertise or promote the agency services, fundraisers, and need for volunteers and practicum students on television, radio, newspapers, magazines, or on the web). **Nonprofit agencies** are more apt to help poor clients than **for-profit organizations**.

Common positions in social service and mental health agencies: The highest **paid employee in an agency** usually holds the title of **executive director** or **president**. A **development director**, or **director of development**, helps raise money for the agency through grants, fundraisers, individual giving campaigns, etc. If this person only creates fundraisers, he or she could simply be called a **fund raiser**. Putting together a fundraiser is a long process (especially if celebrities or local celebrities are used, say a local television news anchor) and could take a year or more to put together. Individuals who donate to the organization are dubbed **contributors or donors**. Donations can be **monetary (money) or gifts-in-kind (e.g., a computer or desk; actual items)**. If the employee's sole job is to write grants, the term **grant writer** will often describe the position. A **clinical director** will oversee the assessment, treatment, and intervention staff. The job title of **program director**

or program coordinator is used for the professional who's in charge of overseeing the actions of one or more programs. A **volunteer coordinator** can help secure new volunteers and practicum students, and keep existing ones happy and scheduled for the best results. Agencies that act as a referral bank often have a **resource and referral coordinator.** In some agencies, an **intake worker** assesses the client's needs, while a **treatment worker** takes over after the assessment process is complete. Workers often base their treatment strategies on a **three-phase approach to problem solving: 1. Accurately identify the problem or difficulty, as well as the client's strengths; 2. Provide intervention; and, 3. Problem resolution.**

The money or resources to run an agency or agency program is called an **allocation.**

Human services practitioners often refer clients to:

Psychiatrists, or medical doctors (e.g., MD or DO) who prescribe psychiatric medicine. **Psychiatrists** also refer patients to hospitals and can administer **electroconvulsive shock therapy (ECT).**

Clinical or counseling psychologists who have a doctorate (e.g., PhD, PsyD, or EdD) and are licensed in the state where they practice. **Psychologists** can diagnose clients; take managed care or insurance payments; perform psychotherapy (aka therapy and counseling); and give psycho-educational, vocational, and personality tests. In a few states, psychologists can legally prescribe psychotropic/psychiatric medicine (aka **prescription privileges or RxP**) if they're properly trained.

Licensed master's or doctorate level counselors (e.g., MEd, PhD, or EdD degrees) who are licensed (e.g., Licensed Professional Counselor, or LPC) in the state they're practicing. Counselors can often diagnose clients, take managed care or insurance payments, do psychotherapy or counseling, give some psycho-educational and personality tests, and provide career counseling and testing. Counselors who meet **department of elementary and secondary education (DESE)** certification requirements could work in K-12 schools as guidance counselors.

Licensed master's level or doctoral level social workers (e.g., MSW, PhD, or DSW degrees), such as Licensed Clinical Social Workers, or LCSW. These professionals can usually diagnose, take insurance, and perform psychotherapy and counseling in the states where they're licensed. Social workers can be licensed at the bachelor's level (e.g., the Licensed Bachelor Social Worker or LBSW), but can't provide the aforementioned advanced services. Unlike psychology, a doctoral degree isn't required for clinical social work practice. A doctoral level social worker will often teach, conduct research, or go into administration.

Chapter 7

Vignettes from the Experts

Here's your chance to learn some key information and wrestle with some vignettes (case histories) that might be very similar to what you could come face-to-face with on the actual exam. So you could get novel points of view that were different than my own, I purposely asked noted textbook authors to contribute. Please remember that on the real exam, each vignette will have 10 questions for you to answer. In this chapter, however, I allowed my panel of specialists to determine the number they felt was necessary.

Julie Birkenmaier is an associate professor at Saint Louis University School of Social Work. She teaches a range of courses at the undergraduate and graduate levels focused on community, organizational, and policy practice, as well as financial capability practice. She is the co-author of *The Practice of Generalist Social Work* (Routledge) and *Financial Capability and Asset Development: Research, Education, Policy, and Practice* (Oxford University Press).

Marla Berg-Weger is a professor at Saint Louis University School of Social Work, and executive director at the Geriatric Education Center. She teaches in the baccalaureate social work program. She is the author of *Social Work and Social Welfare: An Invitation* (Routledge), and she co-authored *The Practice of Generalist Social Work* (Routledge) and *The Practicum Companion for Social Work: Integrating Class and Field Work* (Pearson).

Macro Case Vignette

Michael is a human services worker at a community mental health agency. He has been working for the agency for 3 months as a caseworker for 12 clients with chronic mental illness. As part of his orientation, he has "shadowed" several other caseworkers, and has learned that part of the services required of caseworkers is to help clients with their finances, yet he feels unqualified to assist in this manner since he has only recently become financially independent from his parents. He understands a few basics—that he should spend less than he earns; that he needs to pay his monthly rent, utilities, and cell phone bill on time; and he is trying to save some money each month. However, he does not understand much about the payroll taxes that he has noticed in his pay stub, Social Security retirement, or the retirement saving options he has been presented with from his employer. He has had a savings account at one bank for years, uses ATMs to get cash when he needs it, and has just applied for his first credit card.

To his dismay, Michael thinks he may have seen staff give inaccurate guidance about finances to their clients. For example, one client had been saving up money to buy a new television, and the staff member suggested that he purchase a US savings bond with the money to earn more interest than what he is earning in his savings account. Michael is not sure that the client is willing to wait years before buying the television, and may incur fees if he tries to get his money back too soon, which would negate any interest earned. In another example, he has seen caseworkers take their clients to ATMs where they incur higher costs for accessing cash than at ATMs owned by their banks. Although the fees are not much, they add up quickly.

Michael has asked every staff member that he has shadowed, as well as his supervisor, how they came to learn financial knowledge and skills, and each one of them has responded that they have only learned informally—no one has had a financial education class, and the agency has not offered training about this area. Michael is beginning to think the agency should offer formal financial education to its staff, either at orientation or as ongoing training, or both. When he casually mentioned the idea of financial education for staff to his immediate supervisor during a regular supervision meeting, he was met with a lukewarm response at first, and after more discussion, the supervisor agreed that not every staff member knew as much as they needed to know about finances. However, for now, he was encouraged to learn on the job, and just ask questions of other caseworkers.

Questions

1. What is the best option for the Michael?

    a. Design a proposal for a bank to provide free financial education.
    b. Speak with his supervisor and ask about the idea of financial education.
    c. Continue to assess the organization in terms of training needs with more conversations with staff about financial education.
    d. As a new staff member, keep quiet.

The correct answer is "c." Michael is fairly new to the agency, and further organizational assessment is needed to determine whether other staff members and administrators perceive a need for financial education and, if so, to begin to build support for the idea of training in this area.

2. Due to a series of events, Michael has received support from his supervisor to explore the idea of financial education for the staff. What is the best initial step for Michael?

    a. Communicate with the executive director to get his/her feedback.
    b. Create a group of staff members interested in this idea to explore the problem and possibilities.
    c. Write a grant to raise money for financial education.
    d. None of the above.

The correct answer is "b." Any organizational change effort needs a group effort to consider all possibilities, identify opposition to the idea, and to gain support for any proposed change.

3. Michael has determined that he needs more information about the problem, whether staff and administrators think there is a problem, and what to do about it. What could Michael do to gather more data about the (alleged) absence of financial education information?

    a. Survey staff, clients, and administrators.
    b. Survey staff and clients.

    c.   Survey staff, clients, administrators, other collaborating organizations, and members of the board of directors.

    d.   Survey staff, clients, administrators, and other collaborating organizations.

The correct answer is "d." Collecting data from all sources about perceived weaknesses or gaps in services is appropriate, with the exception of the board of directors. The board of directors is responsible for setting policies and hiring the executive director, but is not supposed to be involved in smaller details of the organization.

4.   Who is ultimate decision-maker about providing financial education at the agency?

    a.   The board of directors.
    b.   The executive director.
    c.   The program directors.
    d.   None of the above.

The correct answer is "b." The board of directors is responsible for setting policies, hiring the executive director, establishing the budget, and other high level decisions. The executive director is responsible for programming and personnel within the organization, including types of training.

5.   If the organization decides to provide financial education training on a one-time basis, and then decides whether or not to repeat it again in the future, this type of a response would be called a

    a.   project.
    b.   program.
    c.   policy.
    d.   practice.

The correct answer is "a." A project is a one-time event, typically paired with evaluation to assist in the decision-making about whether to repeat the effort.

6.   The following statement adequately states a working hypothesis for a change effort to persuade the agency to provide financial education:

    a.   "Because of poor financial education, the result has been that clients' finances have not been maximized. If financial education training is provided, things will improve."
    b.   "Because of poor financial education, the results have been that clients' finances have not been maximized."
    c.   "Because of poor financial education, the results have been that clients' finances have not been maximized. If financial education training is provided, clients will have higher credit scores and more savings than they currently have."
    d.   None of the above.

The correct answer is "d." The working hypothesis should include specific results, such as a target goal of improvement.

7.   After the agency administration agrees that financial education is important for staff, creating a group to examine alternative ways to deliver different sources of financial

education training is better than arranging for training the same way that all training is delivered.

a. True
b. False
c. It depends on whether the current administration is interested in other methods besides face-to-face training.
d. It depends on whether the current administration has ever offered financial education in the past.

The correct answer is "a." Creative ideas and possibilities should be generated about organizational interventions that appear to be relevant before making a decision about method and source of delivery of the intervention.

Ethics, Technology, and Field Education

Samantha is a 24-year-old student completing her human services practicum in an alternative school that serves teens who have dropped out of high school. She has been assigned to work with Daniel, an 18-year-old, who lives in a transitional housing program. He was disowned by his parents when they learned he is gay.

Samantha connected immediately with Daniel. They shared many interests and came from similar backgrounds. They had both experienced depression and Samantha felt she had insights and empathy regarding the struggles of battling chronic depression. Daniel had considerable difficulty relating to the other students and staff, so everyone was pleased that he was opening up to Samantha. Daniel reminded her of her younger brother with whom she had always been close, almost in a maternal way at times when life was chaotic in their home.

Without checking with her supervisor, Samantha gave her cell phone number to Daniel so he could contact her in case he needed to talk to someone. In the beginning, Daniel phoned Samantha infrequently and just when he was feeling low. The calls became more frequent and he began to text her regularly. They then became friends on Facebook. Samantha did not share any of this information with her supervisor, or document the contacts in Daniel's case record, because she feared that Daniel could be expelled from the school and she could fail her practicum. Samantha believed the staff had not been as caring and supportive of Daniel as they could have been. She felt she was the only one who truly understood him.

While Samantha only occasionally responded to Daniel's texts or Facebook postings, she did answer his phone calls. These exchanges continued for several months. They continued to have a professional relationship at the school, but neither mentioned the outside contacts to the school's faculty or staff. As Samantha was preparing to complete her practicum, she let Daniel know that she would be leaving the school. She was also preparing to graduate from her program and move to a new city, where she will be pursuing another degree.

Last week, after learning that she was leaving the school and the area, Daniel became suicidal and was hospitalized after telling another resident at the housing program, "I just want to die." It was during the hospitalization that he shared with the hospital staff that he became suicidal because, he said, "the only person who has ever loved me is leaving and I can't live without her." Today, Samantha is called in to her supervisor's office to discuss her actions in working with Daniel. She is asked to describe the course of events that have occurred throughout the duration of her practicum experience and to consider if she has made any ethical misjudgments about the way in which she has related to Daniel.

Questions

1. What is the best option for the Samantha?

    a. Fully disclose to her supervisor the extent of the relationship she has had with Daniel.
    b. Disclose the fact she provided her cell phone number, but not the fact that she "friended" him on Facebook.
    c. Meet privately with Daniel and offer to find him another confidante if he does not disclose the full extent of their interactions outside of the school.
    d. Talk with the hospital staff to learn about Daniel's status.

The correct answer is "a." Being completely honest with her supervisor will be in the best interest of the client.

2. What is the best initial step for the human services supervisor in working with Samantha?

    a. Inform Samantha of the concerns about her violation of boundaries and dismiss her from her practicum.
    b. Consult with the school's legal counsel to determine if the school can be held liable for Daniel's suicidal threat.
    c. Meet with Samantha to gather relevant information about the situation from her perspective.
    d. Contact Samantha's human services program to inform the faculty about the situation.

The correct answer is "c." Gathering information is the first step in determining an appropriate response to this situation. While one or more of the other options may be considered in the future, having as much information as possible from multiple sources is critical for a response that is in the best interests of Samantha, Daniel, and the school.

3. Which of the following is an example of exhibiting inappropriate professional-client boundaries?

    a. Providing your personal cell phone number to the client.
    b. Connecting with a client through social media.
    c. Meeting the client outside of the agency setting and work hours.
    d. All of the above.

The correct answer is "d." Unless agency policy explicitly permits providing personal contact information, including through social media or meeting with a client outside of the professional context, choices a, b, and c are not appropriate professional boundaries to maintain.

4. Based on your understanding of appropriate ethical behavior for human services practitioners, has Samantha committed an ethical violation?

    a. Yes
    b. No
    c. It depends on the rules of the high school.
    d. It depends on the rules of Samantha's human services program.

The correct answer is "a." Providing personal information without her supervisor's approval or knowledge, and having contact through social media, are ethical violations.

5. Which of the following is the best approach that Samantha might have considered?

    a. Inform Daniel at the outset of their work together that she would be leaving the school and the area.
    b. Check school policy regarding sharing personal contact information.
    c. Talk with Daniel on the phone, but not meet with him outside of the school setting.
    d. Choices a and b, but not c.

The correct answer is "d." Each of the approaches noted in choices a and b are appropriate for a practicum student to consider, particularly when working with a vulnerable adolescent.

6. While Samantha acted inappropriately in the situation, which of the following would have been appropriate actions taken by Samantha in response to her concerns?

    a. Discuss with Daniel the situation at school where he does not connect with other staff members and encourage him to work harder at connecting with others, so as not to rely too heavily on one staff member or student.
    b. Discuss with Daniel's school-based therapist his inability to connect with other staff members.
    c. Discuss with Daniel's parents and other students his inability to connect with other staff members.
    d. All of the above except choice c.

The correct answer is "d." As long as Daniel has signed consent forms, practicum students can discuss concerns about a client with other members of their service team. Daniel is legally independent from his parents (at age 18), and, therefore, sharing information about Daniel would be a breach of confidentiality. It would also be a breach of confidentiality to discuss concerns about Daniel with the other students.

7. Which is the most important concern that a human services practitioner should have about Daniel?

    a. Depression.
    b. Isolation from his parents.
    c. Suicidal ideation.
    d. His sexual orientation.

The correct answer is "c." If clients discuss suicidal thoughts, human services workers should prioritize screening to determine whether the client has a plan and the means to commit suicide.

8. The human services practitioner can provide Daniel with information on which of the following resources?

    a. Clinical resources to treat depression.
    b. A suicide hotline.
    c. Support groups for young gay males.
    d. All of the above.

The correct answer is "d." All of the options would be appropriate areas that may be of help to Daniel.

9. Imagine this future scenario: Several years pass, and Samantha goes on to work for a human services agency in a different state. One day while out shopping, she encounters Daniel again. They are glad to see one another, and he asks whether it would be appropriate for them to be in contact—Daniel tells Samantha how much he has missed her. Which of the following is likely to be the best response?

    a. "Sure, that would be fine, now that you are no longer a client."
    b. "Maybe, let me think about it a bit and I'll be in touch with you."
    c. "Maybe, I'll need to check with my agency to see what their policy is about contact with a former client, and I'll be in touch with you."
    d. Any of the above could be an appropriate response.

The correct answer is "c." Even though they worked together in another state, Samantha may work for an agency that has strict guidelines about personal contact with former clients.

Mr. and Mrs. Sherman: Working with Older Adults

Arthur Sherman is a 76-year-old African American male who lives with his wife of 53 years, Lavinia (age 74 years), in a home they own in your community. Arthur is in the early to middle stage of Alzheimer's disease. At the urging of his family, Arthur retired 2 years ago from driving after having had several episodes of getting lost in his community and being escorted home by a law enforcement officer. Before retiring from driving, he had several incidents with the car (hitting the mailbox, curb, and a parked car), resulting in minor damage to his car. He was extremely reluctant to give up driving, but agreed that he did not want to cause harm to anyone else, particularly as they live near an elementary school.

Since Arthur's driving retirement, Lavinia has assumed full responsibility for driving, but has been less than enthusiastic about this role. Arthur had always done all the driving. In fact, Lavinia had not regularly driven since she retired 5 years earlier.

With this new arrangement, the Shermans were able to function well in their community, maintain their usual activities, and even made a trip to their grandchild's high school graduation, which required a 4-hour round trip.

Lavinia has recently been diagnosed with age-related macular degeneration (AMD—a progressive deterioration of the center of the retina, resulting in the loss of central vision and retention of peripheral vision). She continued to drive without incident until she was required to renew her driver's license. She was unable to pass the vision exam, despite three attempts. When questioned by her physician, she confessed that she and Arthur had been "co-piloting" (an arrangement in which she operated the car and Arthur served as her eyes).

Not wanting to leave their home or burden their family, Arthur and Lavinia began a new co-piloting arrangement. Arthur, who holds a valid driver's license, resumed driving. Arthur operated the vehicle while Lavinia navigated, ensuring that Arthur did not get lost or make a wrong turn, or misinterpret a traffic sign/signal. They always travelled together and despite several "near misses," no major incidents or encounters with law enforcement had occurred.

As a human services practitioner working at a community center for older adults where the Shermans attend a weekly meal and education event, you were unaware of their driving arrangement until you happened to follow them out of the parking lot. You were aware of their medical conditions, but not that Arthur had resumed driving.

Questions

1. What is the best option for the Shermans?

    a. Continue the current arrangement, as it seems to be working.
    b. Sell their home and move in with their son and his family.
    c. Explore options for alternative transportation.
    d. Explore options for assisted living.

The correct answer is "c." Continuing the arrangement is a threat to public safety and the other two options may not yet be necessary. Gaining awareness of transportation options may enable them to stay in their own home.

2. What is the best initial step for you (the human services practitioner) in working with the Shermans?

    a. Inform the Shermans' daughter of your concerns.
    b. Ask the Shermans if you may visit them at their home.
    c. Gather more information about Mr. Sherman's driving by watching them as they drive in and out of the center's parking lot.
    d. Report Mr. Sherman to the state licensing authority.

The correct answer is "b." Conducting a home visit will enable the practitioner to assess the couple's situation in a comfortable location and initiate a discussion about their current driving arrangement.

3. How should you (the human services practitioner) prioritize the issues presented by the Shermans?

    a. Transportation needs, public safety concerns, and need for social engagement.
    b. Social engagement, transportation needs, and burden on family.
    c. Public safety concerns, transportation needs, and social engagement.
    d. Evaluation of Mr. Sherman's dementia, public safety concerns, and transportation needs.

The correct answer is "c." As a person with possible mid-stage Alzheimer's disease, Mr. Sherman is unlikely to be medically fit to drive. Need for alternative transportation and social engagement are also of high priority.

4. Who is responsible for ensuring older adults who are unsafe drivers retire from driving?

    a. Physicians.
    b. Law enforcement.
    c. Family members and older adults.
    d. All of the above.

The correct answer is "d." While all the groups are obligated to address an older adult's unsafe driving, the state licensing authority is the entity that determines one's fitness and right to drive.

5. As long as Mr. Sherman has not been ticketed for driving violations, he has a right to continue driving.

    a. True, but he should be tested to confirm that he is safe.
    b. True
    c. False, because he has Alzheimer's disease.
    d. It depends on the extent of his cognitive impairment.

The correct answer is "a." He legally has a right to drive because he holds a valid driver's license, but he should be tested as soon as possible by the state agency designated to examine drivers, or a driver rehabilitation specialist (typically an occupational therapist with specialized training in driver evaluation), to determine his medical fitness to drive.

6. You (the human services practitioner) are required to report Mr. Sherman to the state licensing authority as medically unfit to drive.

    a. True
    b. False
    c. False, but you are ethically obligated to report.
    d. It depends on the state in which this situation is occurring.

The correct answer is "b." At this time, a small number of states have mandatory reporting laws for medically unfit drivers and, in those states, only physicians are mandated reporters. All other states have voluntary reporting laws.

7. Which of the following is *not* a violation of client confidentiality?

    a. Contacting Mr. Sherman's primary care physician for information on the progression of his dementia.
    b. Making a report to the state licensing authority.
    c. Informing Mr. Sherman's children of your concerns.
    d. Registering Mr. Sherman for a driver evaluation.

The correct answer is "b." Making a report to the state licensing authority is considered to be within the interest of individual and public safety.

8. Which of the following concerns should you (the human services practitioner) have regarding the Shermans in the event Mr. Sherman retires (again) from driving?

    a. Depression and social isolation.
    b. Continued driving.
    c. Choices a and b.
    d. None of the above.

The correct answer is "c." Depression and social isolation may occur following driving retirement, as the older adult perceives a loss of independence and autonomy and may be unable to remain socially engaged. There should always be a concern about the older adult returning to driving in the event a viable alternative transportation plan is not developed and implemented.

9. You (the human services practitioner) can provide the Shermans with information on which of the following resources?

    a. Alzheimer's Association.
    b. Public transportation options, creating an account with a local taxi cab company, or donating their car to a non-profit organization.

    c.   Area Agency on Aging.

    d.   All of the above.

The correct answer is "d." All of the options would be appropriate areas that may be of help to the Shermans.

10. As a human services supervisor, you are asked by one of your employees if she can offer to provide transportation for the Shermans on the days they attend activities at the center, as she drives right by their house. Which of the following is likely to be the best response?

    a.   "Sure, that would be a nice gesture."

    b.   "While I am sure they would appreciate your generosity, what would they do when you are not available to pick them up?"

    c.   "That is thoughtful of you, but our agency policy does not allow employees or volunteers to transport our clients in their personal vehicles."

    d.   Any of the above could be an appropriate response.

The correct answer is "c." While any of the others could be practiced in some agencies, most organizations have policies regarding client transport.

Dr. Ed Neukrug is a professor of Counseling and Human Services at Old Dominion University. He is the author of eight books on counseling and human services (Cengage), editor of the *Encyclopedia of Theory in Counseling and Human Services* (Sage), and producer of an animated website entitled *Great Therapists of the Twentieth Century*. He has been involved in a wide variety of professional activities and is currently editor of the *Journal of Human Services* for the National Organization of Human Services.

    Hannah Neukrug is a student at the University of Virginia where she plans to double major in Psychology and Public Policy. She interned at a resource and referral call center for those who are homeless or at risk of being homeless in the summer of 2013. As an intake specialist there, she was introduced to the field of human services.

Heidi: Intervention Involving Possible Homelessness, Addiction, and Abuse

Heidi is a 45-year-old single female who has an 18-year-old daughter and 9-year-old son. Her daughter has a 2-year-old daughter by an ex-boyfriend who is no longer involved in parenting the child. Heidi, the daughter, the son, and the granddaughter all live together. Heidi tends to be a warm and caring parent but, periodically, has explosive episodes toward her children. At times, she has hit her children so hard that she has left marks on their bodies. She recently lost her job of 2 years where she was a sales associate at a local department store, causing her to fall behind in her rent and face eviction. Her eviction is imminent. She has few family members or friends she could turn to for help and, thus, will soon have nowhere to live. In order to find emergency housing, Heidi comes to your agency, which helps the homeless and those at-risk for homelessness. Based on this scenario, answer the following questions.

1.   As you are talking with Heidi, you notice welts on her son's arms. After inquiring about them, she tells you that her son was in a fight at school. Which of the following reflects the best course of action to take?

    a.   Nothing—you inquired and she told you that it was due to a fight at school. Therefore, you did what was required of you.

b. Call the police, as you suspect child abuse.

c. Call your local child protective service agency and explain the situation.

d. Discuss the situation with your supervisor, who suggests that no follow-through is needed.

e. Ask Heidi if it's okay if you contact child protective services.

The correct answer is "c." Generally, human services professionals are "mandated reporters," which means if you suspect child abuse, you must report it. Human services professionals should view Child Protective Services as an agency with whom one can consult, and should always contact them when there is suspected child abuse. Child Protective Services has a policy that they will not reveal those who reported suspected child abuse.

2. Heidi discloses to you that she sometimes sells marijuana to make extra money. What should you do?

a. Tell Heidi that you cannot work with her if she is selling drugs.

b. Work with Heidi to find a place to live, and refer Heidi to another agency to help her secure new job skills.

c. Contact the police.

d. Suggest to Heidi that she might want to go to rehab if she has a drug problem.

The correct answer is "b." According to most ethical codes, client information should be kept confidential, unless there are compelling reasons to break confidentiality. This situation is likely not compelling enough to break confidentiality, although one should always check with state laws. It is probably most helpful to Heidi if you work on her presenting issue, so she can better herself. Furthermore, telling Heidi that you do not think she should be selling drugs, or to refuse services for her because of she is selling drugs, would probably not be helpful to Heidi in the long run.

3. While Heidi is talking with you, she asks you for money so she can feed her children dinner. What should you do?

a. Give her money.

b. Give her money, but have her sign a contract that she will repay you.

c. Give her money, and tell her that she will owe you the money sometime in the future.

d. Don't give her money, as it is likely unethical, but find her a referral to a local food bank.

The correct answer is "d." Although you should, of course, be concerned about the well-being of Heidi and her children, you also have to be concerned about boundaries with clients. Ethical codes suggest that we should not blur boundaries; therefore, it is best to not give her money. This is because the blurring of boundaries leads to the development of unusual alliances that can interfere with the level of trust between the helper and the client. However, helping her find food in another venue would solve her immediate problem.

4. Heidi becomes angry and defensive when you explain to her what she needs to do to get housing. How do you react?

a. Tell Heidi that she seems angry and defensive, and that she should learn more effective ways of handling her feelings.

b. Tell Heidi she is not a good model for her children when she becomes angry and defensive, and that she might want to monitor her feelings more effectively.

    c.   Suggest to Heidi that she may need counseling and medication to deal with her intense feelings.

    d.   Use empathy and be nonjudgmental with Heidi, so you can hear the entirety of her situation.

The correct answer is "d." Giving large doses of advice and being judgmental are some of the attitudes that human services professionals should stay away from, as they tend to turn off clients and make them more resistant to help or treat. Using empathy and being nonjudgmental can help Heidi feel comfortable enough to talk about this situation and other situations that she may not have yet opened up about.

5.   You inform Heidi that her 18-year-old daughter, and her daughter's child, cannot enter a homeless shelter with Heidi because of a state law that disallows placement of children with their family if they are 18 years old or older. Hearing this, Heidi refuses to go to a shelter and insists she find a place to rent. After analyzing her situation, you realize that Heidi cannot afford a place on her own and that her only option is a shelter. What should you do? (Identify the *best* answer.)

    a.   Be firm with Heidi, telling her that she must go to a shelter, or else she is putting herself and her son in danger.

    b.   Accept Heidi's refusal of shelter and do not push her any further.

    c.   Ask Heidi's daughter to try to convince her mother to go into a homeless shelter.

    d.   Be realistic with Heidi about the likelihood of her not finding an affordable place to rent, and reaffirm that a homeless shelter is the best option at this time. Give her the information for housing that she requests, and let Heidi make the decision about what to do next.

The correct answer is "d." Although you may feel that Heidi will not be able to afford a place of her own, the decision is ultimately up to her. Thus, it is important that you convey your best understanding of the situation to Heidi in a nonjudgmental way. Being realistic with Heidi and offering her options allows Heidi to make an informed decision about what to do while showing respect for her decision-making process.

Henry: Responding to a Schizophrenic Client

Henry is a 22-year-old man who was diagnosed with schizophrenia a couple of years ago. Since his first acute schizophrenic episode, he has been in and out of the inpatient psychiatric treatment center a number of times. Recently, he began attending a mental health day-treatment center at which you are his psychiatric aide. At the day center, he receives counseling, learns job skills, receives career counseling, and works on coping and social skills. Henry does not have a good relationship with his family, and after his first acute schizophrenic episode, his family kicked him out of their house and refused to help him. He has a very limited support system outside of the employees at the day treatment center. He has been drinking heavily since he was 16, which complicates his treatment. Henry is unemployed and in urgent need of a job, particularly because his parents have decided to stop supporting him financially. Henry takes medication for his schizophrenia, which helps to control his delusions and hallucinations. His drinking and mental state contributes to his sense of despair, and he lacks drive and motivation to make positive efforts in his life. Although in-depth counseling is left to the licensed therapists, you are charged with providing supportive care, encouraging him to take his medications, and helping him focus on his treatment plan. Based on this scenario, answer the following questions.

1. Henry tells you he is broke and requests that you contact his parents to ask them to loan him some money for food. Which is the best response to Henry?

    a. Tell him that one of his goals is to gain a sense of independence, and he should know better than to ask his parents for money.
    b. Say you will call them to see if they are willing to lend the money to him, and you will try to repair the dysfunctional relationship he has with them.
    c. Suggest that he obtain a job so he is no longer in this situation.
    d. Lend him money yourself.
    e. Suggest that in your role as helper, it would be inappropriate for you to ask his parents for money, but you are there for him in other ways.

The correct answer is "e." Asking Henry's parents for money removes the responsibility that Henry needs to take for himself if he is to be actively involved in making a change in his life. In addition, asking his parents for money would be blurring boundaries, as you should not be revealing information about your clients to your clients' parents, unless they are actively involved in treatment and have permission from the client. In fact, talking with his parents could potentially be a violation of the *Health Insurance Portability and Accountability Act* (HIPAA), which, amongst other things, protects confidentiality of client information.

2. Henry comes to the day center and you strongly suspect that he has been drinking heavily. The day center has a strict no-substance use policy. Which would be the best way to respond to Henry?

    a. Tell Henry he has broken one of the primary rules of the center, he should be ashamed of himself, and he should know better.
    b. Don't say anything, and allow Henry to stay at the treatment center. As long as he doesn't admit to his drinking and acts relatively normal, there is no problem.
    c. Ask Henry if he has been drinking. If he says yes, remind him of the rules about drinking and politely ask him to come back when he is sober.
    d. Ask Henry if he has been drinking. If he says no, tell him you strongly believe he has been because of the way he is acting and that you smell alcohol. Remind him of the rules of the center and politely ask him to come back when he is sober.
    e. Choices a or b.
    f. Choices c or d.

The correct answer is "f." Ultimately, you have to follow your best judgment. If there is a rule at the agency that you strongly believe is being violated, you need to take action. There is a purpose for the rules. If you do not believe the rules are worthwhile, then you should actively advocate to change them. However, it is important that you follow them until they are changed.

3. You have been providing Henry with all the information and skills that he needs to apply for a job, but he has put in no effort and, thus, made no progress in attaining employment. What should you do?

    a. Partly due to Henry's schizophrenia and drinking, you realize that Henry is not motivated. Thus, you stop helping him obtain a job.
    b. Suggest to Henry that he needs to increase his self-esteem, so he will feel better about finding a job.
    c. Refer Henry to another aide who might be more effective than you. After all, you have not had any success with him.

d.   Be committed to Henry's situation, seek supervision, and continue working with him.

The correct answer is "d." Clients work at their own speed and sometimes it takes time to change. They need to know that the human services professional is committed to them—even when they don't actively change. Although answer "c" would be correct if you had some personal issue that prevented you from working effectively with Henry, or if your skills were preventing him from changing, it is not the best answer in this case. Answer "a" is not correct because it assumes that Henry cannot change due to his mental health issues. Although answer "b" may be correct, self-esteem is not directly related to finding a job, and he could raise his self-esteem and still not want to find a job.

4.   Henry has not been doing well; you notice that his delusional thinking has increased. You think that he might need a change in his medication. Which of the following is your best course of action?

a.   Believing that Henry is not taking the most effective medication to treat his symptoms, suggest to Henry that he try another type of medication.
b.   Document your concerns in your case notes, discuss the situation with your supervisor, and, if appropriate, discuss how your concerns can be communicated to the right person (e.g., the psychiatrist).
c.   Believing that his medication is correct, but that he is not taking a large enough dosage, suggest that Henry increase his dosage.
d.   Seek out the psychiatrist and tell the psychiatrist your concerns regarding Henry's medication.

The correct answer is "b." Human services professionals should not be telling clients directly their concerns about their medication. However, if they do have concerns, they need to communicate that to the appropriate people. In this case, the appropriate person is likely one's supervisor. However, if one does not have a supervisor, "d" would be the next best choice.

5.   While working at the day-treatment center, you realize one of the licensed professional therapists is using a technique that you don't believe she is trained in, and that could be harmful to her clients. What should you do?

a.   Report the therapist to her licensing board.
b.   Report the therapist to your supervisor.
c.   Talk to the therapist directly about your concerns, and if you are not satisfied, talk to your supervisor and possibly report her to the licensing board.
d.   Discuss the situation with your colleagues at a case conference meeting and decide the best course of action.

The correct answer is "c." Almost all ethical codes suggest that the first step to take when you believe someone is practicing unethical behaviors is to talk directly with that person. If one is not satisfied with the response one gets, then the professional should take it to the next level. Although there are some exceptions to this rule (e.g., a client will be harmed if you talk with the professional directly), in this case, the best answer is to report directly to the therapist.

Tricia McClam and Marianne Woodside are professors in Counselor Education at the University of Tennessee, Knoxville, where they teach a variety of graduate counseling courses. They are the authors of *Introduction to Human Services, 8th edition* and its companion text, *Introduction to Human Services: Cases and Applications*, as well as several other human services texts.

Case Study: From a Counselor's Point of View

The following case study is told from the point of view of the counselor, Delores Fuentes. Her narrative is in italics.

People Involved in the Case

Delores Fuentes	Counselor, community health and human services clinic
Mr. and Mrs. Ruiz	Parents of Juan
Dr. Hidalgo	Pediatrician
Ms. Brown	Nurse, Health and Rehabilitation Services, Georgia
Mrs. Marcos	Guardian in Minneapolis
Mexican Consulate	Atlanta
Mr. Sanchez	Lawyer, Mexican Consulate, Georgia
Dr. Stapleton	Physician in Minneapolis
Mexican Consulate	Minneapolis
Police—first encounter	Minneapolis
Mr. Gluckey	Staff member, Mexican Consulate, Minneapolis
Police—second encounter	Minneapolis

My name is Delores Fuentes, and I am a counselor at a community health and human services clinic in rural Georgia. Since I work with a diverse group of clients, including migrant farm workers, my work is very challenging. One problem we face is the client's lack of understanding of the culture here, of the standards of living in this country, and of the laws that govern relationships, such as marriage and child custody. Let me share a recent case in which there was such a misunderstanding.

Mr. and Mrs. Ruiz came to the clinic to see the pediatrician, Dr. Hidalgo. Mr. Ruiz asked the doctor if he was willing to take care of his baby, Juan.

DR. HIDALGO: I know you want me to see Juan. Where is he?

MR. RUIZ: Oh, I need you to sign these papers saying that you are willing to take care of him so they can release him from the hospital in Minneapolis.

DR. HIDALGO: Okay, but why is he there?

MR. RUIZ: Oh, he was sick.

DR. HIDALGO: So, he is there in the hospital?

MR. RUIZ: No, he is with a translator. The nurse from Health and Rehabilitation Services (HRS) needs to have a paper from you because if not, we will lose our baby.

DR. HIDALGO: I don't understand this. Do you mind talking to Ms. Fuentes?

Dr. Hidalgo asked me to look into this case so he could understand the situation better. The scrap of paper Mr. Ruiz gave the doctor had a phone number and a name on it—that was it. From there, I started trying to figure out the case. First, I called the HRS in the state capital and said, "I have this family here and I need to speak to the director of nursing." Eventually, I spoke with a nurse, Ms. Brown.

MS. BROWN: Don't even bother to take on the case. It is a lost cause. It was referred to me by a hospital in Minneapolis [where Mr. and Mrs. Ruiz had recently been living]. They wanted to make sure that the family has a suitable home for the baby. I made a visit; they live in a house with no electricity and no phone. There are three or four people living with them, so that is not a healthy environment for the baby. So I signed that Juan cannot be released into their care.

I asked her Juan's location now. She reported that he had already been released to a guardian. I needed the name of the guardian, and finally she gave it to me. I reported to the pediatrician, and he told me that he would call the guardian. He reported this conversation.

DR. HIDALGO: My name is Dr. Hidalgo and I am a pediatrician working at a community health clinic. I need some information about Juan Ruiz. Could you tell me what is going on with Juan?
MRS. MARCOS: Don't even bother asking questions of the parents. They don't have any more right to be trying to fight for him. I have custody of Juan.

I wondered, "How is that possible?" She should have been able to describe why she had custody. She could have said, "I have custody because the father mistreated the wife, and I was able to remove that kid from that unhealthy environment."
I called Mrs. Marcos back and told her that the pediatrician had spoken to me. I asked her what the issues are, and she told me not to assess the situation. She explained that she had observed the interaction between Mr. and Mrs. Ruiz. According to her, Mr. Ruiz is the only one who talks—his wife always looks down, she cannot face you. Mrs. Marcos concluded that it was a typical case of abuse.
In Mexican culture, it is a mark of respect for the lady not to look her in the eyes, and it is the man who answers the questions. I told the pediatrician what I had learned and that I would visit Mr. and Mrs. Ruiz to determine whether it was an abusive situation. I talked with them and their neighbors and friends and found no evidence of abuse.
I then called the Mexican Consulate for help, explaining that one of our clients had a problem and describing the details I had uncovered so far. I said that I thought the family needed a lawyer. They agreed. After investigating the case, the lawyer, Mr. Sanchez, called me.

MR. SANCHEZ: I found out that the couple signed custody papers for a Mrs. Marcos to take care of the baby, Juan, while he was in the hospital. The hospital released the baby without permission from the parents to this person who actually, at least initially, had the good will to help. She was a translator and spoke Spanish well, so the family thought she would help them. I think initially that was what she really intended. Later, she became attached to Juan.

I called Mrs. Marcos back. I explained that the case is complicated and I had found a lawyer for the family. I told her that she would receive a call from a lawyer working for the Mexican Consulate. He was exploring the issues and wanted her to tell him more about the situation. She said that Mr. Sanchez had already called her. I think she was becoming nervous because she called Dr. Hidalgo. She told him she wanted to take care of the baby and that Juan had extensive special needs. Dr. Hidalgo asked me to contact the Minneapolis hospital for the name of the doctor. I talked with the doctor, Dr. Stapleton, who confirmed that nothing was wrong with the baby when he was released. I gave his name and phone number to the lawyer, Mr. Sanchez. Dr. Stapleton told Mr. Sanchez what he told me: "There is nothing wrong with the baby." Then Mr. Sanchez told me about his conversation with Mrs. Marcos.

MR. SANCHEZ (to Mrs. Marcos): The doctor said that the baby must go home to Georgia.
MRS. MARCOS: Oh, no. I will not release the baby.

Eventually, an agreement was reached that the baby, the guardian, the family, and the lawyer would all see Dr. Stapleton. Meanwhile, Mr. and Mrs. Ruiz learned that Mrs. Marcos had been seen putting some boxes in her car, and they called me at home at 2:00 a.m. I called Mr. Sanchez, who said that we needed to send the couple to Minneapolis immediately. In the meantime, he would call the police.

We sent the parents to Minneapolis in a van. While they were on the way, we made sure the family had a home in Georgia to return to, as well as work, a pediatrician for the baby, and a phone. They arrived in Minneapolis the next morning. The family reported that the translator, Mrs. Marcos, was very nice.

MR. RUIZ: She gave us a piece of cake and a coffee, and let us play with the baby. Then she disappeared. About ten minutes later, the police came in, and the police literally chased us out, and said, "If you come back here, we will put you in jail."

Mr. Ruiz called me from a gas station to report what had happened. I called the Mexican Consulate to report on the situation. The Consulate here called the one in Minneapolis and asked them to have someone meet the family at the gas station. We called the police to tell them what was going on. The police agreed to check on it.

The police sergeant found a report with the correct time and date, stating that the parents were removed from the home of Mrs. Marcos, but he did not have the full report of what happened. So a member of the Mexican Consulate in Minneapolis and their lawyer, Mr. Gluckey, went to see Mrs. Marcos to get custody of Juan. All agreed to meet at the doctor's office the next morning, and if he said the baby could travel, then Mr. and Mrs. Ruiz could take Juan home.

This case took three weeks to resolve.

Questions

1. Ms. Fuentes' assessment of the Ruiz situation, her plan of action, and its implementation best represent her skills in

   a. ethical decision-making.
   b. problem solving.
   c. evaluation.
   d. confrontation.

The correct answer is "b." These are the three steps in problem solving. Choices a and c are incorrect because while ethical decision-making and evaluation are important, they are not steps in the problem solving process. Choice d, confrontation (usually thought of as a challenge), is a way to communicate with a client, it is not a step in the problem solving process.

2. Mrs. Marcos' assessment of the relationship between Mr. and Mrs. Ruiz illustrates

   a. a lack of cultural understanding.
   b. her understanding of Spanish.
   c. her abilities as a translator.
   d. her inexperience with human services.

The correct answer is "a." Mrs. Ruiz' behavior is appropriate in Mexican culture. Mrs. Marcos might understand Spanish (choice b) and how to be an effective translator (choice c), but lacks an understanding of the Mexican culture. Although experiences in human services delivery (choice d) might help Mrs. Marcos understand a client's relationships, it does not insure this understanding.

3. The involvement of Ms. Fuentes, Dr. Hidalgo, Mr. Sanchez, Dr. Stapleton, and Mr. Glukey is an example of

   a. ethical and legal issues.
   b. professionals and nonprofessionals.
   c. collaboration among professionals.
   d. managed care.

The correct answer is "c." All of the individuals mentioned above are professionals, not nonprofessionals, as in choice b. Consideration of ethical and legal issues (choice a) includes involving consideration of the client perspective. Choice d is incorrect because the professionals involved would not all be involved in the managed care system of service delivery.

4. As physicians in this case, Dr. Hidalgo and Dr. Stapleton are

   a. administrators.
   b. nonprofessionals.
   c. professionals.
   d. volunteers.

The correct answer is "c." Physicians are professionals with medical degrees, and are paid for their services.

5. Mrs. Marcos' role as translator and eventually guardian is an example of what ethical violation?

   a. Confidentiality
   b. Dual relationship
   c. Competence
   d. Beneficence

The correct answer is "b." Mrs. Marcos' two roles and their potential conflicts represent the ethical standard considering dual relationships. The remaining choices are incorrect because, although confidentiality, competence, and beneficence are important ethical standards, this case does not illustrate these standards or the lack of them.

Note. From "Thriving and Surviving as a Case Manager," by M. Woodside and T. McClam, 2013, *Generalist Case Management: A Method of Human Service Delivery* (4th ed.), pp. 374–377. Copyright 2013 by Brooks/Cole, a part of Cengage Learning. Reprinted with permission.

About the Author

Dr. Howard G. Rosenthal, EdD, a founding Human Services-Board Certified Practitioner (HS-BCP), received his master's degree from the University of Missouri, St. Louis and his doctorate from St. Louis University. He is the author of the best-selling exam prep book and audio program of all time: the *Special 15th Anniversary Edition of the Encyclopedia of Counseling* and the *Special 15th Anniversary Edition of the Vital Information and Review Questions* for the NCE and CPCE. He also authored the first-ever *Human Services Dictionary,* which is unique because the definitions help the reader answer typical or prototype exam questions. In 2010, all three of the aforementioned materials made it into the Routledge Counseling and Psychotherapy *Top Ten List* for the US and overseas, with the *Encyclopedia* taking the number one slot.

His book, *Favorite Counseling and Therapy Techniques* (a publisher's best seller), and the companion book, *Favorite Counseling and Therapy Homework Assignments,* include contributions from many of the top therapists in the world.

Dr. Rosenthal's humorous, reader-friendly writing style landed him an interview—along with other influential authors, such as Barry Sears of *Zone Diet* books and Mark Victor Hansen, co-author of the *Chicken Soup for the Soul* series—in Jeff Herman's book, *You Can Make It Big Writing Books: A Top Agent Shows You How to Develop a Million-Dollar Bestseller.*

Some of his other popular books include *Not With My Life I Don't: Preventing Your Suicide and That of Others; Before You See Your First Client: 55 Things Counselors and Mental Health Providers Need to Know; Help Yourself to Positive Mental Health* (with Joseph W. Hollis); and his *Therapy's Best, Practical Advice and Gems of Wisdom From Twenty Accomplished Counselors and Therapists.* Dr. Rosenthal has lectured to over 100,000 people, making him one of the most popular speakers in the Midwest.

He holds the national record for winning the most "teaching tips of the year awards," given by the publication, *Teaching for Success.* He has been inducted into the St. Louis Community College Hall of Fame, is an Emerson Excellence in Teaching Award Recipient, and a winner of the Missouri Wayne B. McClelland Award. He is listed in *Who's Who in*

America, and Samuel T. Gladding's *The Counseling Dictionary* in the "Prominent Names in the Counseling Profession" section. He has written over 20 articles for *Counselor, The Magazine for Addictions Professionals* alone, and is one of the leading bloggers for Victor Yalom's *Psychotherapy Net*. His website is www.howardrosenthal.com.

He currently serves as professor and coordinator of the Human Services and Addiction Studies Program for St. Louis Community College Florissant Valley.

Printed by PGSTL